The Politics
of Contraception

Carl Djerassi

W · W · NORTON & COMPANY

New York · London

Library of Congress Cataloging in Publishing Data
Djerassi, Carl.
The politics of contraception.
(The Portable Stanford Series)
Bibliography: p.
Includes index.
1. Contraception. 2. Contraception—Research.
3. Oral contraceptives. I. Title.
RG136.D57 1979 613.9'4 79-21845
ISBN 0-393-01264-6 pbk.

This book was published originally as a part of THE PORTABLE
STANFORD, a series of books pulished by the Stanford Alumni
Association, Stanford, California. This edition first published by W. W.
Norton & Company, Inc. January 1980 by arrangement with the
Stanford Alumni Association.

1 2 3 4 5 6 7 8 9 0

CREDITS

All tables and figures were prepared by The Design Quarter, San Diego, California.

Page 28. Figure redrawn with permission of L.S. Burnett et al. "An Evaluation of Abortion: Techniques and Protocols," *Hospital Practice,* x:3, August 1975; original figure by A. Miller.

Pages 40–41. Norinyl® 1+50 egg poster reprinted with permission of Syntex Laboratories, Inc.

Pages 108–14. "Studies on a New, Peerless Contraceptive Agent: A Preliminary Final Report" by Julius S. Greenstein. Reprinted from *Canadian Medical Association Journal* 93:1351–1355, December 25, 1965. By permission of The Canadian Medical Association.

Special thanks to the World Health Organization for permission to quote extensively from their 7th Annual Report and various Technical Reports.

All pre-Columbian pottery figures throughout this volume and on the cover are from the collection of the author and were photographed by Robert A. Isaacs, Sunnyvale, California.

Steroid notations in the Author's Postscript were prepared by Instructional Media, School of Medicine, Stanford University.

Permission to quote material from various books was obtained from the following sources:

Pages 155–56. Reprinted from page 30, John F. Marshall, in *Fertility Control Methods—Strategies for Introduction,* edited by G.W. Duncan. Copyright © 1973 by Academic Press. By permission of John F. Marshall and Academic Press.

Pages 171–72. Reprinted from pp. 10, 11, 138, 139 in *Brave New World Revisited* by Aldous Huxley. Copyright © 1958 by Aldous Huxley. By permission of Harper & Row, Publishers, Inc.

Pages 174–75. Reprinted from pp. 23–24 in *The Voice of the Dolphins, and Other Stories* by Leo Szilard. Copyright © 1961 by Leo Szilard. By permission of Simon & Schuster, a division of Gulf & Western Corporation.

Pages 177–79. Reprinted from pp. 168–69 in *Are Our Descendents Doomed?*, edited by Harrison Brown and Edward Hutchings Jr. Copyright © 1970, 1972 by California Institute of Technology, all rights reserved. By permission of Viking Penguin Inc.

Pages 183–213. Special thanks to The Population Council for permission to quote extensively from "Fertility Limitation Through Contraceptive Steroids in the People's Republic of China" by Carl Djerassi, in *Studies in Family Planning*, vol. 5, no. 1, January 1974.

Page 225. Reprinted from page 265, "The Pure Good of Theory," in *The Palm at the End of the Mind* by Wallace Stevens. Copyright © 1971 by Wallace Stevens. By permission of Alfred A. Knopf, Inc.

For Pamela, who would have liked this book

For Dale and Vocalissima

Acknowledgments

THIS BOOK WOULD NEVER HAVE BEEN STARTED without the encouragement and support of Professor Diane Wood Middlebrook, nor would it have been completed without the heroic tape transcription efforts of Guynn Perry and Ingeborg Kuhn and the editorial perseverance of Cynthia Fry Gunn. Thanks are due to Zoecon's librarian, Carolyn Erickson, for much-needed assistance in locating obscure references and to Dean Julius S. Greenstein (Shippensburg State College, Pennsylvania) for providing me with correspondence relating to his article from the *Canadian Medical Association Journal,* which is included in Chapter 6. I am greatly indebted to Professor Egon Diczfalusy (Stockholm) as well as to the following individuals for prompt replies to my numerous inquiries: Dr. Richard E. Edgren (Palo Alto, Ca.), Dr. Thomas Fingar (Stanford), Mr. Paul E. Freiman (Palo Alto), Dr. Milan Henzl (Palo Alto), Dr. Liang Huang (Peking), Dr. Stanley Kaplan (Nutley, N.J.), Dr. Armand M. Karow Jr. (Augusta, Ga.), Dr. John F. Marshall (Geneva), Dr. Malcolm Potts (Research Triangle Park, N.C.), Dr. R.T. Ravenholt (Washington, D.C.), Dr. Eugene J. Segre (Palo Alto), and Dr. Roger V. Short (Edinburgh).

Contents

CHAPTER ONE   Introduction   1

CHAPTER TWO   Current Contraceptive Hardware   7

CHAPTER THREE   The Pill: Use and Concerns   33

CHAPTER FOUR   The Fear of Cancer   51

CHAPTER FIVE   The Road from Laboratory to Consumer   67

CHAPTER SIX   The Public's Right to Know   91

CHAPTER SEVEN   Future Prospects in Male Contraception   121

CHAPTER EIGHT   Future Prospects in Female Contraception   143

CHAPTER NINE   Birth Control à la 1984   169

CHAPTER TEN   Birth Control in China:
                     The Contraceptive Supermarket   183

CHAPTER ELEVEN   Strategies for the Future   215

AUTHOR'S   The Chemical History of the Pill   227
POSTSCRIPT

READER'S GUIDE   256

The Politics of Contraception

Authoritarian male figure. Veracruz, *ca.* A.D. 200–500.

1

Introduction

OVER THE YEARS I HAVE BECOME progressively more disturbed by the demands of the public—citizens, legislators, and journalists alike—for black-and-white answers to grey questions. This demand was illustrated by Senator Edmund Muskie's call during a Senate hearing in 1975 for "one-armed scientists" because most of his scientist witnesses hedged their replies to his questions with "on the one hand the evidence suggests . . . , but on the other hand. . . ." I know of no field that better illustrates this problem—the desire for conclusive answers to ambiguous questions—than does contraception.

Birth control affects nearly everybody—people either have used it, will use it, or, at the very least, are against it. Birth control illustrates the dilemma that modern science and technology have created—fear of new developments accompanied by the demand for even newer and "better" methods. It raises urgent questions of public policy—consumer concerns, individual rights, and the impact of U.S. technology not only upon the highly developed countries but upon the three fourths of the world's population that lives in poverty and frequently in ignorance of modern medicine.

By 1968 I had written alone or coauthored half a dozen books and a hundred times as many articles in various fields of chemistry. All of them were directed to my scientific peers. My initial involvement in the birth control field in the early 1950s, as one of the participants in the very beginning stages of the discovery of the birth control pill, was purely technical. However, in the 1960s I became more interested in all aspects of human fertility control as a result of my participation in various international projects that addressed themselves to the ever-widening technological gap between the highly developed countries and the Third World. I realized then the importance of communicating with a much wider public in a comprehensible way. As a result, in the last ten years I have written articles on occasion and have given numerous talks addressed to the general public which dealt with the many ramifications of fertility control.

The contents of this book have thus been simmering within me for more than a few years. The simmering finally reached the boiling point, and this book was written as a concentrated, personal outpouring. It is not a scholarly treatise, but the distillate of the conclusions and opinions of a person who for over 20 years has lived a bigamous professional life in serving simultaneously as a professor carrying out basic research and as an industrialist who has had to concern himself with finding worldwide applications for laboratory discoveries. Not many scientists have lived in both worlds *simultaneously* for so long, and as a result I have acquired a perspective from both the basic and applied research viewpoints that is especially necessary when considering *practical* new birth control approaches.

This book germinated in an article I wrote in 1970 entitled "Birth Control After 1984," the most important article that I have written about the public policy context of fertility control. The title was purposely ambiguous because the article dealt with two different problems—the time required for research in new birth control methods to come to practical fruition and utopian expectations about the outcome of such research. My basic conclusion in 1970 was that fundamentally new birth control procedures in the female or in the male probably would not be developed until the middle 1980s at the earliest and then only if major steps of the type outlined in the article were instituted in the early 1970s. Although I realized from private conversations at that time that other individuals in the field felt similarly, I seemed to be the only one willing to commit such dismal predictions to cold print. Nine years have now passed. On March 9, 1978, Dr. Donald Kennedy, then Commissioner of the Food and Drug Administration, made the following statement at hearings before the House Select Committee on Population of the 95th Congress: "I would just parenthetically say that of Dr. Djerassi's remarkable set of predictions back in 1970, it occurs to me to observe that we're more than halfway to 1984—and that's a little troublesome—but his crystal ball was, in almost all respects, pellucid."

I am not quoting Dr. Kennedy out of braggadocio but rather to put the book—especially the chapter dealing with my recommendations for the future—into the proper perspective for the layman. My 1970 article contained actual or implied criticisms of the FDA as well as numerous suggestions for a changed modus operandi regarding the current procedures for drug approval. I discussed these proposals in early 1970 at a meeting with the Assistant Secretary of Health, Education and Welfare, the Commissioner of the FDA, the Surgeon General, the Assistant Secretary of HEW for Population Problems, and the head of the National Institutes of Health's Population Program. None of them agreed with me at that time, and it is therefore not unimportant that even in the eyes of the head of one of the agencies that I criticized, the validity of many of the predictions has now been acknowledged.

This is not a "how to" book—a guide to contraceptive practice or family planning—but rather a "why, when, and whether" exploration of the critical issues surrounding birth control, not only as it affects the individual but, more broadly, as it affects the world. I am addressing the citizen, legislator, and journalist who want to understand the current state of affairs in contraception and what improvements might be possible by the turn of the century.

When discussing the broad topic of human fertility control I find it helpful to use computer terminology to differentiate between contraceptive "hardware" and "software." In computer language the former term refers to the actual computer equipment and the latter term refers to the programs needed to solve problems. Neither item alone will do. In the context of contraception I use the term "hardware" to refer to the actual means of birth control—condoms, oral contraceptives, abortion, coitus interruptus, and so forth. (I find this computer term especially appropriate given our society's almost pathetic belief in the "technological fix" as a solution to all of the problems that beset us.) I use "software" to cover all the complicated social, cultural, political, religious, and legal issues that must be dealt with before any "hardware" research can be implemented.

I first cover the hardware aspects of current birth control so that the reader understands what methods we have now and how they might possibly be improved. Because of the enormous impact of the Pill—in terms of its effect not only on contraceptive practice but also on sexual mores, women's emancipation, religion, etc.—I devote an entire chapter to it. I then move to the fear of side effects, especially of cancer, since carcinogenicity has become a key concern that governs much of our thinking about short- and long-term exposure to innumerable chemicals, natural or synthetic, of which contraceptives are only one. The complexity and "greyness" of this greyest of all questions—"Will it cause cancer?"—must be understood in order to appreciate why most contraceptive hardware development time must now be measured in decades rather than in years.

Contraceptive "software" issues have become inextricably intertwined with politics; hence the title of this book. The increasingly stringent controls on research in contraception, imposed by the FDA and other government agencies under pressure from consumer groups, and the resulting spillover into the international arena are unusually sensitive topics, as is the quality and scope of journalistic and congressional coverage of the extraordinarily complicated and multifaceted components of human fertility control. Even future prospects for male and female contraception are dependent on politics and policy questions, since virtually all contraceptive research requires clinical investigation involving thousands of human guinea pigs in a climate that is increasingly inhospitable to such work.

In the words of Dr. Malcolm Potts, in his 1970 Darwin Lecture in Human Biology in London, "Too much emphasis has been placed on what might be called contraceptive Cadillacs, when the need in many countries is for contraceptive bicycles." In my opinion, the present climate in the biomedical field worldwide is such that with relatively few exceptions the development of contraceptive bicycles is not much simpler than the development of contraceptive Cadillacs. Instead we may have to spend more time teaching people how to "ride" and "drive" the currently available contraceptive vehicles. Learning how to ride and drive is, of course, precisely what I mean by software.

The term "population explosion" had its maximum impact in the 1960s and led to dire predictions that within a few centuries there would not be enough room for people to lie down. The relative success of family planning programs in several countries during the 1970s is now leading to an equally unrealistic response in that many people in the highly developed countries have begun to believe that the pressure of the population explosion will not be felt. Although it is true that on a global scale a decline in the *rate* of population growth has become noticeable, on an absolute scale the world's population is increasing and will continue to do so for decades. Take just one example—Mexico, our closest neighbor to the south. At the current annual growth rate of 3.4 percent, Mexico's population will increase from 67 million in 1979 to 600 million in a mere 70 years. Even if the birth rate is reduced in accordance with Mexico's *most optimistic* family planning objectives, there will still be a staggering 300 million people in Mexico in 70 years.

Efforts in the field of human fertility control must be increased and widened, regardless of whether there is a *global* population explosion or not. Unless one believes passionately that child spacing or sex without concomitant procreation is bad, most people at some stage of their lives use some sort of birth control, and the majority of people in the affluent countries use it throughout their reproductive lives. Few people will argue that present methods of birth control should not be improved.

Thus, I discuss the critical need for strategies for the future and set forth my own recommendations. Many readers are likely to disagree with some, or possibly even the majority, of my conclusions. However, simply disagreeing is a luxury that we cannot afford. What other alternatives are offered? If none are presented and implemented, birth control—not just in 1984, but also in 1994, and in 2004—will not differ much from what we have today.

I felt it would be incomplete for me to write this book without including a discussion of the early history of the Pill, the scientific development with which I am most closely associated. First of all, I believe it is worthwhile to present my recollections as one of the participants in the very beginning stages of this discovery. These early developments have not been presented before to the layman; even the technical reviews addressed to specialists have been rewritten so many times by people who have had only second- or third-hand knowledge that the border between fact and fiction has become very blurred. Second, the development of oral contraceptives illustrates the complexity of the research that will be required to develop a future "Pill"—be it for males or for females. The public—including consumer advocates and regulatory agencies—has a tendency to look at the 1950s through 1979 glasses, which is both preposterous and counterproductive. But looking at 1979 through 1951 glasses may be of more than historical interest, since the discoveries were made and implemented then, and do not seem to be now.

Affectionate couple. Mayan, *ca.* A.D. 700–900.

2

Current Contraceptive Hardware

BEFORE TALKING ABOUT THE FUTURE, we need to know what birth control methods we have now, how they work, and who uses them. In other words, what is the status of current contraceptive hardware?

It is remarkable how far we have progressed with birth control during the past 20 years. In 1959, oral contraceptives had not yet been approved anywhere in the world; IUDs, developed in the 1930s but quickly abandoned, had not yet been reintroduced; sterilization, especially vasectomy, was minimal; and abortion was illegal outside of Japan, Eastern European socialist countries, and (with major restrictions) Sweden.

Precise figures about the current use of existing contraceptive methods—old and new—are unobtainable but the best recent estimates are shown in Table 2-1 on page 8.

Coitus Interruptus and Rhythm

Coitus interruptus is, of course, not a contraceptive hardware item in the sense that other birth control methods are—indeed, that is its greatest virtue. Its greatest drawbacks are that it clearly detracts from sexually satisfying intercourse and its success depends heavily on practice and sexual discipline.

TABLE 2-1

Estimated Worldwide Use of Fertility Control Methods

Millions of Users

Coitus Interruptus	?
Rhythm	?
Prolonged Lactation	50-100
Abortion	30-55
Condoms	15-20
Diaphragms	2-3
Intrauterine Devices (IUDs)	15
Oral Contraceptives	50-80
Sterilization	15-30

SOURCE: Data for oral contraceptives, IUDs, and abortions from World Health Organization. *Special Programme of Research, Development and Research Training in Human Reproduction,* 7th Annual Report, November 1978, Geneva.

A charmingly graphic prescription for effective coitus interruptus was provided in the early nineteenth century by the founder of the British birth control movement, Francis Place: "The most convenient and easy, as well as the most effectual method is for the man at the moment of spending to throw himself on his left side by which motion he not only in some measure extricates the part, but gives it also a slanting direction with respect to the woman, so that the seed being thrown not directly but in a side-long manner it is perfectly impossible for the womb to receive it."

The rationale for some of the precise instructions—the man throwing himself on his *left* side or the seed being thrown in a *side-long* manner—is not difficult to understand. In Francis Place's time, only the "missionary" face-to-face sexual position (with the man on top of the woman) was considered acceptable, and it was assumed that the vigor of the man's final thrust during ejaculation propelled the sperm toward the waiting egg. Thus, even if the man could not withdraw his penis completely prior to ejaculation, moving backward rather than forward presumably slowed down the speed of the sperm's movement so that it would not reach the egg. This prescription, of course, was written at a time when nothing was known about the inherent motility of sperm or about the fact that its fertilizable lifetime extends over several days. As far as Place's emphasis on the man's throwing himself on the left side is concerned, one can probably assume that the author was right-handed and thus would use his stronger arm to push himself away from the woman.

Even though coitus interruptus is frequently unsatisfying or even ineffective at the microscopic individual level, it nevertheless has a significant macroscopic demographic impact. The falling population growth rate in Europe during the nineteenth century was, for example, to a large extent due to the wide use of coitus interruptus, and a large but undeterminable number of couples to this day still depend on it as their sole method of family planning.

In contrast to coitus interruptus, there is no question that technical improvements could make the rhythm or periodic abstinence method more reliable. Those improvements, which are related to accurate prediction of the time of ovulation, will be covered in Chapter 8. Suffice it to say here that the length of time requiring sexual abstinence by the couple depending solely on the rhythm method is based on two criteria: the first is the fertilizable life of the freshly shed human ovum, which is *shorter than one day;* the second is the fertilizing life span of the human sperm deposited in the female genital tract (even when using Francis Place's "side-long manner"), which may be *as long as five days.*

The rhythm method has recently been included in the generic category of "natural family planning," and with our predilection for acronyms it is now called NFP among professionals in the field. The World Health Organization as part of its Special Programme on Research, Development and Research Training in Human Reproduction has initiated a number of studies on the use of this method in various clinical centers in lesser-developed countries. But, as its November 1978 report illustrates, there are inherent disadvantages in natural family planning. The first problem is to actually persuade people to become motivated enough to try it:

> The recruitment figures of the study give some indication of the demand and acceptance of NFP in Colombia. As of September 1978, 9,378 potential users attended orientation lectures given for the purpose of finding volunteers for the study. Of these, only 514 women (5.5%) were sufficiently interested and complied with the selection criteria to be randomized into the study. The investigators have experienced more difficulty than they anticipated in recruiting subjects for this study due to lack of confidence in the methods by the population because they are thought of as "rhythm," which has been discredited in Colombia; the fact that the methods themselves require the support and continued cooperation of the husband/partner and abstinence during the fertile period, which renders them unattractive to many people; the general scepticism of the medi-

cal profession in Colombia toward NFP; and intensive campaigns and community services which promote the use of other methods by national and nongovernmental agencies. Thus, one must question the actual demand for NFP services in Colombia.

The other problem is the lack of efficacy of the method among couples who use it. The results of a five-center trial in Auckland, Bangalore, Dublin, Manila, and San Miguel showed the unacceptably high annual rate of 19.4 pregnancies per 100 women. What are the reasons for this poor *use effectiveness* (to be contrasted with the considerably higher *theoretical effectiveness* if this method is followed scrupulously)? The WHO report explains:

> The majority of the pregnancies experienced so far appear to be the result of couples knowingly "taking a chance" during the fertile phase, despite the fact that during each follow-up interview they declared their continued interest in participating in the study and using the method during the next cycle to avoid pregnancy. It appears that almost all of the women entering the study could be taught to identify the mucus symptoms associated with ovulation, that the ovulation method enables women to detect the fertile days of the menstrual cycle and that *failure to implement the abstinence required* [my italics] during the fertile phase rendered the method relatively ineffective in general use for preventing pregnancy.

Prolonged Lactation

The precise hormonal mechanism whereby breast feeding delays renewed conception is not completely understood, but both the hypothalamus and the pituitary glands appear to be involved in this complex sequence of events. We do know that neural stimulation from the breast is an essential component. Thus, a baby who is carried by the mother all day and fed on demand exerts a much more noticeable inhibitory influence on renewed conception than does a child who is fed on a rigorous schedule at specific times.

It is likely that even now, when considered on a global scale, *more births are prevented by breast feeding than by any other method of contraception.* Dr. Malcolm Potts of the International Fertility Research Program estimates that between 50 and 100 million women a year are protected from conception by breast feeding. This is truly natural family planning. Dr. Roger Short, head of the Medical Research Council's unit on reproductive biology in Edinburgh, discussed this topic in an extraordinarily interesting manner at a 1976 meeting of the Royal Society of London:

> It is no wonder that social changes which reduce the contraceptive efficiency of lactation have had such a staggering demographic impact. Petros-Barvazian (1975) has listed some of the factors that have led to a decline in the incidence of breast feeding in the West: these include urbanization and industrialization, mothers working outside the home, attitudes of health workers, the availability of easy-to-use, safe and attractive breast milk substitutes, and the influence of marketing, advertisements and the mass media. To these should be added Western woman's shame at the idea of having to breast feed in public, and her fear of "losing her figure," and by inference her sexual attractiveness, in our breast-conscious society. But powdered milk and baby foods are one thing for the emancipated, hygienic, pill-taking Western career girl, but quite another matter for the socially deprived inhabitant of some squalid favella. The more unfavourable the environment, the more infant survival and birth spacing both become dependent on breast feeding. It is often said that we cannot expect people in developing countries to wish to control their fertility until their infant mortality rates have been reduced to an acceptable level. *If we could develop contraceptives that promoted breast feeding, they would increase the birth interval and reduce the infant mortality at the same time* [my italics].

Short also reviewed some of the recent work carried out in Africa on the relationship between socioeconomic levels and conception during lactation. In a study of rural and urban Rwandese females who were solely dependent on breast feeding for contraception, the malnourished rural mothers, who carried their babies continuously and fed them whenever they cried, showed in 50 percent of the cases a 23-month elapsed interval before conception occurred again. On the other hand, 50 percent of the better-nourished urban mothers, who fed their babies on a specific time schedule, conceived within nine months of the last birth. Among women who did not breast feed at all, the differences between the rural and urban mothers disappeared completely, and 50 percent of each group was pregnant again within three months. As Short points out, "Although it is not possi-

ble to disentangle the relative importance of nutrition and the frequency of the suckling stimulus in bringing about post-partum infertility in these Rwandese women, the study does emphasize how
the process of urbanization, with its attendant social and nutritional
changes, can have a major impact on human fertility."

Unfortunately, most trends in modern life, including increasing
urbanization, are likely to reduce the overall extent of breast feeding
in the world, and this will be particularly noticeable in those lesser-
developed countries where mothers will start to enter the organized
labor force. Nevertheless, breast feeding remains an important subject for research—not only because of its impact as a child-spacing
device, but also because of the impact other contraceptive methods
may have upon it. For example, take the greatly increased use of oral
contraceptives among women in lesser-developed countries: what
effect does the Pill have on the breast-feeding performance of the
mother and on the nutritional quality of her milk? Perhaps even more
serious is the question of whether the hormonal components of the
Pill are transferred through the milk to the infant, and if so what the
short- or long-term effects on the infant might be. (This question
must be asked of any systemic medication—be it for contraceptive or
therapeutic purposes—that a lactating mother might take.)

Detailed studies on this topic have appeared in the scientific
literature, notably from Sweden, only since 1977. Trace quantities of
the progestational and estrogenic components of the Pill have been
detected in the mother's milk, but according to a summarizing report
by Drs. Stefan Nilsson and Karl-Gösta Nygren in the January 1979
issue of *Research in Reproduction,*

> Since the start of oral contraception in the middle fifties,
> very few side effects in breastfed infants have been re-
> ported. Indirect effects on the growth of babies have been
> reported because of a decreased milk volume [known to be
> caused by the estrogen component of the Pill], but the only
> direct side effect on infants to date is, to the best of our
> knowledge, the development of gynaecomastia [breast
> growth] in a very few cases. This condition has not been
> found in systemic studies and it is obviously very rare. It
> could possibly be caused by the oestrogen component in
> oral contraceptives. If hormonal contraception is to be
> used during lactation, low-dose gestagens [progestational
> hormones] may be preferable, in order to avoid any side
> effects due to the oestrogens. This form of contraception
> seems to be highly effective during lactation in women.

The effect of a contraceptive upon both the quality of the mother's milk and the health of the infant becomes even more important with injectable or other long-acting systemic contraceptives currently under investigation, because they are designed particularly for use by women in lesser-developed countries, where there is likely to be a high proportion of lactating mothers.

Lactational amenorrhea—inhibition by breast feeding of ovulation and hence of menstrual bleeding—not only plays an important role in natural child spacing, but its absence clearly also must have some more subtle effects on modern woman. The reduction in long-term breast feeding has happened so quickly that no evolutionary adaptation could possibly have compensated for it as yet. The consequences are illustrated dramatically by Short's comparison of a woman of the African !Kung hunter-gatherers with a woman from a typical developed country. During her reproductive life span, Short notes, the average !Kung woman will experience 15 years of lactational amenorrhea, four years of pregnancy, and *a total of only about 48 menstrual cycles.* Contrast this with the reproductive life span of the average modern woman: because she begins to menstruate earlier, goes through menopause later, has fewer pregnancies, and does not breast feed, she may menstruate for 35 years, with a total of approximately 420 menstrual cycles—*372 more* than her primitive African sister!

Short's conclusion in his 1976 Royal Society article is not only thought-provoking but staggering:

> An increased number of menstrual cycles is the inevitable consequence of any form of contraception that interferes with fertility after ovulation, be it a male-oriented method, like the condom, or a female-oriented method, like the intrauterine device. It is curious that even with the one really effective form of contraception that acts before ovulation, the combined contraceptive pill, we have still chosen to mimic the monthly menstrual rhythm, in the belief that it is more "normal" than amenorrhoea, and hence more acceptable. More acceptable it may be, but more "normal" it certainly is not. Perhaps the ingrained gynaecological prejudices of Western medicine have unwittingly dictated the development of forms of contraception that are ill-adapted to the past experience or future needs of the developing world. And even in our own society, there is growing evidence that women would welcome a form of contraception that produced amenorrhoea.

As a result of his conclusion "that women would welcome a form of contraception that produced amenorrhoea," Short and his collaborators in 1976 offered on an experimental basis a "tri-cycle pill regimen" to a group of Scottish women. The women menstruated only every third month. No pregnancies occurred, but the usual side effects of monthly oral contraceptive regimens, such as weight gain and occasional headaches, were present. The great majority of the women welcomed the reduction of menstrual periods, but most of the women and their attending physicians were concerned about the possibility of undetected pregnancies during the three-month intervals.

Though there is nothing magic or even "natural" about a monthly menstrual period, its periodicity is the greatest assurance a woman has that she is not pregnant. Thus, to be widely accepted, a contraceptive regimen that reduces monthly menstrual periods to trimonthly or possibly even semiannual occurrences should probably be accompanied by a simple pregnancy test to offer reassurance to both the woman and her physician.

Condoms

With the exception of coitus interruptus, condoms are the only currently available method of reversible fertility control for men. They are still used very widely—by some 15 to 20 million males—though their relative importance has shrunk considerably over the last ten years owing to the popularity of the Pill. (In 1968 worldwide condom and oral contraceptive use was estimated to be identical—18 million each; today use of the Pill is three times that of the condom.) One of the greatest perceived advantages of the Pill is its total independence from coitus; the condom, on the other hand, is the birth control method most directly related to intercourse.

The use of a condom prototype was first documented in the sixteenth century when the Italian anatomist Gabrielle Fallopio (after whom the Fallopian tubes are named) recommended a linen sheath as a prophylactic against syphilis: "I tried the experiment on eleven hundred men, and I call immortal God to witness that not one of them was infected." By the late nineteenth century, condoms (known as "French letters" in England, presumably because they were washed up on the beaches from France) were used widely in Europe.

An interesting and little-known historical gem is that Marie Stopes—one of the most enthusiastic proponents of birth control in England during the early part of this century—strongly disapproved of the condom because of its presumed detrimental effect *upon the woman!* In her book *Contraception* (1923) she wrote that "women absorb from the seminal fluid of the man some substance, 'hormone,' 'vitamine' or stimulant which affects their internal economy in such a way as to benefit and nourish their whole system." It obviously never occurred to her that if semen were so healthy for women, fellatio alternating with condom use would be the ideal prescription. Nevertheless, even Dr. Stopes saw some occasional benefit in the condom:

> When asked, as I frequently am, what course should be pursued by a young couple with good reasons to take contraceptive measures on the bridal night I generally recommend that for the first few weeks of marriage the man should use the ordinary condom or sheath. This has a double advantage because it not infrequently happens, particularly with men who have lived honourable lives, that at first the man may be inexperienced and hence a little clumsy and thus fail in the proper placement of the ejaculate. The use of the sheath prevents accidents which, unless guarded against, cause such revulsion on the part of the bride that the effect may be life-long and ineradicable.

At present, approximately 75 percent of all condoms (outside of the People's Republic of China) are manufactured in Japan and the United States, which divide the market approximately equally. But American condoms are used primarily within the U.S. (if one excludes condoms purchased for use in government-sponsored projects abroad under the aegis of the Agency for International Development). Japanese condoms are more popular abroad because they are thinner than their American counterparts and are available in imaginative shapes (e.g., the "Japanese Pagoda"). The Japanese have always been much more interested in condom use; colored condoms, for instance, were introduced in Japan long before American manufacturers followed suit. The use of condoms in Japan alone is equal to that in all of Western Europe, even though the latter has 50 percent more people. Japanese usage is also equal to American usage even though our population is double theirs. Certainly much of the condom's popularity in Japan is attributable to innovative marketing and materials, but it is also related to the fact that abortion plays a very important role in contraceptive practice in Japan and that *officially* the Pill is still not approved there.

The use of condoms in the U.S. and elsewhere could no doubt

increase, but if this is to be achieved it will depend not only on creative marketing approaches but on the selection of logical target populations to which these approaches are directed. For instance, although condom use in Arab countries is minimal, this is largely attributable to cultural factors, and Arab men would not be a particularly receptive target population for condom marketing efforts; they are, generally speaking, simply not interested in taking responsibility for fertility control. The same can also be said of men in many Latin American countries, including Mexico. In other lesser-developed countries, however, condoms are used relatively widely. Thus, in 1979 AID will distribute approximately 200 million condoms, of which 82 million will go to Bangladesh, 15 million to Haiti, and 4 million to Ghana—to cite just three examples from three different continents.

In the United States and Western European countries, increased use of condoms can certainly be achieved, and for certain segments of the population this could have important beneficial effects. The condom is one contraceptive method that could have an early and important impact on the sexually active teenage population—which is sorely in need of simple, nonsystemic contraceptives requiring no medical participation or advice. Condom use may even accustom some males—during the most impressionable period of their lives— to bearing part of the contraceptive responsibility.

Although it is surely appropriate for women to give men advice in this regard since the reverse has been true for so long, I doubt whether greatly increased condom acceptance will occur as a result of proposals like the ones that follow. Valerie Jorgensen, for instance, in discussing adolescent contraception at a symposium organized by the Women's Center at the University of California, recommended: "The condom is one of the safest methods of contraception for the female. . . . Adolescent males commonly believe that the condom causes a back up of the semen and sperm and may impair their fertility. Express firmly that this is not so! If they insist on proving this to themselves, encourage them to plan trials without the condom during the menses!" [exclamation point mine].

Barbara Seaman, author of *The Doctors' Case Against the Pill* (1969) and *Free and Female* (1972), at the March 9, 1978, hearings of the House Select Committee on Population suggested:

> We also think—and I'm sorry, gentlemen, if this disturbs any of your egos—that condoms should be marketed in three sizes, because the failures tend to occur at the extreme ends of the scale. In men who are petite, they fall off, and in

men who are extra well endowed, they burst. Women buy brassieres in A, B, and C cups and pantyhose in different sizes, and I think if it would help condom efficacy, that we should package them in different sizes and maybe label them like olives: jumbo, colossal, and supercolossal so that men don't have to go in and ask for the small.

I am not certain to what extent different sizes of the type recommended by Ms. Seaman will increase condom usage, but she clearly has a case with respect to absurdly rigid condom standards in the U.S. The FDA's condom requirements essentially guarantee condoms free from minor defects, but as a result lead to the manufacture of the thickest condoms produced *anywhere in the world.* That this is counterproductive should be obvious to any man who has ever refused to use a condom because of reduced sensation. In 1966 an interesting calculation was made which showed that if the FDA's standards were relaxed to permit an increase of *one* percentage point in pinhole incidence—thus permitting manufacturers to make condoms only half as thick—the increased risk in pregnancy would be equivalent to *one per 2.5 million to 5 million instances of coitus.*

Even the regulations with respect to condom length are amusingly rigid and involve no international coordination. From a 1972 review in *Family Planning Perspectives* one learns the intriguing information that "the shortest permissible teat-ended condom in the American standard is at least 1 cm. longer than the longest permissible Hungarian teat-ended condom." In other words, U.S. condoms would be illegally long in Hungary!

What we ought to concentrate on is enhancing the acceptability of condoms and overcoming their bad press—their "undercover" aspects that until recently prohibited any type of advertisement, and the continuing emphasis on the negative, namely the prevention of venereal disease and pregnancy. Condoms are not part of dinner conversation, in contrast to the Pill, which made contraception an acceptable social conversational topic. And though *Playboy* and similar magazines now carry condom advertisements, you will not find them in the *New York Times.* What is wrong with having condoms advertised in a serious manner in places like the sports section of newspapers? What is wrong with having condom dispensers available in all restrooms of gas stations and in high school gyms? Are anybody's sexual mores really going to be contaminated by such availability or advertising? If some readers of newspaper sports sections have never heard of condoms, then it is high time that they learn about them.

The key way to increase the use of condoms is to emphasize their possible relation to sexual pleasure rather than to venereal disease or contraception—a fact the Japanese began to recognize some time ago. This may not be easy to do, yet the remarkable acceptance of colored condoms indicates that they are not necessarily used in pitch-black darkness under blankets. It is interesting in this regard that in the early 1970s, when colored condoms were first widely distributed, a survey indicated specific color preferences in different population groups (for example, black condoms are more popular in Sweden and white ones in Kenya).

Marketing approaches should take advantage of sexual fantasies. Some of the recent American promotional literature, though somewhat suggestive, seems to me a step in the right direction, at least as far as the teenage and more "swinging" portions of the male population are concerned, which incidentally are precisely the groups with the highest incidence of venereal disease. An advertisement for one American colored condom, for instance, states: "Color is a powerful sexual stimulus. In ancient civilizations experienced women excited their partners by painting their vulvas in the lush colors of the natural surroundings. Tahiti lets you excite your partner with condoms that are Morning Blue, Sunset Gold . . . etc." Calling the condom colors "Dawn Pink," "Siesta Green," "Midnight Black," or "Black Cat for the Bold" is by no means as tasteless as many of the advertisements for other items we see every day in magazines and on television.

The woman partner is not ignored in such promotional literature, as can be seen from one advertisement that begins "It's like hundreds of tiny fingers urging a woman to let go" (promoting recently introduced American condoms with patterned ribs, something that the Japanese introduced years ago). The advertisement continues, "Now you can reach a level of sexual pleasure that only months ago was unheard of. A condom delicately ribbed to give a woman gentle, urging sensations. Yet, with a shape and thinness that let a man feel like he's wearing nothing at all." In my opinion, extending the use of condoms would be societally so beneficial that I advocate relaxing restrictions that apply to condom promotion at least to the level of that permitted for deodorants or brassieres.

Diaphragms

The diaphragm is the contraceptive hardware item with the least potential for technical improvement because any "failure" with this device is largely attributable to improper size, faulty insertion, or lack of motivation to use it. Although not quite as coitally related as a condom since a woman can insert the diaphragm hours before intercourse, it is difficult to visualize how one could increase the diaphragm's acceptability by associating its use with aspects of sexual foreplay, as has been suggested with the condom. Yet, even here one may be surprised; when I made this point to a woman panel member at a TV roundtable discussion in Canada, she retorted that her male companion invariably inserted her diaphragm.

The diaphragm is unlikely ever to become a very significant method of fertility control in lesser-developed countries, especially where women have very little privacy, no bathroom, no running water, and often no place even to store the diaphragm. Furthermore, one cannot overlook the many cultural barriers that exist in societies where women are not supposed to handle their genitalia or where contraceptive protection has to be hidden from the man. Still, the diaphragm has enjoyed a certain amount of renewed popularity recently among a select middle-class group of women, a group I would characterize, only partly facetiously, as one frequenting organic food stores rather than supermarkets. I do wish to emphasize that on safety grounds the diaphragm is clearly the best female contraceptive and for those women motivated and able to use it properly, it should get a very high rating.

Intrauterine Devices

The modern history of IUDs is interesting. I emphasize "modern" because in ancient times pebbles were inserted in camels' vaginas during long caravans as a means of contraception and the writings of Hippocrates mention introduction of foreign bodies into the female genitalia. The use of IUDs in their present form started in the late 1920s and early 1930s when Ernst Gräfenberg in Germany and shortly thereafter T. Ota in Japan introduced the use of metal (e.g., silver) rings inserted into the uterus as a means of contraception. Even though they reported good contraceptive protection in several thousand patients, the method was not accepted by the medical profession because of fear of uterine injury and pelvic infection.

However, in 1959 when W. Oppenheimer in Israel and Atsumi Ishihama in Japan reported on satisfactory long-term use with IUDs, they received a much more sympathetic hearing. The advent of oral contraceptives in the early 1960s gave birth control devices a degree of scientific and even social respectability that they had not previously enjoyed. Concern about the "population explosion" became an everyday topic, and in theory the IUD appeared to be the ideal answer to fertility control in the Third World. (Many people believed then that oral contraceptives—partly because of cost and partly because of the need for daily pill taking—were unsuitable for semiliterate or illiterate women. No one imagined that in the year 1979 a monthly-cycle preparation sold to AID would cost 15¢.)

Until the middle 1970s medical devices did not fall within the control of the FDA, and therefore IUDs could be introduced almost with impunity. A wide variety of materials, initially metal but subsequently primarily plastic, was examined, and at least 25 differently shaped IUDs have been tested or introduced on the market. Their names range from the confidence-instilling "Silent Protector" (Indonesia) and the charming "Flower of Canton" (China), to "Massouras Duck's Foot" and the "Lippes Loop," which in the late 1960s and early 1970s became the most widely used IUD.

A problem with research in the IUD field is that, because animal models are not comparable, almost all IUD research must involve human females. Now that medical devices such as IUDs are monitored (both for safety and efficacy) by the FDA—appropriately so in my opinion—the development time for IUD improvements has clearly lengthened by several years.

Proper placement of the IUD within the uterine cavity is extraordinarily important; it has a direct bearing on the contraceptive efficacy of the device, which is somewhat inferior to the Pill but nevertheless very high. Therefore, the ease with which an IUD can be correctly inserted, along with the experience of the medical or paramedical personnel performing this operation, is crucial. Research has concentrated on developing shapes and materials that are less likely to be expelled or cause perforation or excessive bleeding. In particular, advances in design have been made so that IUDs can now be inserted in women who have never delivered a child, and a great deal of work is under way to develop IUDs that could be inserted immediately after a woman delivers a child or has an abortion. Clearly these are two times when a woman might be most receptive to contraceptive advice. And, especially in developing nations, they may be the only times that she visits a hospital or clinic.

Research during the last ten years has led to the introduction into clinical practice of two types of "medicated" IUDs—that is, IUDs whose effectiveness is caused not just by the foreign body reaction in the uterus but also by the release of a chemical. The first one was the copper IUD, developed by Dr. Jaime Zipper in Chile, who found that winding fine copper wire around the IUD increased its efficacy. The so-called Copper-T and Copper Seven are simply plastic T-shaped and 7-shaped IUDs with fine copper wire wound around them. Much more complicated and sophisticated in design is the "Progestasert," a plastic T-shaped device consisting of a very carefully engineered membrane that permits the daily release of minute amounts of progesterone (a natural female sex hormone) contained in it. The amount of progesterone released daily is probably insufficient to enter the general circulation; it acts primarily on the uterine lining. The principal difficulty with this device is that it needs to be removed every year, although work is now under way to develop an IUD that could contain a three-year progesterone supply.

At least 15 million women throughout the world use IUDs. The WHO is currently conducting a series of multicenter trials with several different IUDs in order to assess their comparative efficacy, acceptability, and, especially, incidence of side effects. The most common side effect of the IUD is excessive bleeding, but spontaneous expulsion (particularly when not detected by the user), perforation of the uterine wall, and infection are also of concern, as are serious side effects such as pelvic inflammation and ectopic pregnancy (pregnancy outside the uterus), which is relatively rare. Among these side effects, increased blood loss may be particularly significant in lesser-developed countries, where there is a higher incidence of anemic and malnourished women—in whom the consequences of excessive bleeding are more severe.

All of these side effects must be studied in large-scale clinical trials involving humans since, as indicated earlier, there are no comparable animal models. Extensive research in this field will continue for several years before a consensus can be reached as to which of the various IUD shapes is preferable and whether medicated or unmedicated IUDs eventually become the items of choice. For instance, copper IUDs appear to increase blood loss, whereas IUDs medicated with progestational hormones of the type present in the Pill may reduce increased blood loss by as much as 80 percent.

Sterilization

The most significant trend in human fertility control that has been observed in recent years has been the worldwide increase in sterilization. For anatomical reasons, sterilization is clearly easier in men, since vasectomy involves a very minor operation outside the body wall that can be performed quickly and painlessly using simple local anesthesia. Tubal ligation (severing and tying of the Fallopian tubes) in women is more complicated, and hysterectomy (removal of the uterus) is not recommended for contraceptive purposes, though there has been an explosion in elective hysterectomies among affluent women in the United States.

An analysis of sterilization practice by sex shows interesting trends. In the United States among the white population, sterilization is almost equally divided between males and females, whereas among blacks the ratio is at least ten to one in favor of women. Similarly, in many Latin populations, for instance, in Puerto Rico (where female sterilization is frequently referred to as "la operación") men hardly undergo sterilization at all. In China, where sterilization has rapidly increased, no segregation between sexes is indicated in any of the statistics, but from my personal inquiries at various meetings in 1973 in China I had the distinct impression that sterilization was predominantly occurring among women.

The topics of simpler female sterilization, notably by nonsurgical means, and of reversibility of vasectomy and tubal ligation will be discussed in later chapters in the context of future research. Clearly the stability of marriage and the age of the individual play an enormous role in determining a person's attitude toward sterilization, particularly among younger people. In countries where the divorce rate is high, even middle-aged parents are probably more reluctant to undergo sterilization, which at this stage should be considered irreversible (especially in males). This is less true in countries where the divorce rate is minimal (for example, China). An assured method of reversal of vasectomy could have an enormous impact in the field of male contraception and might significantly shift the burden of responsible family planning to the male.

Abortion

In 1966 the Chilean demographer M.B. Requena, in attempting to explain the high incidence of abortion in Chile, constructed a qualitative picture in which he related fertility control to the socioeconomic-cultural level of that population (see Fig. 2-1). The poorest, least educated, and economically most disadvantaged persons have the highest uncontrolled fertility (stage 1); as one moves up the socioeconomic-cultural scale, births decline until, presumably, optimum family planning is achieved.

Requena made the important point that fertility control is accomplished first by induced abortion (stage 2) and that the incidence of effective contraception increases gradually and finally surpasses that of abortion only when the population has reached the highest socioeconomic-cultural level (stage 3). This picture is obviously only a qualitative one since the extent of such abortion, which is likely to be largely self-induced and illegal, would hardly be accurately reported.

Nevertheless, there is some real justification for assuming that this

FIGURE 2-1

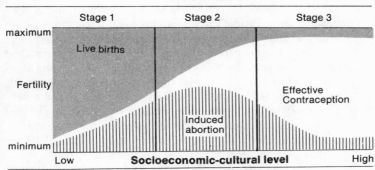

SOURCE: M. B. Requena. *Revista Medica de Chile,* vol. 94, 1966, p. 714.

picture is generally correct for most countries, notably lesser-developed ones. When a population is first exposed to medicine it turns to *curative* medication for a disease already incurred before it accepts the more sophisticated concept of *preventive* medication for a disease that it may never get. The same generalization applies to fertility control, with the "disease" being equated to an unwanted pregnancy. Here, the only "cure" is abortion. It is not surprising then that at the lower socioeconomic-cultural levels (stages 1 and 2), where populations have not generally been exposed to preventive medicine, curative birth control is implemented first, and this accounts for the high incidence of abortion. Indeed, after the Pill and prolonged lactation, abortion is the most widely practiced form of birth control in the world today. And of all available fertility control methods, abortion is the only one that might be called curative; other methods fall into the preventive category.

At times special factors may enter that create exceptions to Requena's model. For instance, Japan clearly falls into the category of a population high on the socioeconomic-cultural scale (stage 3), yet the incidence of abortion has been very high (as in stage 2). Why? After World War II the government instituted a deliberate policy to control Japan's population, which was achieved primarily through legal abortion conducted by the private medical sector. Similarly, a number of Eastern European socialist countries, though relatively high on the socioeconomic-cultural scale (stage 3), also can be placed into Requena's stage 2 abortion rate. In these countries, the high abortion rate is the result of the relative unavailability of contraceptives or sterilization because of pronatalist policies of the state.

The Eastern European socialist countries had the highest abortion rate in the world until 1974, when their record was surpassed by that of Cuba—the only socialist country in the Western hemisphere. With the exception of the People's Republic of China, a communist state and a high incidence of abortion seem to go hand in hand.

Until 1966, Rumania had the dubious distinction of reporting the largest number of legal abortions in any country—nearly four abortions for each live birth. In that year, the Rumanian government, concerned about the rapidly falling birth rate, introduced a very restrictive abortion law, whereupon births skyrocketed by 150 percent in one year. Ever since that time, however, the birth rate in Rumania has declined. The Rumanian population required only about a year to adjust to the changed circumstances; they quickly shifted to other means of birth control and to illegal abortions. Because the latter carry with them a much higher mortality rate, one could have predicted that the maternal mortality associated with abortion would increase in Rumania. It did. Fig. 2-2 demonstrates graphically the tragic rise of abortion-related deaths that began one year after the restrictive abortion law was introduced. American antiabortion groups would be well advised to register this reality.

FIGURE 2-2

Birth rate per 1000 population and number of deaths from abortion, Rumania, 1961-1972

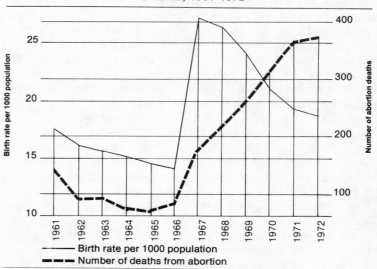

SOURCE: *World Health Statistics Annual* for the years concerned.

In an important review in 1977 of the global incidence of legal abortion, Dr. Christopher Tietze of the Population Council presented a number of interesting analyses that illustrate how abortion is used for different purposes and under different circumstances in various countries. I cite a few here to indicate some of the patterns that emerge which relate to a country's political system and its level of economic development.

In the U.S., Canada, and Sweden, for instance, abortion is primarily practiced by the unmarried; by contrast, in India, where abortion was only recently legalized under certain restricted conditions, and in the Eastern European countries, it is primarily married women who turn to abortion (see Table 2-2). When the distribution of legal abortion is analyzed in terms of the number of children of the mother, one again sees the same pattern (see Table 2-3). American,

TABLE 2-2

% Distribution of Legal Abortions by Marital Status (1975)

Country	Married	Not Married (or Previously Married)
Canada	32.3	67.7
Czechoslovakia	76.0	24.0
England	40.6	59.4
Hungary	69.6	30.4
India	92.8	7.2
Sweden	35.8	64.2
USA	27.4	72.6

TABLE 2-3

% Distribution of Legal Abortions by Parity (1975)

Country	Parity 0	1	2	3	4	5-	Total Number of Abortions	Abortion Rate/1000 Women Age 15-44
Canada	58.5	14.6	14.8	7.1	2.9	2.1	49,300	9.5
Czech.	15.5	17.0	41.4	17.8	5.0	3.3	81,700	25.9
England	49.0	12.2	18.7	11.5	5.2	3.4	140,500	N.A.
Hungary	24.2	21.9	35.1	11.8	— 7.0—		96,200	41.9
India	11.1	13.6	22.4	20.9	—32.0—		97,700	0.8
Sweden	40.0	18.7	23.6	11.8	4.0	1.9	32,500	20.3
Tunisia	4.3	8.8	12.0	13.3	13.8	47.8	16,000	13.9
USA	47.1	20.2	15.5	8.7	4.3	4.2	854,900	18.1

SOURCE (both Tables): C. Tietze. "Induced Abortion: 1977 Supplement." *Reports on Population/Family Planning*, no. 14, December 1977.

Canadian, and Swedish women who resort to abortion predominantly have no children or one child; in Czechoslovakia and Hungary the highest incidence of abortion occurs among women with two children. In Tunisia, where 48 percent of the women having an abortion have five or more children, abortion is clearly an act of desperation, resorted to in the absence of other alternatives. Finally, when the breakdown of legal abortion is made by age (see Table 2-4), we notice that the bulk of the women in the U.S., Canada, and Sweden are under 24; whereas in Czechoslovakia and Hungary appreciable proportions of the women are between the ages of 30 and 39. The first column of Table 2-4—the incidence of abortion among women under age 19—leads to another conclusion, namely, that premarital sex begins earlier in the U.S. and Western Europe than in Eastern Europe, Japan, or a typical Moslem country (i.e., Tunisia).

TABLE 2-4

% Distribution of Legal Abortions by Age of Woman (1975)

Country	-19	20-24	25-29	30-34	35-39	40-
Canada	31.3	29.1	19.5	10.6	6.5	3.0
Czechoslovakia	7.6	23.7	28.3	21.5	13.5	5.4
England	26.5	24.4	19.2	14.3	10.5	5.1
GDR (E. Germany)	12.7	21.8	17.7	22.2	18.9	6.7
Hungary	10.7	23.5	21.0	19.7	17.0	8.1
Japan	1.8	16.6	27.5	26.4	18.4	9.3
Sweden	23.8	22.9	21.2	16.1	10.5	5.5
Tunisia	1.6	14.9	24.5	24.2	23.0	11.8
USA	33.1	31.9	18.3	9.7	5.0	2.0

SOURCE: C. Tietze. "Induced Abortion: 1977 Supplement." *Reports on Population/Family Planning*, no. 14, December 1977.

In sum, in affluent Western countries abortion is generally used by young, unmarried women who have not yet started to use contraceptives but who clearly switch to contraceptives as they mature and/or marry. In socialist countries, with the exception of the People's Republic of China, abortion still appears to be the chief method of fertility control.

Abortion Procedures

In terms of maternal mortality, abortion early in pregnancy in a proper medical setting is quite safe and the incidence of death very low. The mortality rate rises quickly as the length of gestation prior to abortion increases (see Fig. 2-3). Unquestionably, if a woman is going to have an abortion she should do so in the first trimester or early in the second trimester. Restrictive legislation or the need for illegal abortion often leads to delays that bring a woman into the more dangerous period of late second-trimester pregnancy before the abortion is actually performed.

FIGURE 2-3

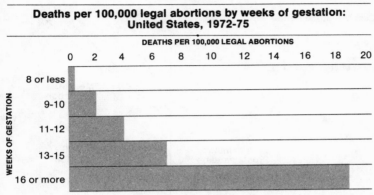

Deaths per 100,000 legal abortions by weeks of gestation: United States, 1972-75

SOURCE: C. Tietze. "Induced Abortion; 1977 Supplement." *Reports on Population / Family Planning*, no. 14, 1977.

With this in mind, let us look at the types of abortion procedures that are employed at various stages of pregnancy (Fig. 2-4, page 28). Until the late 1960s, by far the most common abortion method was dilatation and curettage (D & C), scraping of the uterine wall. Today this method has been largely superseded by vacuum or suction evacuation, which during the first trimester is the safest abortion method. Originally introduced in the Soviet Union and improved in the late 1950s in China, the suction method has been used in the West only during the last 15 years.

A more recent procedure, menstrual extraction (or menstrual regulation), is a variation of the suction method that is carried out within 14 days of the missed menses. Frequently performed without anesthesia, menstrual extraction is an outpatient procedure that takes only a few minutes and has a postoperative recovery time of less than an hour. It can be performed with a simple hand syringe. Though it is frequently done without a pregnancy test (especially in developing countries), this is definitely undesirable since less than 10 percent of missed menses are due to pregnancy. As newer and more accurate pregnancy tests are introduced (those currently available are already reliable within one week of fertilization, that is, before

FIGURE 2-4

Abortion Procedures Used During 24 Weeks of Pregnancy

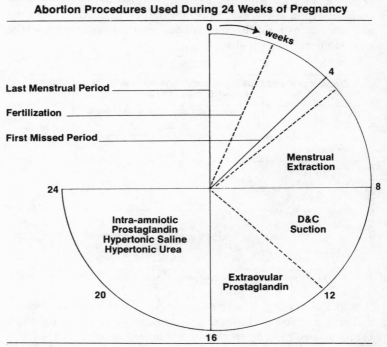

Reprinted with permission from L. S. Burnett et al. "An Evaluation of Abortion: Techniques and Protocols." *Hospital Practice*, X:8, August 1975.

the first missed menstrual period), menstrual extraction should be performed only after a positive pregnancy test is obtained.

Second-trimester abortion requires hospitalization and until fairly recently was performed by injecting into the amniotic fluid a hypertonic solution of salt or urea, which kills the fetus and eventually leads to its expulsion. The potential side effects of this procedure are sufficiently serious that Japan, the country that first utilized abortion as a countrywide fertility control method, for all practical purposes has discontinued use of this method in second-trimester abortion.

Prostaglandins, initially discovered in Sweden by Sune Bergström, are naturally occurring compounds related to the fatty acids and, because of their wide-ranging biological properties, comprise one of the most exciting areas of biomedical research today. They may be employed during the later stages of the first trimester as well as during the second trimester to terminate pregnancy. Prostaglandins are not orally active and therefore have to be administered intravaginally or by intravenous or intraamniotic instillation to stimulate contraction of the uterus and thereby bring about expulsion of the fetus. Both natural and synthetic prostaglandins can be used to terminate pregnancy, and though for early abortion they offer no particular advantage over the standard suction procedures, they are becoming the method of choice for second-trimester abortion because of their greater safety.

Facing Reality

The incidence of abortion worldwide is still increasing, because on a global scale we are at best at Requena's stage 2. The ultimate aim is, of course, to reduce induced abortions to a minimum, but there will be great variations in the mix of birth control approaches needed to achieve this goal in countries that currently rely on abortion as the primary means of fertility control. In the meanwhile, it is essential to study carefully the various consequences of abortion, both psychological and physiological. Concurrent abortion and sterilization is receiving more and more attention, with respect both to the safety of performing the two procedures together (as opposed to performing the abortion first and sterilization at a subsequent time) and to the woman's mental state at the time of the abortion (when she might agree to a sterilization that she would later regret).

The most important consequence of abortion, which can only be studied with large groups of women in countries where abortion is legal and practiced widely, is the long-term risk that follows the procedure, especially repeated abortion. Here I am referring to the adverse effects of abortion on subsequent pregnancies—including premature birth, low birth weight, and increased incidence of spontaneous abortion—which are related to the age at which the woman has an abortion (consequences are more serious in older women) and even to the method used. Preliminary indications suggest, for instance, that an early second-trimester prostaglandin-induced abortion may have fewer side effects in terms of subsequent normal births than a first-trimester vacuum aspiration.

Contraception is clearly preferable to abortion, just as prevention of a disease is obviously preferable to a subsequent cure. However, the lack of prevention of many diseases does not restrict scientists from working on cures; similarly, the lack of "perfect" contraceptives should not prevent scientists from working on improved abortion procedures. Over the short and the medium term, the availability of induced abortion, be it surgical or chemical, is likely to be a crucial component of any fertility control program; consequently, much greater financial and technical resources should be allocated to improvements in this field.

No degree of moral outcry or restrictive legislation—usually by male rather than female legislators—will change the fact that abortion is practiced widely. When 8 percent of the world's fertile women have abortions in a given year, irrespective of religion, economic status, or location, unfilled contraceptive needs obviously exist. Legislating abortion out of existence without offering suitable alternatives will not make abortion disappear. The experience of Rumania provides a vivid example. If governments wish to increase the birth rate, as is the case in several Eastern European countries, this can be achieved only through appeals to nationalism or by means of financial or material incentives.

The perseverance of a highly motivated and frequently desperate woman seeking termination of an unwanted pregnancy crosses all socioeconomic and developmental levels, and her ingenuity far surpasses that of legislatures and law enforcement bodies. Similarly, once a population has reached the stage of motivation where birth control is practiced freely, no degree of repressive legislation will lead to significant long-term increases in the birth rate.

Of all the birth control methods listed at the beginning of this chapter, only oral contraceptives have not been discussed. Since they are currently the most widely used item of contraceptive hardware and involve the most complex array of software components—social, political, and ethical—I have devoted a separate chapter, which follows, to the Pill.

Kneeling pregnant woman. Nayarit, classic, *ca.* A.D. 100–400.

Worried woman. Nayarit, classic, *ca.* A.D. 100–400.

3

The Pill: Use and Concerns

IN A PERIOD OF LESS THAN 20 YEARS the Pill has become the most significant hardware component of man's contraceptive armamentarium. According to recent estimates from the World Health Organization, somewhere between 50 and 80 million women are currently using steroid oral contraceptives. Even though the use of the Pill is unequally distributed throughout the world and depends on many factors, affluence is no longer a key one: the cost of oral contraceptives in large government projects has now been reduced to approximately 15¢ per woman per month (as compared to $3 to $4 when bought with a doctor's prescription in a U.S. drugstore).

Most merchants realize that bargain prices alone are not enough. One must also bring the customers to the store, and convince them to buy. The situation is not very different in birth control. It is the cost of the educational and delivery components, including the paramedical and/or public health aspects, as well as the sociocultural factors—in other words, the software—that plays the crucial role in determining the acceptance and use of the Pill. Therefore it is worth looking at a few countries to examine how use of the Pill compares with that of other contraceptive methods.

Pill Consumption

In the United States, consumption of the Pill has essentially stabilized at approximately ten million women, which accounts for nearly half of all couples practicing birth control in the U.S. Of the remaining couples who use contraceptives, about half use condoms or IUDs, and the rest employ another half-dozen methods as outlined in detail in Table 3-1. This table also outlines the trends in contraceptive usage by different age groups in the U.S. in 1973 and 1976. Particularly noteworthy are the increase in sterile persons from 24 percent in 1973 to 30 percent in 1976 and the decrease in contraceptive users from 53 percent to 49 percent during that same time. Within the latter group, the Pill is still the overriding contraceptive favorite. Its highest use (43 percent) occurs among the youngest women (between the ages of 15 and 24), whereas its lowest use (8 percent) occurs among women between the ages of 35 and 44— understandably so, since the risk of cardiovascular side effects, especially among smokers, is greatest for women of that age group or older.

TABLE 3-1

Percentage distribution of currently married U.S. women, aged 15-44, by contraceptive status

CONTRACEPTIVE STATUS	Ages 15-44 1973	Ages 15-44 1976	Ages 15-24 1976	Ages 25-34 1976	Ages 35-44 1976
Number	26,646,000	27,185,000	5,941,000	12,014,000	9,230,000
Total	100.0%	100.0%	100.0%	100.0%	100.0%
STERILE	23.8	30.2	4.3	27.7	50.2
Intrinsic	0.9	1.9	0.4	1.5	3.3
Surgical	22.9	28.3	3.9	26.2	46.9
Noncontraceptive	6.5	9.0	0.4	6.3	18.0
—Female (e.g., hysterectomy)	6.3	8.2	0.4	5.5	16.8
—Male	0.2	0.8	—	0.8	1.2
Contraceptive	16.4	19.3	3.5	19.8	28.9
—Female (tubal ligation)	8.6	9.6	2.5	10.6	13.0
—Male (vasectomy)	7.8	9.7	1.0	9.2	15.9
FERTILE	76.1	69.8	95.7	72.3	49.9
Noncontraceptors	22.9	21.1	31.1	21.1	14.6
Pregnant, postpartum	7.3	6.9	14.9	7.4	1.1
Seeking pregnancy	7.0	6.5	10.4	8.1	2.0
Other nonusers	8.7	7.7	5.9	5.7	11.5
Contraceptors	53.2	48.6	64.5	51.2	35.2
Pill	25.1	22.3	42.9	23.3	7.9
IUD	6.7	6.1	6.2	7.2	4.6
Diaphragm	2.4	2.9	2.5	3.1	2.9
Condom	9.4	7.2	4.9	7.5	8.3
Foam	3.5	3.0	2.9	3.2	2.9
Rhythm	2.8	3.4	2.5	3.1	4.3
Withdrawal	1.5	2.0	1.6	2.0	2.4
Douche	0.5	0.7	0.3	0.6	1.2
Other	1.3	0.9	0.6	1.2	0.7

SOURCE: Modified from K. Ford. "Contraceptive Use in the United States 1973-1976." *Family Planning Perspectives*, vol. 10, no. 5, 1978, p. 264.

Using the United States as a reference point for a typical highly developed country, let us turn now to a few lesser-developed coun-tries. In Mexico, for instance, 85 percent of all contraception is divided almost equally between just two hardware items, namely, the Pill (44 percent) and IUDs (41 percent). Singapore, a ministate that is undergoing rapid development, also depends chiefly on two methods, the condom and the Pill (of those people who began contraceptive use there in 1977, 52 percent chose the condom and 46 percent the Pill). In Indonesia, which has an aggressive birth control program and the fifth largest population in the world, Pill use pre-dominates (71 percent), followed by the IUD (17 percent), and the condom (9 percent). And in Thailand Pill consumption predomi-nates (59 percent), followed by sterilization (15 percent—nearly all among females); interestingly, use of injectable steroid contracep-tives (8 percent) essentially equals that of IUDs (9 percent) and condoms (8 percent).

I do not cite these figures to suggest that the Pill is the final answer to world population problems or indeed that it is universally ac-cepted. For instance, in Nigeria, the most populous nation in Africa and one of the most rapidly growing, Pill and IUD use is negligible (5.4 and 1.5 percent, respectively), as is use of other modern birth control methods (1.9 percent). However, demographics of Pill con-sumption do show that statements that the Pill is useful only for highly affluent, highly educated women are utter nonsense.

The Pill plays an ever-increasing role in family planning programs around the world, including programs in countries that do not have an elaborate medical care system. No prescription is required for oral contraceptives in Bangladesh or Pakistan, to cite just two examples, and in other countries, such as the Philippines and Sri Lanka, paramedical personnel are permitted to dispense oral contraceptives. In 1975 the Birth Control Trust in Britain urged that the Pill be taken off prescription because even though there are measurable risks associated with the Pill's use, "The important thing is to appreciate that unpredictable side effects are not made more common or less common by the system of distribution. Since nobody can predict such side effects, the expensive diagnostic skills of doctors are being wasted for this purpose."

Compare this with the statement of Dr. Herbert Ratner, a vocal opponent of the Pill, who testified as follows in March 1970 at the Nelson hearings in the U.S. Senate on the safety of oral contracep-tives: "The Pill is actually a rich man's contraceptive since it needs so much medical follow-up and routine access to the doctor. Life for the poor is miserable enough without adding to it the miserable and depressing complications associated with the Pill." These are the words of a public health official, and one wonders what would now be the lot of millions of poor women all over the world if his words were actually heeded.

The realization that the Pill can be used without the kind of sophisticated medical system that exists in the U.S. and other highly developed countries has led to an ironic situation with regard to the current *rate* of Pill consumption in the world. In certain highly developed countries such as the U.S., which initially showed a very rapid acceptance of the Pill, the consumption level has stabilized or has even declined slightly. This is the result of the overriding concern about negative side effects, which have received enormous publicity. (I discuss the fallout of such publicity at greater length in Chapter 6.) By contrast, many of the lesser-developed countries, which initially either did not practice contraception or tried other less convenient methods, have started to shift largely or at least partly to the Pill for the sake of convenience and efficacy. They have done so with the understanding that though there are serious side effects, they occur in a very small proportion of the population and are more than offset by the enormous direct and indirect health benefits associated with child spacing and responsible family planning.

The most important contribution that the Pill, together with the various IUDs, has made worldwide is to teach people that reversible contraception can be completely separated from coitus by a method that for the first time permits the woman herself to decide whether and how to control her own fertility.

Safety and the Pill

The Pill's efficacy is no longer a subject of debate since oral contraceptives, if used properly, are widely acknowledged to be the most effective method of reversible fertility control, with the exception of total abstinence. Today the hotly debated issue about the Pill is that of "safety"—presumably meaning the absence of negative side effects—and in many respects this issue cannot be resolved. The demand for a "safe" Pill has no operational meaning because "safe" is not an absolute term. This is well illustrated by the following exchange between Senator Gaylord Nelson of Wisconsin and Dr. Charles C. Edwards, then Commissioner of the FDA, at the March 4, 1970, Senate hearings on the safety of oral contraceptives.

> DR. EDWARDS: . . . our [the FDA's] position is that the oral contraceptives are an effective and safe method of birth control, but as with other potent drugs there are both contraindications and complications.

Women whose history and present medical condition include thromboembolic disorders, impaired liver function, known or suspected cancer of the breast, estrogen dependent tumors, and abnormal bleeding should not take oral contraceptives.

SENATOR NELSON: Doctor, may I ask a question at this point?

DR. EDWARDS: You certainly may.

SENATOR NELSON: On the use of the word "safe" in respect to the oral contraceptives, I think that there is considerable confusion within the medical profession and the public alike as to how the word "safe" was being used . . . [when the FDA agreed to refer to oral contraceptives as] "safe within the intent of the law." . . . Would you mind elaborating on that?

DR. EDWARDS: Certainly. In categorizing this drug as safe, I do not want to imply, by any stretch of the imagination, that this is an innocuous drug. It is a very potent drug, and when arriving at this decision to call it a safe drug we [the FDA] had to utilize the same standards we use for all other drugs.

As you well know, most of the other "safe" drugs, the powerful drugs, have certain contraindications. There are certain dangers in taking any drug, and they have to be taken under the conditions which are stated very clearly in the labeling.

So again, I would like to emphasize that in establishing this classification, we applied the same standards for the oral contraceptives as we have for all other drugs in categorizing them as safe.

SENATOR NELSON: The use in this context, then, was not in the ordinary dictionary use of the word?

DR. EDWARDS: It certainly was not. *It was a Food and Drug Administration description of the word "safe," which really is "safe under the conditions of labeling," and which perhaps is a more accurate definition* [my italics].

In sum, "safe" does not mean safe. If it is not possible to develop a Pill without side effects, let's talk about what these side effects are. Probably no modern drug has been studied as extensively as the steroid oral contraceptives—deservedly so because so many healthy women have taken and are taking this potent medication for long periods of time. (For example, of how many drugs can one make the statement that the amount of wax in one's ear will be reduced upon taking the drug? Yet the single largest study dealing with side effects of the Pill—conducted by the Royal College of General Practitioners in England and involving approximately 46,000 women—reports a significantly lower rate of ear wax.)

Side effects of the Pill can really be divided into two categories. The first is that of so-called minor side effects, including weight gain, nausea, libido changes, and headaches. These may be minor to the clinician or even to most women, but they are nevertheless serious to certain individuals. That what is minor to most becomes major to some is true of all drugs and, for that matter, applies to foods we eat (e.g., almost every food has been shown to cause allergic reactions in some sensitive individuals) and activities we engage in daily (e.g., certain tennis players develop painful "tennis elbow"). Clearly, an individual must make a personal decision whether or not to utilize a particular drug, just as she or he decides whether to eat a particular food or engage in a particular activity.

Within this category of minor side effects, one may also find an entire range of imagined side effects. In an interesting Swiss clinical trial in 1969 in which various oral contraceptive preparations were tested for minor side effects, women were put on oral contraceptive regimens that were changed every six months. To quote the Swiss researchers: "The importance of the psychic influence [on the perception of side effects] is shown by the fact that the incidence of nausea is increased every sixth cycle, when the woman is transferred to another preparation and then obviously loses her confidence in the Pill and/or her doctor. Libido changes are following a similar pattern: whenever the preparation is changed, more women show an increase in libido, fewer women a decrease."

In addition to minor side effects, there are several serious or potentially serious side effects that must be taken into consideration. Cancer is of such overriding importance that I will discuss it separately in the next chapter, but other serious side effects include an increased incidence of various circulatory disorders—abnormal blood clots, strokes, and heart attacks—which seem to be associated with the estrogen component of the combination oral contraceptive pill. To minimize such risks a woman should select a Pill with the lowest possible estrogen content that still provides her acceptable menstrual cycle control. Based on an analysis of vital statistics in Britain, it has generally been accepted that the risk of dying from cardiovascular diseases is increased fourfold among Pill users. A detailed reevaluation of these data, both for the U.S. and 21 other countries, published in 1979, failed to confirm these results and suggests that the risk is considerably smaller than had been assumed originally.

Other significant side effects are an increased risk of gall bladder diseases (which doubles after four to five years of oral contraceptive therapy) and the occurrence of certain metabolic changes, such as a decrease in glucose tolerance, which could be dangerous in diabetic women. Elevated blood pressure, mental depression, worsening of migraine headaches in migraine-prone women, and an increase in birth defects if oral contraceptives are ingested during early pregnancy are some of the other serious, though infrequent, side effects associated with Pill use. The administration of oral contraceptives, as well as of many other drugs, during early pregnancy is definitely unwise, and though oral contraceptives are unlikely to be taken deliberately by pregnant women, accidental ingestion can occur. (In this regard, it is important that a woman use some other method of birth control until she has her menstrual period before beginning to use the Pill.)

America is the most litigious society in the world; it is for this reason that drug manufacturers and regulatory agencies protect themselves by emphasizing the negative. Most package inserts and advertising copy for oral contraceptives are written these days by lawyers. Page 40 shows a recent advertisement that was obviously generated by advertising professionals. It is equally obvious that the reverse side of this advertisement, on page 41, was prepared by lawyers. In fact, *every* oral contraceptive advertisement by *every* American manufacturer now carries similar "fine print," which is nothing other than the fine print of an insurance policy.

Do physicians really read the fine print, and are women helped by this information? Information about such side effects must, of course, be disseminated, but I wonder whether this all-encompassing, virtually undifferentiated list, presented in such a highly unreadable fashion, is a reasonable way to provide a woman with information about contraceptive risks. The basic purpose of such legalistic materials is for the manufacturer to be able to say that the physician was informed of every conceivable side effect. The package insert for oral contraceptives (see Chapter 6, pages 101-3) suffers from these same drawbacks.

Benefits of the Pill

In 1976 Dr. M.P. Vessey and Sir Richard Doll of Oxford Univer-

TIME TESTED

Norinyl® 1+50 21-Day tablets
(norethindrone 1 mg with mestranol 0 05 mg)
Norinyl® 1+50 28-Day tablets
(21 norethindrone 1 mg with mestranol
0 05 mg tablets followed by 7 inert tablets)

ORAL CONTRACEPTIVE (O.C.) AGENTS

INDICATIONS O.C.s are indicated for the prevention of pregnancy. *DOSE-RELATED RISK OF THROMBOEMBOLISM FROM O.C.s.* Studies have shown a positive association between the dose of estrogens in O.C.s and the risk of thromboembolism. For this reason, it is prudent and in keeping with good principles of therapeutics to minimize exposure to estrogen. The O.C. product prescribed for any given patient should be that product which contains the least amount of estrogen that is compatible with an acceptable pregnancy rate and patient acceptance. It is recommended that new acceptors of O.C.s should be started on preparations containing 0 05 mg or less of estrogen.

CONTRAINDICATIONS 1 Known or suspected pregnancy (see Warning No 5) 2 O.C.s should not be used in women who have or have had any of the following conditions a Thrombophlebitis or thromboembolic disorders b Cerebral vascular or coronary artery disease c Markedly impaired liver function d Known or suspected carcinoma of the breast e Known or suspected estrogen dependent neoplasia f Undiagnosed abnormal genital bleeding

WARNINGS: Cigarette smoking increases the risk of serious cardiovascular side effects from O.C.s use. This risk increases with age and with heavy smoking (15 or more cigarettes per day) and is quite marked in women over 35 years of age. Women who use O.C.s should be strongly advised not to smoke.

The use of O.C.s is associated with increased risk of several serious conditions including thromboembolism, stroke, myocardial infarction, liver tumor, gall bladder disease, visual disturbances, fetal abnormalities, and hypertension. Practitioners prescribing O.C.s should be familiar with the following information relating to these risks.

TABLE 2. Smoking habits and other predisposing conditions - risk associated with use of O.C.s

	Age	Below 30	30-39	40+
Heavy smokers			B	A
Light smokers		D	C	B
Nonsmokers				
(No predisposing conditions)		D	C D	C
Nonsmokers				
(other predisposing conditions)		C	C B	B A

A—Use associated with very high risk   C—Use associated with moderate risk
B—Use associated with high risk   D—Use associated with low risk

TABLE 1. The annual number of deaths associated with control of fertility and the number per 100,000 nonsterile women by regimen of control and age of women are

	15-19	20-24	25-29	30-34	35-39	40-44
No method	5.6	6.1	7.4	13.9	20.8	22.6
Abortion only	1.2	1.6	1.7	1.7	1.9	1.2
Pill only—nonsmokers	1.3	1.6	1.9	2.2	4.5	7.1
Pill only—smokers	1.5	1.6	1.6	10.9	13.4	58.9
IUDs only	0.9	1.0	1.2	1.4	2.0	2.1
Traditional contraception only	1.1	1.6	2.0	3.6	5.0	4.2
Traditional contraception and abortion	0.2	0.2	0.3	0.3	0.3	0.2

INFORMATION FOR THE PATIENT (See Patient Package Insert)

sity, two of the most experienced and best-known investigators of the hazards and benefits of oral contraceptives and other birth control methods, listed the following potential benefits of Pill usage: 1. suppression of menstrual disorders; 2. inhibition of benign lump development in the breast, thus reducing the need for surgical biopsies; 3. less-frequent occurrence of ovarian cysts; 4. diminished risk of developing peptic ulcers. Yet the benefits of oral contraceptives, aside from the obvious ones of preventing unplanned pregnancy and affording contraceptive protection separate from coitus, are not adequately promoted.

Of particular importance in lesser-developed countries, where malnutrition and anemia are common, is a benefit of Pill usage not mentioned directly by Vessey and Doll—and one that we in affluent parts of the world tend to ignore. In contrast to IUDs, whose most common side effect is increased bleeding, use of a standard combination oral contraceptive pill leads not only to more regular menstrual cycles but also to decreased blood loss. In the large-scale British study of the Pill's side effects, the Royal College of Practitioners in 1974 reported that "use of the Pill is associated with a highly significant protective effect against iron deficiency anemia and anemia of unspecified etiology." In fact, it has been suggested in some lesser-developed countries that oral contraceptives should contain iron supplements so as to offer even greater protection against iron-deficiency anemias.

Speaking at the Women's Center at the University of California in 1977, Dr. Elizabeth Connell of the Rockfeller Foundation summarized well a risk/benefit evaluation of the Pill: "When compared to many of the risks of everyday living, the complications [of Pill use] have been found to be comparatively quite low. In fact, it has been suggested, only partly facetiously, that given their relative risks of producing disease and death, pills should be sold over-the-counter and cigarettes placed on prescription."

I would now like to turn from the discussion of risks and benefits of the Pill to possibly even more significant software issues—the effect of the Pill on sexual mores, on religion, on women's rights, and on the economically disadvantaged millions in the Third World.

The Pill and Sexual Mores

The effect of oral contraceptives on sexual mores has been enormous, and it is likely never to be equalled by newer or better contraceptive agents, since by the time such methods are introduced the so-called sexual revolution will have almost run its course. The Pill's impact on sexual mores has been both damned and praised, and I have often been asked in public and private discussions how I felt about this consequence of the scientific discovery with which I was associated. In my opinion, establishing standards for sexual mores should be a personal or family decision. If parents, religious leaders, or educational authorities believe that premarital or early sex is immoral, then they should make that case on moral grounds and not hide behind the horrible fear of an unwanted pregnancy and its consequences. Essentially, is this not identical to proclaiming "do not kill" and then justifying the statement by pointing out not that killing is immoral and cruel but rather that, if caught, one might end up in the electric chair? I firmly believe that the fear of pregnancy is not the proper vehicle for enforcing sexual morality, whatever that term means to different people.

In spite of the many comments, frequently negative ones, about the effect of oral contraceptives upon the sexual mores of the young, we should never forget that the Pill has enriched the sex lives of millions of couples in ways that were unheard of 20 years ago. The two main reasons for the enormous positive impact of the Pill are its unsurpassed efficacy and, more important, the fact that it can be taken in privacy and separate from coitus. One need not be an inhabitant of Huxley's "brave new world" to appreciate this daily benefit of the Pill.

Religion and the Pill

Sexual mores and religion are invariably intertwined, but contraceptive practices themselves are becoming increasingly secularized. Today an edict by a higher (usually male) religious authority forbidding the use of the Pill (or any other contraceptive hardware) will simply not ensure widespread adherence. Even the Catholic Church's vocal opposition to abortion is disregarded widely and leads to an obvious estrangement, especially among women who carry the brunt of the physical and psychological consequences of an unwanted pregnancy, be it within or outside marriage. Consider that in 1967 when abortions were illegal, in Austria, Argentina, Belgium, France, and Italy—countries in which the population is largely or overwhelmingly Catholic—*abortions either nearly equalled or exceeded the number of live births!*

If so many women were willing to commit a mortal sin, should it be surprising that a Church edict against taking the Pill tends to be ignored? The gap between Church doctrine on birth control and the contraceptive behavior of Catholics is dramatically illustrated in

Table 3-2, which compares the contraceptive use of white American Catholic women with that of non-Catholics for the years 1965, 1970, and 1975. In the use of the Pill, non-Catholics greatly exceeded Catholics in 1965, but within ten years the two groups were indistinguishable. Conversely, the rhythm method was used by 31.8 percent of Catholics in 1965, but by 1975 its use had dropped to 5.9 percent.

The authors of this 1977 study, C.F. Westoff and E.F. Jones from Princeton University, concluded: "Except for sterilization, Catholic and non-Catholic contraceptive practices are now quite similar. Within several years, even sterilization will probably be adopted by the same proportion of Catholics as non-Catholics, and the rhythm method is destined to be of historical interest only. The wide gulf between official Catholic doctrine and the birth control behavior of Catholics can only deepen in the next few years."

The advent of steroid oral contraceptives has, I believe, accelerated this secularization of U.S. Catholic birth control practices, but I am certain that it would have happened sooner or later even without the Pill.

The Women's Movement and the Pill

What about women's emancipation and the Pill? Although "emancipation" has many components, an indispensable one is the ability of a woman to decide for herself whether and when to become pregnant. In many countries or sectors of a given country's population, the Pill has had an enormous positive impact on providing women greater control over their own fertility—particularly in those situations where the man does not care about birth control or even actively opposes it. It is ironic that a radical fringe of well-meaning, affluent, middle-class members of some women's rights movements now condemn the Pill, seemingly without any awareness of how culture-bound their arguments are. Let me cite a typical diatribe of the radical fringe which contains threads of objections often heard; this anonymous article, entitled "Birth Control in Amerika" [sic], appeared in *Science for the People* (December 1970):

> How is birth control practiced in our society? . . . It's a familiar story to women. We go to a doctor and lowering our eyes, embarrassed at our dependency, with a mixture of fear and anger we stumble through that horrible sentence, "What do I do not to get pregnant?" Remember, we are asking this of a male doctor, behind whom stands the whole power-penis-potency complex (PPP). What do you think he's going to tell us? Right! "Get high on our latest special,

TABLE 3-2

Current Contraceptive Exposure of White, U.S. Non-Catholic (NC) and Catholic (C) Married Women Younger than 45 (1975, 1970, and 1965)

Type of exposure	1975 NC	1975 C	1970 NC	1970 C	1965 NC	1965 C
Total number	2,434	895	2,780	1,004	1,975	851
Percent total	100.0	100.0	100.0	100.0	100.0	100.0
Using contraception (%)	79.9	76.4	69.2	63.2	70.0	58.5
Not using contraception (%)	20.1	23.6	30.8	36.8	30.0	41.5
Number of users	1,938	679	1,923	635	1,396	505
—Wife sterilized (%)	17.5	12.9	7.5	4.6	5.5	2.5
—Husband sterilized (%)	15.6	13.1	8.3	3.6	5.1	1.3
—Pill (%)	34.3	34.2	36.2	33.1	30.7	21.8
—IUD (%)	9.0	7.6	7.1	8.8	1.2	0.8
—Diaphragm (%)	4.1	3.5	6.5	3.5	12.8	4.2
—Condom (%)	9.6	14.9	15.3	13.2	23.4	18.3
—Withdrawal (%)	1.8	2.4	2.0	3.5	3.4	5.7
—Rhythm (%)	1.7	5.9	3.6	17.8	4.2	31.8
—Other (%)	6.4	5.5	13.6	12.0	13.6	15.5

SOURCE C.F. Westoff and E.F. Jones. "The Secularization of U.S. Catholic Birth Control Practices." *Family Planning Perspectives*, vol. 9, 1977, p. 204.

the PPP's Pill!" Great new wonder drug! It launches frontal attack on the pituitary gland (fondly known as the master gland of the body—which means that our entire hormonal system is assaulted) and "saves us from pregnancy" in exchange for a two-page long list of side effects—nausea, edema, vomiting, bleeding, cramps, mental depression, bloating, changes in menstrual period, etc., with risk of thrombophlebitis, pulmonary embolism, cerebral thrombosis, etc., etc.—which our male pharmacist or male doctor threw in the waste basket, and which we will never see. What we do see are little booklets from the drug companies decorated with roses, tulips, and peach blossoms full of reassuring babbling.

And what do these anonymous authors recommend? They continue:

Where does this leave us? The responsibility for birth control has to be shared by the reproductive unit: female and male. There is at present only one method available which shares the responsibility, doesn't have dangerous side effects, and doesn't require reliance on the medical establishment. This is the use of a condom by the male and a spermicidal foam by the female. [I can just see the consequences of some poor Egyptian woman following this precious American advice with her husband, who would not dream of using a condom even if he had seen one.] Research into other methods that meet these three requirements must be begun at once. Those of us who have been harmed while being used as human guinea pigs must be compensated. This includes the women in Puerto Rico, Haiti, Yugoslavia, Thailand, and other countries, and all women in prisons and ghettoes. The experimentation that is currently being conducted on all of us must stop.

A similar message, though couched in much more reasonable terms, was expressed by Barbara Seaman, author of *The Doctors' Case Against the Pill,* when she testified on March 9, 1978, before the House Select Committee on Population in Washington, D.C.:

There was a popular song in the 1950's that went, "It's what you do with what you got. And never mind how much you got." Many of us are willing to return to the 1950's contraceptive technologies and make them work, but we are not being well served by today's physicians and clinics.

We urge you to consider a whole new paramedical approach, which would not be costly. Welfare mothers, for example, could be excellent at instructing other welfare mothers in safe contraception, and such employment would also get them off welfare. Feminists can instruct other feminists at our rapidly burgeoning women's health centers. The Couple-to-Couple League, a Catholic group which instructs wives and husbands in the optimum use of rhythm methods, also deserves support.

The Larger Issues

The point that these opponents of the Pill really miss is that the Pill as well as all other methods of fertility control should be available for any woman who is willing and able to use them given her particular circumstances. The diaphragm may be ideal, for instance, for the motivated American woman willing to use it, but it is totally unsuitable for the impoverished woman living in a hovel lacking running water, toilet, and privacy. The reality is that for many women throughout the world, the Pill is the best contraceptive method currently available. It is this last factor that is ignored totally by some feminists and by many other affluent, middle-class Americans.

Shortly before his death, Frederick S. Jaffe, president of the Alan Guttmacher Institute, addressed this point eloquently when he stated in 1977 at the Women's Center of the University of California:

Two of the most profound social changes of the last twenty years have been the increasingly more effective regulation of fertility and the widespread movement for altering the roles and status of women. . . . Both of these processes have been facilitated in the last fifteen years by the emergence of a new contraceptive technology, based primarily on the oral contraceptive. . . . The medical risk framework carries with it an implicit assumption that other methods of contraception could be substituted for the Pill, thus rendering the risks from the Pill unnecessary. This assumption is true for some persons, but not for all. *It is a particularly class-bound assumption, which ignores the difficulties low-income women had with traditional contraceptives before the advent of the Pill and their quite different experience with it subsequently* [my italics]. Those who advocate replacing the Pill with a diaphragm, the condom, or other coitally related methods may be speaking for themselves, but on the record of the last fifteen years, they are not addressing the needs of the bulk of low-income women in the U.S. They have every right to make that choice for themselves, but they should be careful to avoid imposing their values on others.

Jaffe's words bring me to a broader issue—the impact of oral contraceptives upon millions of women in some of the poorest countries in the world. I will not quarrel with the statement, heard on occasion, that the Pill is being "pushed" upon ignorant women for the convenience of the dispenser rather than for the exclusive benefit of those women. But, in many instances, this is simply not the case, and the extensive use of the Pill in many lesser-developed countries is dramatic testimony to its importance in global human fertility control.

How can an affluent American female recommend to her impoverished sister in some Asian country that she use a diaphragm when this woman has not even any storage place for it or the jelly? What about the woman living in an Arab country where the use of the diaphragm or an IUD is minimal because touching one's genitals or allowing a male doctor to demonstrate proper insertion of a diaphragm or to insert an IUD is proscribed by Moslem custom, and men for cultural reasons are disinterested in using condoms? It is in such countries that the Pill plays an extraordinarily important human and humane role in the lives of women.

In some countries, such as the People's Republic of China with its 900 million people, the Pill is one of many available contraceptive methods. But in other countries, the Pill is the dominant or even the essential method in current family planning programs. Again, this does not mean that the Pill is for everyone the ultimate answer or even that the Pill is the best answer, but, in many instances, it is the best answer we have currently.

From an even broader perspective, the most important impact of the Pill may not be in human fertility control but as a prototype of the kind of medication that will be needed in the future in health areas other than birth control. I am referring here to the prevention of diseases associated with the aging process—the killers that will be with us long after effective treatments for most acute diseases have been found. If the aging process is ever to be treated in a preventive manner, it may have to be done through the long-term administration of certain agents to healthy men and women in their prime of life. A simple example would be the prevention of atherosclerosis, so common among men above the age of 60, where preventive treatment may well have to start by administering to men in their twenties an agent inhibiting cholesterol deposition.

The development of oral contraceptives and their clinical evaluation, retrospective and prospective, is teaching us much about the extraordinarily complicated problems surrounding when, how, and whether a potent agent should be given to healthy persons for long periods of their lives. (Though the potential toxicology problems are of a different order of magnitude, a case in point is the indiscriminate use of vitamins for many years by healthy individuals, who either do not need them or who could get them easily through appropriate diets.) It would be folly to ignore these lessons of the Pill, just because it was developed by men and is consumed only by women.

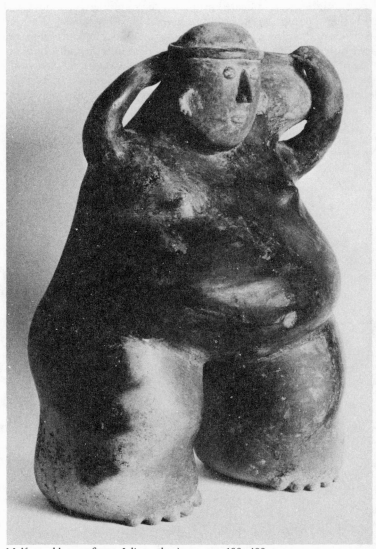

Malformed human figure. Jalisco, classic, *ca.* A.D. 100–400.

4

The Fear of Cancer

LET'S NOT BEAT AROUND THE BUSH. Cancer has become the overriding health concern in today's world. With relatively few exceptions—tobacco being the most striking—today's affluent society is not even willing to put up with *potential* cancer risks; to be more precise, we are *especially* unwilling to put up with potential cancer risks. I have segregated the cancer issue from other concerns about side effects because of its importance, its enormous complexity, and its particular relevance to chemical and other methods of birth control that involve long-term exposure (for instance, IUDs).

Contraceptives and other drugs are not a select category singled out for special scrutiny; our fear of cancer extends to food additives, pesticides, gasoline additives, aerosol can propellants that may cause ozone depletion in the atmosphere, and innumerable other chemicals that have become part of modern life. While we focus our attention on cancers caused by our exposure to synthetic chemicals and other by-products of modern technology, we have a tendency to forget that there are also many naturally occurring carcinogens (e.g., aflatoxins in peanuts, corn, chili peppers, etc.; nitrites in soil which eventually are converted into carcinogenic nitrosamines in the intestines; cycasin in cycad nuts eaten in Africa, etc.).

We also tend to ignore two factors that have a great deal to do with the apparent increase in certain types of cancer in the last few decades. First and foremost is the longer life expectancy that people enjoy in the twentieth century. Since cancer is primarily a disease of the elderly or at the very least the middle-aged, it is not surprising— given the increasing proportion of older people in our society—that the incidence of cancer is rising. Second, during the last few decades there has been a great increase in epidemiological studies concerned with cancer as well as major advances in diagnostic procedures for detecting cancer. These epidemiological studies have demonstrated that a very long lag time can exist between the initial exposure to a carcinogen and the actual appearance of malignancies. A particularly dramatic recent example of this lag effect is the appearance of otherwise rare vaginal tumors in young women exposed *in utero* some 20 years earlier to the nonsteroid estrogen drug *diethylstilbestrol* (DES), which in the early 1950s was frequently prescribed to pregnant women in the mistaken belief that it would help prevent miscarriages (DES administration presumably caused no damage to the mothers to whom the drug was given).

The fear of cancer—justified or imagined—has obvious public policy implications. In its crudest form, such fear is often used to justify panic responses without any rational consideration of their consequences. Consider for instance the headline "Why Would the U.S. Ban Cyclamates and Not the Pill?" which appeared in the *St. Louis Globe-Democrat* (November 5, 1969) under the byline of Morton Mintz, a well-known journalistic opponent of the Pill. His point was that when either product is given in high enough doses, one can find some animal species that ostensibly shows increased malignancies. Suppose the U.S. government actually had followed Mintz's simplistic reasoning and had banned the Pill?

Banning cyclamates, even though subsequent studies indicated that the scientific rationale behind this step was at best dubious, did not really have a major global impact. However, does anyone believe that such a statement could be made if the Pill were suddenly banned because of some questionable results from animal testing? There is no doubt that if the Pill were formally prohibited in the U.S., then most other countries in the world—especially the lesser-developed ones—would have to follow suit.

It is for this reason that I address myself here in detail to the question of cancer and the Pill by examining some of the currently available data, both from animal studies and from studies of women who have taken the Pill over a number of years. Let me emphasize at the outset that the answers will not be black and white, because the question—Will it cause cancer in humans?—is the most ambiguous and greyest of all questions. For many aspects of this cancer issue, one can find recognized experts taking diametrically opposite positions.

The Ambiguity of Animal Studies: The Beagle Story

Nobody wants to expose humans to undue experimental risk; this is probably truer in the cancer field than in almost any other toxicological area. That is why we initially conduct toxicity experiments on animals. But one question that remains unanswered is the extent to which animal data can be extrapolated to human experience. Although every agent that causes cancer in humans also does so in some other animal species, the converse has not been demonstrated. Since testing for potential carcinogenicity is such an urgent issue, much effort has gone into developing quick, short-cut screening methods that provide at least some indication of potential carcinogenicity of a given agent before animal experiments are begun. Only one such rapid screening method so far has been introduced—the so-called Ames test, which is based on the observation that substances causing mutations in bacteria frequently cause cancer in animals and humans as well. The reliability of this correlation between bacterial mutation and the appearance of cancers in higher animals was originally believed to be on the order of 80 to 90 percent, but more extensive recent experience suggests that the correlation may be lower. So far no steroid has shown a positive result for potential carcinogenicity in the Ames test. Even DES (a nonsteroid estrogen) does not respond to the Ames test, since in this instance the agent is toxic toward the bacterial cells and kills them before mutagenicity can be examined. Thus, since we have no reliable, rapid test to screen steroids for their potential carcinogenicity, we must turn to animal models.

This brings us to the single biggest bottleneck in fertility control research: the lack of a satisfactory test animal, other than the human, for evaluating contraceptive efficacy and safety. Because of the enormous diversity in the reproductive processes of animal species and the widely divergent effects of steroid sex hormones on different species, it is exceptionally difficult to extrapolate to humans data gained from administering steroid drugs to experimental animals.

Despite this uncertainty, in 1968 the FDA imposed very special requirements for animal testing of female contraceptive agents (requirements that are far more stringent than those for any other drugs)—one of them being the stipulation that two-year toxicity studies in rats, dogs, and monkeys must be completed before large-scale clinical trials can be undertaken, at which time seven-year toxicity studies in dogs and ten-year studies in monkeys must also be initiated. The *motivation* for the unprecedented length of these toxicology studies is understandable on political and even humane grounds—after all, we are talking here about drugs that may be given to millions of healthy women for prolonged periods of time and therefore should carry minimal risk. Nevertheless, the *scientific rationale* for the FDA's selection of these very specific animal species is highly debatable.

The FDA selected monkeys because of their presumed close evolutionary proximity to humans, and dogs because they had been used for decades as the subject of pharmacological and toxicological studies and hence a great deal was known about their response to various drugs. However, it was also known that the bitch is enormously sensitive to female sex hormones and that her semiannual heat cycle is not comparable to a woman's monthly menstrual period. It is these differences that allow hardly any meaningful extrapolation from dogs to women.

In the same year that the FDA imposed its very rigorous and inflexible toxicology requirements, a World Health Organization scientific group reached the following conclusion about animal studies with steroid contraceptives: "The extrapolation to women of data derived from dose and duration studies in experimental animals is of questionable validity and may be misleading, particularly when it is impossible to assess the comparability of dosages and lifespans. In the light of these considerations, the interpretation of such data is extremely difficult. *There is no evidence to justify recent emphasis on the presumed advantages of observations in subhuman primates and in canines* [italics mine]."

In spite of the scientific doubts surrounding the validity of extrapolating these dog data to women, the FDA's insistence that long-term tests be performed in dogs, in addition to monkeys, has resulted in the discontinuance of advanced clinical trials of several progestational steroid compounds. In 1970 the FDA's practical power to determine detailed scientific protocols led one of the largest American drug companies (which does not market any contraceptives) to discontinue virtually all research on contraceptive agents chemically related to female steroids. Such a self-imposed restriction may not have been regretted by competitive drug firms, but it was certainly unfortunate as far as general scientific advances in fertility control were concerned because this company's research organization was internationally recognized as one of the very best.

As a result of such testing on dogs, one important oral contraceptive drug actually had to be withdrawn from the market. Specifically, in early 1970 the FDA required that because of the appearance of breast nodules in beagles, advanced clinical studies on the *chlormadinone acetate minipill*—an innovative, progestin-only, low-dosage regimen that presumably obviated the clinical side effects associated with estrogens—be stopped. The FDA's banning of this clinical work in the U.S. was particularly serious because chlormadinone acetate was a highly effective agent which had already been used commercially for several years abroad (e.g., in England and Mexico). Because further clinical experimentation in the U.S. was halted, Syntex, the company that developed chlormadinone acetate, had no choice but to withdraw it from all foreign markets, since it would otherwise have been in the untenable position of *selling* an agent in certain countries which could not even be *tested* clinically in an experimental mode in the U.S. Ironically, at the same time the FDA banned the continued use of the chlormadinone acetate minipill, it permitted continued experimentation with a closely related compound, *medroxyprogesterone acetate,* the active ingredient in an injectable steroid contraceptive (called Depo-Provera) being developed by the Upjohn Company, even though this substance produced exactly the same type of breast nodules in beagles.

In 1973 the WHO organized a symposium for the express purpose of determining the most appropriate animal models for testing toxicity and side effects in contraceptives used in humans. This meeting was attended by nearly 50 participants from all over the world, including academicians, industrialists, and representatives of the major national regulatory agencies. The proceedings were published in a 494-page volume, but it is fair to say that on the controversial issues, notably the FDA-imposed dog studies, no consensus was reached. The wide divergence of views became particularly noticeable when the discussion turned to the logic behind the FDA's decision to allow continued experimentation with medroxyprogesterone acetate, but not with chlormadinone acetate. In the words of Dr. V.R. Berliner of the FDA, "A different stand was taken by the agency in the case of the [sustained-release] injectable preparation of medroxyprogesterone acetate [Depo-Provera]. *Even though this compound too is implicated by its action in beagles as being potentially carcinogenic* [my italics], the uniqueness of this preparation and its high efficacy as a contraceptive, no matter by which pathway this contraceptive effect is obtained, provides it with a benefit-risk ratio which permits its use in the U.S. albeit for a very special patient population." (Dr. Berliner was presumably talking about women who could not or would not take oral contraceptives.)

Dr. Berliner's view on this issue was very much in the minority at that WHO meeting, as can be judged from two typical comments from the published discussion following the presentation of his paper. The first comment came from Dr. Roy Hertz, formerly of the National Cancer Institute and neither a proponent of the Pill nor a person ever accused of laxity in terms of his concern for potential cancer dangers. He had served as a member of the FDA's Advisory Committee on Obstetrics and Gynecology, which consisted exclusively of academic and government physicians and had been convened by the FDA in the late 1960s to provide outside advice in the field of oral contraceptives:

> I think it should be a matter of record that not all members of the Advisory Committee of the Food and Drug Administration felt that these [beagle] studies were indicated or would be particularly fruitful. . . . *I feel that we must make clear that we do not have the scientific basis for our decisions and that we cannot have with the tools that we have available. Hence a great deal of emphasis must be put on improving those tools and developing them on a sound scientific basis and on not deluding ourselves into somewhat arbitrary, if I may say so, presumptuous, administrative conclusions which are poorly based* [italics mine].

Dr. G.A. Overbeek, of the Dutch pharmaceutical company Organon, made a further observation on the FDA's dog requirement:

> I fully understand the difficulties of decision-making, and certainly the difficulties of making decisions under the conditions under which the regulatory bodies have to work. . . . I can also fully understand that the beagle was chosen as the most suitable animal at the time that the first regulations and guidelines for using the beagle were made known to the companies and to the public. But I have no understanding for the fact that, when quite a substantial amount of evidence became available to the effect that apparently this was not a good choice, they could not come back on such a decision.

In further beagle studies conducted in the early 1970s, researchers discovered that *even the natural female sex hormone progesterone, which is secreted during part of each menstrual cycle and continu-*

ously during pregnancy, produces similar breast nodules in beagles when administered in high doses. One would have thought that by now the FDA would have given up insisting on this particular animal model and would admit having made a mistake—or at least a poor choice. Yet on March 9, 1978, before the House Select Committee on Population, FDA Commissioner Dr. Donald Kennedy testified, with respect to my earlier criticism of the FDA's dog requirement, that "One may not like it, but the fact is that gradually . . . the beagle has become a widely accepted model, one accepted by the World Health Organization, as well as by most national drug regulatory agencies, and I think it's on solid ground."

I cannot agree with this conclusion and I am by no means alone on this. Indeed, a few months later, in September 1978, the WHO convened a meeting of its Toxicology Review Panel in order to examine once more all of the information on the effects of progestational steroids on the beagle. The panel concluded: "Considerable reservations must be expressed over the relevance of the findings in the beagle to possible toxicity of long-acting progestogens in humans. Significant differences in response to progestogen treatment between dogs and women have been demonstrated . . . and the available evidence suggests that all investigated progestogens, including progesterone itself, are able to promote mammary tumors in the beagle dog." As summarized in another WHO report dated November 1978, *"The Panel strongly recommended that there should be a search for an alternative, appropriate, animal model for the testing of carcinogenicity of progestogens* [italics mine]."

Why have I belabored in such detail the use of beagles in animal studies undertaken to ascertain possible carcinogenicity of contraceptive drugs? I have done so because although I am a firm believer in the importance of regulatory agencies, I do not believe that they are infallible. Yet it seems almost impossible for a government agency to admit publicly that it might have erred! In this particular instance, the error is a very serious one because, as was stated in a recent lecture by Dr. Egon Diczfalusy, director of the WHO Collaborating Center for Research and Training in Human Reproduction in Stockholm, "This policy [use of the beagle in oral contraceptive toxicology studies] also led to a significant discouragement of the pharmaceutical industry and to a drastic reduction of research on new contraceptive steroids at a time when the demand for improved and safe contraceptives was considerably increasing."

It is difficult for the layman or even the nonspecialist scientist to appreciate fully the negative impact of these beagle studies on future contraceptive development. But as I said in 1969 and believe firmly today, there is little doubt that if the present climate concerning testing of oral contraceptives had existed in the 1950s, the Pill would never have seen the light of day.

Human Studies

Having shown how ambiguous extrapolation of animal studies to humans can be, let us look first at some of the general methods available for measuring possible carcinogenic effects of a drug in humans and then examine what we know specifically about steroid oral contraceptives.

A first-class review dealing with steroid contraceptives and cancer risks was published by the WHO in 1978, and data in the following section, unless specifically indicated otherwise, are derived from this report. To determine whether a steroid contraceptive or any other drug produces cancer in women, one can undertake either an *experiment* or an *observational study*. In general one would prefer to conduct experiments because they can be controlled more rigorously, but not many women are likely to volunteer to participate in an experiment that would require them to accept a random allocation of markedly different methods of contraception. In general, therefore, one is reduced to *observational studies* and these can be classified in two categories.

The first is a *case-control study*, which is particularly helpful when one is looking for occurrences of relatively rare tumors. In a case-control study, individuals with the disease under investigation are compared with one or more control individuals selected according to certain matching criteria. Typical criteria for a contraceptive study are sexual activity, age, race, and number of children, and if these factors are not taken into consideration tremendous bias can be introduced into the study's conclusions.

Consider the following example. If one wants to study the incidence of breast cancer among oral contraceptive users, one cannot simply compare the Pill-taking women to non-Pill-taking women. Other criteria must be taken into account. Whether or not a woman has ever given birth is an important factor. Nuns, a non-child-bearing group, are known to have a higher incidence of breast cancer than do women who have borne children. Among child-bearing women, the chief correlating factor is the age at which the woman bore her first child (rather than the total number of children borne or the extent of breast feeding). Women who give birth before age 18 are one third as likely to develop breast cancer as those who have their first child at age 35 or older. (Thus, one should match Pill-taking women who had their first child at an early age with non-Pill-taking women who, similarly, had their first child at an early age. Alternatively, one should compare two groups of childless women.)

The other observational method is the *cohort study*. Here women on different contraceptive regimens are studied over time, and tumor occurrence is noted directly. Since tumors are relatively infrequent, especially among younger women, very large numbers of women must be observed over a long period of time in order to obtain meaningful results.

At times, the magnitude and complexity of such epidemiological studies are truly staggering. Women who on the one hand complain that little is known about possible cancer risks associated with the Pill, yet at the same time object to being human guinea pigs, should carefully examine Table 4-1.

TABLE 4-1

Minimal Samples Required to Detect Differences in Disease Rates Between Oral Contraceptive (OC) Users and Controls in Prospective Study

Disease	No. of Years After Onset of Study	Annual Incidence Rate in Controls per 10,000	Persons Required in Each Group	
			Incidence Two Times in OC Users	Incidence Five Times in OC Users
Cancer of the breast	1	2.2	85,000	11,000
Cancer of the corpus uteri	1	0.3	600,000	80,000
Cancer of the cervix	1	3.1	60,000	7,500
Cancer of the breast	10	7.5	25,000	3,000
Cancer of the corpus uteri	10	1.3	140,000	20,000
Cancer of the cervix	10	5.6	35,000	5,000
Diabetes	1	20.0	9,000	1,200
Malformations	1	300.0	600	100
Thromboemboli	1	20.0	9,000	1,200

SOURCE: D. Seigel and P. Corfman. "Epidemiological Problems Associated with Studies of the Safety of Oral Contraceptives." *Journal of the American Medical Association*, vol. 203, 1968, pp. 950-54.

Take, for instance, cancer of the uterine body (corpus uteri). If the natural incidence rate of this type of cancer is 1.3 women per 10,000 *nonusers* of oral contraceptives, then to determine whether this "natural" rate of cancer occurrence is doubled after ten years of oral contraceptive use, no fewer than 140,000 women would have to be studied for that period of time! To determine whether the incidence of that form of cancer is quintupled among Pill users, 20,000 women rather than 140,000 would have to be examined over a ten-year period. The obvious lesson to be learned from Table 4-1 is that before even embarking on such a study, one must be sure to include enough subjects (often tens of thousands) in order to have a reasonable chance of detecting a cause-and-effect relationship between the drug and cancer. This is a classic "Catch-22" situation, because there is no way to involve such large numbers of people in studies of this sort until the product to be studied is actually on the market and used extensively.

Does the Pill Cause Cancer?

Before evaluating what we know currently about the relationship between oral contraceptives and tumor formation in humans, one must understand the concept of *relative risk* and how to measure it. Relative risk is determined by comparing the incidence of cancer among persons exposed to the possible carcinogen and persons not exposed. Though the severity of the tumor (e.g., the extent of associated disability and possible risk of death) must be considered, from a public health standpoint the most important concern is the frequency of tumor occurrence. For instance, assume there is a cancer incidence of one per million among nonusers of a contraceptive and that use of a given Pill increases the relative risk of cancer tenfold. One would then expect ten cancer cases per million users of that Pill. This is tragic for these ten women but not of enormous consequence to a large population. However, if the natural incidence of a given cancer is 100 per million and exposure to the drug only doubles the risk, then one would expect 200 cases per million among its users. Even though this latter case shows a smaller *relative risk* to the individual user, the public health problem is clearly ten times greater.

Geographical variations in the natural incidence of certain cancers complicate the picture enormously; conclusions from data obtained in one country cannot necessarily be applied to another unless one first knows something about major geographical differences. Table 4-2 presents data (collected in the late 1960s and early 1970s) for three types of cancer common among women. Note for instance that the U.S. has the highest incidence of breast and uterine (body) cancers. Yet we see an almost total reversal with regard to the incidence of cervical cancer: Colombia has by far the highest incidence and the U.S. the second lowest.

In the case of breast cancer some of the major known determinants of risk include the woman's age at the birth of her first child (mentioned earlier); age at first menstruation (decreasing age being associated with an increased incidence of cancer); age at menopause (increasing age leading to increased breast cancer risk); and genetic factors as demonstrated by family history of breast cancer. Furthermore, surgical removal of the ovaries, especially when performed at a relatively early age, lowers the incidence of breast cancer. The great geographical variations summarized in Table 4-2 are apparently associated with environmental influences (such as dietary factors) rather than with genetic or reproductive behavioral ones.

TABLE 4-2
Age-Standardized Annual Incidence Rate of
Certain Cancers per 100,000 Women

Country	Breast	Uterus (Body)	Uterus (Cervix)
USA (Connecticut)	71.4	17.8	9.8
Switzerland	70.6	16.3	16.1
Israel (Jews)	55.5	10.8	4.5
Denmark	49.1	11.4	31.6
England	48.0	8.0	14.0
Yugoslavia	28.3	9.1	18.1
Colombia	27.8	5.1	62.8
India	20.1	?	23.2
Singapore	17.6	3.8	11.6
Japan	13.0	1.3	13.8

SOURCE: "Steroid Contraception and the Risk of Neoplasia." *World Health Organization Technical Report Series*, no. 619, 1978.

Given this simplified background I would now like to summarize briefly what we know at the present time about the possible relation between combination oral contraceptives (i.e., those pills that contain both a progestational and an estrogenic component) and tumor growth.

In the case of *benign breast tumors,* consumption of oral contraceptives for more than two years appears to reduce the risk and there is even some evidence that a residual protective effect persists after discontinuance of oral contraceptive therapy. This apparent protective effect seems to be associated with the progestational component rather than with the estrogen.

Thus far we have no clear evidence from current extensive

epidemiological data to suggest either an adverse or a beneficial effect of oral contraceptives on the risk of *breast cancer* because the period of oral contraceptive exposure and the duration of follow-up are still too short to ascertain possible correlations. As the WHO report succinctly stated, "No inference can be drawn about the long-term effects of oral contraceptives on subsequent risk of breast cancer."

Present evidence suggests that oral contraceptive use decreases *ovarian cancer* but increases the incidence of *liver tumors*. Though the liver tumor correlation seems to rest on fairly firm ground, it should be recognized that in women under 30 years of age the risk is no more than three per 100,000 oral contraceptive users, regardless of length of oral contraceptive consumption. The risk is higher in older women, but all of the data now available apply to oral contraceptives containing relatively high doses of steroids. The introduction since 1974 of lower-dose oral contraceptives seems almost certain to lessen the risk of such liver tumors, but it will take until the mid 1980s before definitive evidence about such possible reduced risk could be demonstrated.

The case of *uterine endometrial carcinoma* (cancer of the uterine lining) is particularly instructive because it demonstrates the complexity and ambiguity of many of the studies. So far there seems to be no clear evidence for any association between combination oral contraceptive use and an increased or decreased risk of uterine endometrial cancer. However, there is some evidence of increased risk among women who have used sequential oral contraceptives (i.e., regimens in which estrogens alone are given during the earlier part of the cycle and are then followed by the administration of the progestational agent), but these have now been withdrawn from use in most countries, including the U.S. If sequential oral contraceptives do indeed increase the risk of cancer of the uterine lining, then this may be associated with the estrogen component.

Indeed, a controversy has raged during the last three years as to whether estrogens administered to women for the relief of menopausal symptoms cause an increased incidence of uterine endometrial cancer. This question is now being studied by Drs. Ralph Horowitz and Alvan Feinstein of Yale University, who believe that estrogen administration to menopausal patients does not lead to a *real increase* in the occurrence of cancer of the uterine lining but only to its *increased detection*. Estrogens are known to induce uterine bleeding in many women, and since such bleeding is frequently taken as a symptom of cancer of the uterine lining, the woman showing such bleeding subjects herself to more diagnostic tests for cancer than do control patients. A recent review of this topic in *Science* points out that the score now stands at 7 to 3 in favor of studies indicating a causal connection between estrogen therapy and uterine endometrial cancer. However, in contrast to sports where, in the absence of cheating, scores define the winner unequivocally, this is not necessarily true of cancer studies based on epidemiological evidence. Another epidemiologist, Harold Dorn, succinctly expressed the innate flaw of such score keeping: "Reproduceability does not establish validity, since the same mistake can be made repeatedly."

The overall public health conclusion that can be reached from currently available human data is that although no firm deductions can be made as yet—because longer studies are required and many variables need to be disentangled—there appears to be no reason for major concern that an epidemic of tumor-producing diseases is likely to arise from the use of currently available combination oral contraceptives. Like any other statement concerning overall rates of incidence of a disease or side effects, assurances on a national or global scale are not necessarily sufficient for the individual person who has the misfortune to incur the disease.

Most of the data cited so far have been obtained from patients who were on relatively high-dosage oral contraceptives, which are rapidly being discontinued since the FDA began to approve lower-dosage regimens in 1974. The question therefore remains: what risks are associated with the present lower-dosage oral contraceptives? With respect to cancer, it will take years to determine the answer to this question and will require the analysis and observation of thousands of women. In fact, these low-dosage regimens will require the reassessment of the incidence of a number of other serious side effects, such as thromboembolic (blood-clotting) complications, hypertension, and reported carbohydrate, protein, and lipid metabolic changes. Most of these complications were uncovered as a result of laborious and lengthy studies with women who have been on the higher-dosage contraceptives. It remains to be seen whether these side effects will be associated with the modern low-dosage varieties and, if so, to what extent.

Generally speaking, the severity and incidence of undesirable side effects of a drug are directly proportional to the dosage; accordingly, it is desirable to use the lowest effective quantity of any active drug. Obviously this principle should apply to Pill dosages and many persons, notably legislators and women, have questioned why reduction in dosage regimen progressed so slowly. Let me offer a partial answer to this seemingly simple, but actually highly complex, question.

The conventional Pill consists of two components—the progestational agent, which through its ovulation inhibition prevents conception, and the estrogen, which is added to overcome menstrual irregularities associated with administration of an "unopposed" progestational drug. A number of undesirable side effects of oral contraceptives are associated with the estrogen component, and minipills containing only small amounts of a progestational agent without added estrogen are now on the market. Injectable contraceptives are also frequently estrogen-free, but their associated menstrual irregularities are a chief reason why they have never found favor in the U.S. and many other countries. Adjusting the ratio between the progestational agent and the estrogen in a combination Pill is not simple because one has to contrast the incidence of certain side effects with beneficial properties (i.e., menstrual regularity) in large studies requiring hundreds and even thousands of women.

The question may also be asked why it took so long to reduce the dosage of the progestational agent, which is primarily used for contraceptive efficacy. (The original dosages of oral contraceptives in the early 1960s ranged from 10 to 5 mg. per day while at the present time the majority fall into the 1 to 0.5 mg. range—a tenfold reduction.) Though it is frequently possible to arrive at very approximate doses of various drugs for humans from animal experiments, it is particularly difficult to achieve this with contraceptive drugs. First, as mentioned earlier, reproduction is extraordinarily species-specific and dosages in rodents and even in lower primates tell us little about efficacy levels in humans. Second, when establishing an effective human dose of a particular drug, one can approach the task in two ways—either starting from a suboptimal direction and working toward full efficacy or commencing with a superactive dose and working gradually downward. In the case of a contraceptive, lack of efficacy means pregnancy. How many women in clinical experiments are willing to expose themselves to that risk? Among those who do, the majority would at the very least demand that contraceptive failure resulting in pregnancy would be corrected by prompt abortion. (Most critics forget that prior to 1969, it was not possible to get legal abortions in the United States. This was one of the reasons why so many clinical studies were first carried out abroad, a situation I have always considered morally and ethically untenable.) When such studies are completed, a laborious FDA review is required even if the manufacturer only wishes to lower the dose—the reason being that since 1962 the FDA by legislative mandate has had to examine efficacy as well as safety data, and the former may be affected by lowering the dose.

Given the crucial importance of dosage, the reader will understand why I conclude with an exchange from the early 1974 hearings for the 1975 appropriations for the FDA between the chairman of the congressional subcommittee, Congressman Jamie L. Whitten, and Commissioner Alexander M. Schmidt of the FDA.

> MR. WHITTEN: He [Djerassi] also says, "If the present climate and requirements had prevailed in 1955, oral contraceptive steroids would still be a laboratory curiosity in 1970." Do you agree with that statement?
>
> DR. SCHMIDT: No, I do not agree with Dr. Djerassi's statement. In my opinion, Dr. Djerassi's statement has no basis in fact. Factually, several oral contraceptives have been approved since 1970, having adequately fulfilled current requirements being much more stringent than those which existed in 1955. Examples: Loestrin, Micronor, Ovrette.

To the uninitiated Dr. Schmidt's testimony seems persuasive. It becomes less so when one discovers that the names Loestrin, Micronor, and Ovrette are simply new trade names of old oral contraceptives which were now approved by the FDA in a lower-dosage form. Thus Loestrin is a lower-dosage variant of Parke-Davis's Norlestrin, which was first marketed in 1964; Micronor is a minipill variant of Syntex's norethindrone, which was first synthesized in 1951 and approved by the FDA in 1963. Ovrette is a similar minipill of Wyeth's Ovral, which was first approved in 1968. I regret that I was not present at these 1974 congressional hearings and, in fact, knew nothing about them until a copy of the appropriate *Congressional Record* was sent to me. If I had been present I would have asked Dr. Schmidt one more question: "Why did it take the FDA so long to approve a low-dose variant of oral contraceptives that had been on the market for years?"

The answer probably would have been along these lines: "We are not prepared to take any chances, and what is your hurry anyway?" This really summarizes the two basic issues: how much safety do we want, and how do we balance innovation with risk? The fear of cancer has a great deal to do with both of these issues, and the cost and consequences of our emphasis on safety are examined in detail in the next chapter. I am not suggesting that Western society's overriding current concern with safety is necessarily inappropriate. I only feel that it is important that we understand its cost, not in dollars and cents, but in terms of lost opportunities and greatly delayed improvements in birth control.

Man and woman. Colima, classic, *ca.* A.D. 100–400.

5

The Road from Laboratory to Consumer

REP. SCHEUER: My assessment of this field has led me to believe that it is American scientists, in American institutions supported by the American Government, who will make the discoveries that will lead to better contraceptives. What are the real needs for better contraception? How do we go about developing them? What resources are needed? How soon can we expect to have better contraceptives? How can we have contraceptives that are not so abusive of the bodies of women?

> Testimony from hearings of the House Select Committee on Population, 95th Congress, March 7, 1978.

DR. DJERASSI: I'm not questioning the utility of basic research. What I'm concerned about is this: in the context of contraception you are talking about drug development that is totally different from any other. Point number one, you're dealing with healthy people, and therefore for very obvious reasons, you're not willing to take the risks that you would be willing to take in many other diseases. Therefore, the clinical trials aspects, particularly when they come to even minor side effects, are much more serious; they take longer and are much more expensive.

The second point is that this is the one single area where, in fact, I think you're dealing with global problems and not with local problems. . . . In spite of everything that you've heard, I know of no really significant example . . . where a noncommercial or nondrug company has really been responsible for the entire process of finally bringing a drug to market. I'm not saying that this is ideal; I'm simply telling you that these are the facts of life. I think it would be extraordinarily more expensive, both in terms of money and time, to try to do it another way. However, to improve the present system is a completely different proposition, and one that I can readily accept. . . . The reason why industry is not putting more of its front-end money into contraceptive research is that they know what the subsequent expenses, both in terms of money and time, will be. It is in that area that incentives have to be provided. And these incentives are not tax incentives—this is not at all what I'm talking about.

> Testimony from hearings of the House Select Committee on Population, 95th Congress, March 9, 1978.

THIS CHAPTER DOES NOT DEAL with basic research uncovering fundamental new concepts in reproductive biology; such breakthroughs are few and far between. Rather, I address here the subject most often ignored by scientists in academia and in government: the really tortuous path that must be traversed in order to convert a laboratory discovery in the biomedical field into something that millions of people can use. If many scientists do not understand the complexity and magnitude of that path from laboratory to consumer, is it reasonable to expect the lay public to do so? Yet this understanding is crucial in order to evaluate the resources needed and the time required to bring new approaches in male and female contraception to practical fruition.

Congressman Scheuer's opening remarks, quoted in the beginning of this chapter, are only slightly chauvinistic in implying that virtually all discoveries that will lead to better contraceptives will originate in the United States. Though not all such discoveries will come from the U.S., most of them will—not because we in the U.S. have a monopoly on brains but rather because of our overpowering resources in the biomedical field, particularly in contraception. According to the latest figures available, during the five-year period ending in 1974, the United States expended from 77 percent (1969) to 68 percent (1974) of all worldwide funds allocated to reproductive research—compared to the 21 percent to 30 percent spent by 15 other industrialized nations and the less than 2 percent spent by lesser-developed nations. Our dominance in contraceptive research, together with the fact that the private contraceptive market in the U.S. is still the largest in the Western world, suggests that we should pay special attention to the conditions governing the technical process of contraceptive drug development in the United States, from the standpoint of both providing incentives and removing hindrances.

The Role of the FDA

To understand what it takes in the U.S. to bring a biomedical discovery from the laboratory to the consumer, it is absolutely essential to examine the dominant role played by the Food and Drug Administration in this entire process. Let me state at the outset that I do not view the FDA as an agency populated by incompetent bureaucrats who make up rules to complicate life for everyone. Actually the FDA mirrors fairly accurately society's attitudes and concerns about safety and consumer protection, which themselves are shaped by a type of public press coverage that requires separate discussion (see Chapter 6). Although much I have to say here may appear to be implied or implicit criticism of FDA policies, I am not sure that I could act very differently if I had to operate within that agency, given the tremendous constraints imposed by its legal mandate and the insufficient resources it has to fulfill its real or imagined public missions. If the FDA's mandate is to be altered, the need for change must first be perceived by well-informed citizens who then make their views felt through the political process.

Until 1962, the legal function of the FDA was to see that drugs and foods being sold to consumers met certain standards of safety and purity as well as to approve new drugs before they could be marketed to the public (this approval process concentrated almost exclusively on safety considerations). However, in 1962, the FDA by legislative mandate (the Kefauver Amendment) was given an entirely new responsibility: Congress, reflecting the public's concern over the widely publicized thalidomide tragedy, directed the FDA to concern itself with the effectiveness of a drug in addition to its safety. As a result, the FDA took on the additional role of research monitor and inspector through its newly acquired authority to approve all protocols dealing with the *clinical research phase* of a drug development project. (This is the phase that involves administering the drug under investigation to humans and is particularly significant in the field of contraception because, given the extraordinary species specificity of the reproductive process, suitable animal models are extremely difficult to find in the field of reproductive biology.) Irrespective of the sponsor of the clinical work—industry, government, university, or private physician—no new drug can lawfully be administered to humans in the U.S. without an Investigative New Drug (IND) exemption issued by the FDA. The application for an IND exemption must outline the precise clinical protocols for the project and, for all practical purposes, there is no appeal from FDA decisions or inaction during this experimental phase. If the FDA does not agree with the proposed clinical protocols, wishes to change them, delays approval, or denies the IND exemption totally, there is little one can do except possibly go to court.

The original role of the FDA, and one which it must maintain, is that of the policeman. But there is an inherent tension between the policeman's function, however important and indispensable, and that of the researcher attempting to bring a new drug to the consumer. Legalistic inflexibility, extreme caution, aggressive searching for violators, and, most importantly, an intrinsically adversary relationship—all features that many persons, especially consumer advocates, consider important, necessary, and consistent with the public good—are counterproductive when dealing with research. The appropriate stance of the FDA, in fulfilling its current legislative mandate, is to respond to any New Drug Application (NDA) with, "Give me good reasons why I should not say no." For those who operate within the FDA, their reward structure, and indeed their professional promotion, is predicated upon seeing to it that no accidents happen, that no undue risks are taken. Time is of no consequence, safety is the overriding concern, and no medals are awarded for passing a new drug through the regulatory process quickly. Yet in drug research the absence of risk is equivalent to the absence of progress, and time is *the* most expensive commodity. In many biomedical research areas, delays are exceedingly costly—not only in terms of money but also in terms of human lives.

I know of no simple solution to this problem because we must accept the reality of increasing public as well as congressional interest in and concern about the conduct of clinical experimental drug research in this country. It is with great hesitation that I have come to the conclusion that this regulatory/bureaucratic dilemma is probably best solved, if it can be solved at all, by interposing another bureaucratic layer. (A fortune cookie opened in a San Francisco

Chinatown restaurant contained a message that may have been prophetic: "Your problems are too complicated for fortune cookies.")

I would propose the creation of a new government agency whose sole mandate would be to stimulate and facilitate research in those areas where the eventual product must be subject to government regulation, for example, in the field of drugs, pesticides, food additives, and the like. The mandate of that new agency should be a positive one: its employees should be encouraged to say "yes" or at least to ask, "Is there a good reason why I should not say yes?" To put this suggestion into the concrete context of drugs, I would propose that all clinical research (and associated toxicology) through phases I, II, and possibly even III (see Table 5-1) be subject to scrutiny by that new agency—in other words, that the de facto research monitoring function of the FDA be removed. Another important function of this new agency should be to identify those areas of research in which very little is happening currently but which are of societal importance. It should then determine what incentives are needed to motivate greater involvement in those fields by industry or other appropriate research institutions.

The ultimate approval for marketing of drugs and related products would remain with the FDA. However, by channeling the initial research supervision to a separate agency, a great deal of very valuable research that now is simply not even being started very likely would get under way. Under such circumstances, much research would reach a stage where it is not so easy any longer simply to say "no," because the scientific evidence will be sufficiently persuasive to justify its continuation and completion.

FDA decisions, especially in the area of fertility control developments, can have an enormous impact on the rest of the world. The international effects of FDA decisions constitute an indirect area of responsibility that the agency itself largely ignores and that is virtually unknown to the public. Except for the specific ability of the FDA to prohibit the export of drugs manufactured in the U.S. that are not approved here, the agency's jurisdiction ends with the geographic boundaries of this country. However, almost irrespective of the reasons, if the FDA formally disapproves a drug in the U.S. or orders that a drug be withdrawn from clinical trials here, the stigma is sufficiently great that the drug has little chance of being marketed in Europe and many other areas. In essence, the FDA has what often amounts to a de facto veto over the development and use of new methods of contraception on a worldwide scale—the discontinuance of the clinical work with the chlormadinone acetate minipill (described in the preceding chapter) is a typical example. During the 1978 hearings of the House Select Committee on Population, the following exchange on this subject took place between FDA Commissioner Donald Kennedy and myself:

> DR. DJERASSI: [The FDA makes] decisions which have an enormous impact on the rest of the world, particularly in the area of fertility control, because there are so few existing [contraceptive] methods right now that almost anything that you do with them is felt internationally. I think one example is injectable contraceptives. This is totally unimportant in the American context, but it is enormously important, as far as the WHO is concerned, in many lesser-developed countries. Anything that you do in the field of injectable contraceptives here will have essentially no impact on American women because it never did have one, but will have an enormous one on people abroad. Are you really taking that into consideration in your decision [to disapprove the use of the U.S.-developed steroid Depo-Provera as an injectable contraceptive]?
>
> DR. KENNEDY: . . . There are some questions in this world that it's better to turn around before answering, and I think Dr. Djerassi's last point is one of those. Put in the obverse direction, the question is this: Should national drug approval decisions in the United States be influenced by the needs of users of those drugs abroad?
>
> And if you answered that question "Yes," I submit that . . . you would be on the slipperiest public policy slope you can possibly conceive of. You would have to make a global cost-benefit decision for every drug which you are then approving for use in a single national population. I know of no way, nor do my colleagues know of any way, in which such a process could be conducted rationally.
>
> So I prefer a very different kind of solution . . . ; I think many of the people around this table can help significantly in making it clear that national drug decisions are just that: national drug decisions, and that they should not torque the practice of a particular nation.
>
> To do otherwise is to adopt a process that would hopelessly blur real differences in national populations, in national objectives, and in national policies. I think it could not be done sensibly.

Though I appreciate the difficulty of the FDA's dilemma as outlined by Dr. Kennedy, I feel that in the area of fertility control it is impossible for our national drug decisions not to have international effects, whether we like it or not. Specifically, I believe that the U.S. must recognize that our virtual scientific monopoly in the field of reproductive physiology imposes upon us a moral and logical obligation to take a global rather than a parochial view concerning the investigation of novel contraceptive approaches. The pivotal role for future contraceptive developments anywhere in the world is played to a considerable extent by the FDA, whose legal mandate is the protection of national, rather than global, problems. Such a parochial view may perhaps be tolerated in research dealing with specific diseases, but its consequences will be disastrous if applied to a problem like the world's population growth. Therefore, in Chapter 11, which contains my policy recommendations for a strategy for the future, I make a very specific proposal dealing with the problem outlined by Dr. Kennedy insofar as it applies to the field of human birth control.

Phases in the FDA Approval Process

Before considering in detail the path from laboratory to consumer, we must understand the rules of the game as they are currently promulgated and enforced by the FDA. Clinical studies carried out under an IND exemption from the FDA are categorized into three phases, outlined in Table 5-1 (page 74). The purpose of phase I is basically to determine in a few human subjects whether there are any gross, unsuspected toxicological responses that were not detected in prior animal toxicology studies. In phase II more detailed clinical pharmacology is carried out in a few dozen subjects, whereby the appropriate human dose is usually determined. In phase III more extensive studies are conducted to demonstrate the drug's efficacy and to uncover any less obvious, longer-term, and/or rare side effects. (Not mentioned in Table 5-1 is phase IV clinical work, in which continuing clinical trials and supervision are performed after a drug has already been approved by the FDA for marketing.)

Animal Toxicity Studies

For obvious reasons, before the FDA approves an IND exemption for clinical work, the results of animal toxicology studies must first be presented. For drugs other than contraceptives that are subject to long-term administration, the FDA's requirements for animal toxicology are quite reasonable; in particular, the choice of what animal model to use in such experiments is left to the discretion of the investigator.

TABLE 5-1

Food and Drug Administration requirements for animal toxicological studies for steroid contraceptives, estrogens, and progestogens

Clinical Study	Requirements
IND phase I (limited to a few subjects for up to 10 days' administration)	90-day studies in rats, dogs, and monkeys.
IND phase II (approximately 50 subjects for 3 menstrual cycles)	1-year studies in rats, dogs, and monkeys.
IND phase III (clinical trial lasting several months or years depending on drug)	2-year studies in rats, dogs, and monkeys. Initiation of 7-year studies in dogs and 10-year studies in monkeys prior to start of phase III. Reproduction and teratological studies in two species.
NDA (New Drug Application)	No further requirements, but must include up-to-date progress reports on long-term studies in dogs and monkeys.

SOURCE: E.I. Goldenthal. *FDA Papers.* November 1969, p. 15.

However, an entirely different set of FDA toxicology requirements exists for steroid contraceptives, and these requirements have a considerable impact on the time and cost associated with developing new fertility agents. (These toxicology requirements and their correspondence to each of the clinical IND phases are shown in Table 5-1.) In contrast to the requirements for noncontraceptive drugs where the animal to be tested is not specified, contraceptives *must be tested in rats, dogs, and monkeys.* The choice of these three animal species was based on the following rationale. Rodents are standard animals in toxicology because their relatively short life span (about two years) permits life-long observations. The dog was picked as a larger, nonrodent species in which a good deal of *general* pharmacological and toxicological background was available from decades of earlier work. The monkey was selected as a species that presumably resembles humans more closely than any of the others.

Nobody in the contraceptive field disputes the wisdom of the requirement for data on animal toxicity before a drug is administered to humans, even in short-term clinical experiments involving only a few individuals. Nevertheless, the FDA's stipulation of particular animal species to be used in contraceptive research has proved to be extremely unwise. After all, the sole reason for selecting any animal is to provide an appropriate model for extrapolation to humans. As discussed in the previous chapter, the FDA's choice of the dog—notoriously sensitive to steroid sex hormones—as one of the required species for testing oral contraceptives was especially unfortunate. Indeed, even the simple requirement for data on toxicity in the "monkey" may be virtually meaningless in the area of reproductive physiology unless careful attention is given to the choice of the monkey species.

In order to gain as much knowledge as possible from animal studies, a model should be selected that most closely resembles humans in its *metabolic handling* of the particular drug in question. Table 5-2 summarizes data accumulated on the excretion pattern and plasma half-life (i.e., time during which 50 percent of the administered drug is still present in blood circulation), in humans and in seven animal species, for a new experimental nonsteroid drug. These studies were conducted in order to select the best animal model for that drug in humans, who excrete 94 percent of the drug in the urine and in whom the plasma half-life, as established by work with radioactive material, is 14 hours. The studies demonstrate that, for this particular drug, the mini-pig is at least as good an animal model as the rhesus monkey and, even more strikingly, that the differences between the rhesus and the capuchin monkey are almost greater than the differences between any other two animal species in the study! If Gertrude Stein had said "a monkey is a monkey is a monkey," she would have been dead wrong from a metabolic standpoint.

TABLE 5-2

Data on excretion patterns and plasma half-life for an experimental drug

Species	Excretion		Plasma half-life (hours)
	Urine (%)	Feces (%)	
Man	94	1-2	14
Rat	90	2	4-6
Guinea pig	90	5	9
Dog	29	50	23-35
Rhesus monkey	90	2	2-3
Capuchin monkey	45	54	20
Stump-tail monkey	40	60	1
Mini-pig	86	1-2	4-7

SOURCE: C. Djerassi. "Birth Control After 1984." *Science*, vol. 169, 1970, pp. 941-51.

I go into such detail about toxicity requirements and metabolic differences in various animal species to illustrate a crucial point on which most future fertility control research rests. Unless all research is to be performed directly on humans—a suggestion that can hardly be entertained in the case of completely new drugs—much more work needs to be done to identify useful animal models that have some predictive bearing on the biological response of humans to a given agent. Such work will require major efforts on the part of investigators, major financial inputs (notably to establish primate facilities), and, most importantly, some relaxation of the present FDA requirement specifying the rat, dog, and monkey as animal models for toxicology in contraceptive research. Although it is likely that the higher apes (i.e., chimpanzees or gorillas) are the best models for human reproductive physiological behavior, insufficient biochemical work has been done to substantiate this claim. The smaller monkeys, which frequently bear little resemblance to humans in their metabolic response, are used almost exclusively because of ease of handling and lower cost. In addition to the enormous cost differential between monkeys (approximately $200 per animal) and apes (approximately $2,000 for a chimpanzee and $10,000 for a gorilla) one must take into account the very much higher handling and maintenance cost for apes as well as their extraordinarily limited availability. Indeed, the higher apes are now protected species and extensive breeding facilities would be needed to supply the large numbers of such apes required for the type of work outlined in the sections that follow.

Time and Cost Estimates for a New Female Contraceptive Agent

Prior to 1970, newspaper articles and scientific journals were filled with descriptions of prospective new contraceptive approaches, together with extraordinarily loose and optimistic time projections about major advances that were supposedly to occur within a period of five years. However, none of these predictions included any type of "critical path map" outlining each of the necessary developmental steps, along with associated cost and time estimates, that would be required to bring these laboratory discoveries to the consumer. In 1970 I published such a critical path map, which I bring up to date here taking inflation into consideration. This type of detailed presentation illustrates graphically how long it takes and how expensive it is to bring a new contraceptive drug to the public (see Fig. 5-1 and Table 5-3). More importantly, such an analysis also draws attention to the weakness in our present regulatory system, which retards the development not only of new contraceptive drugs but of other drugs as well.

Fig. 5-1 shows the critical path for the development of an important hypothetical new drug—a "once-a-month" pill with luteolytic properties (meaning that the agent will destroy the *corpus luteum,* which is responsible for the continuing secretion of progesterone necessary for the maintenance of pregnancy). Such a once-a-month pill would have at least four advantages over presently used oral contraceptives. First, ingesting a single pill once a month is more convenient than daily pill taking. Second, periodic short-term administration of a drug (once a month) would be expected to give rise to fewer long-term side effects, primarily because the agent is intended to act at a specific time on a well-defined biological process rather than interfere for prolonged periods with the entire hormonal balance. Third, a luteolytic agent would be effective as a contraceptive irrespective of whether fertilization has occurred—it would be a menses-inducer in the nonpregnant woman and an early abortifacient in a pregnant subject. Fourth, such a luteolytic agent might be active any time during the first eight weeks after fertilization; it could then be taken bimonthly.

The overall development process (from the beginning chemical synthesis and biological evaluation in the laboratory, to the metabolic and toxicological studies with animals, followed by the clinical evaluation) is so complicated that it is not feasible to present this material in a form easily comprehensible to the layman. The individual steps and time estimates, assuming optimum coordination and performance of many steps almost simultaneously rather than sequentially, are outlined in Fig. 5-1 (see page 78); a fuller description of the individual steps and the crass financial details are listed in Table 5-3 (see pages 80-81). Most readers can skip this information if they are satisfied with the punch line: it would take 10½ to 17½ years to develop such a new female contraceptive agent and would cost $15 to $46 million—*if everything goes well!*

For those readers interested in the details, three major additional comments are required to evaluate fully Fig. 5-1 and Table 5-3. The first refers to the teratology studies—looking for birth defects in offspring—which are extremely important when dealing with any agent that could affect embryonic development. I assume in the critical path map that the FDA would permit phase I clinical studies without previous teratology studies in animals (because very few women would be exposed and any pregnancy would be aborted, thus eliminating any danger of a malformed offspring). Whether or

FIGURE 5-1

Critical path map for luteolytic "once-a-month" pill

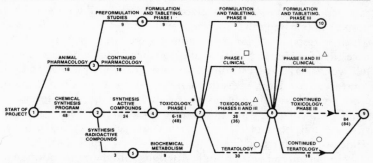

* 25 compounds into toxicology for phase I clinical
□ 15 compounds into phase I clinical (assumes 10 lost from results of toxicology)
△ 1 compound into phase II and III toxicology and clinical studies
○ May not be necessary if all failures are surgically aborted

The circled numbers are step numbers; the numbers below the line are time periods, in months. Thus, for example, ①—⑨ means that the period from the beginning of step 1 to the beginning of step 3 is 18 months. Numbers in parentheses indicate time periods, in months, when the usual FDA toxicological-study requirements for contraceptives are a possible alternative.

SOURCE: C. Djerassi. "Birth Control After 1984." *Science,* vol. 169, 1970, pp. 941-51.

not this assumption is correct, phase I clinical studies and the subsequent phase II and phase III clinical research can be performed only in a location where, in case the method fails, surgical abortion can be employed.

Indeed, the work leading to eventual determination of the clinically effective dose would require progressive lowering of the dose until a level is reached in which failure is observed—that is, pregnancy results. From an investigative standpoint, it would be desirable for human pregnancies resulting from such drug failure to proceed beyond the 14th week before surgical abortion was undertaken, so that the fetus could be examined for evidence of malformation. Yet this would present enormous problems—not only in terms of a woman's overall safety (see the discussion of abortion in Chapter 2) but also in terms of the availability and cooperation of participants. For obvious reasons, many women would be loath to participate in such experiments. In the absence of actual experience with humans, one would have to depend on monkey data, which are much less informative.

The second comment on the critical path map (Fig. 5-1) pertains to the time estimates associated with each step. These are ideal figures, and the aggregate of about 10½ to 17½ years is based on the assumption that saving time rather than dollars is the overriding objective. Therefore, I am assuming the concurrent performance of several steps, which are usually carried out sequentially in ordinary practice. For instance, the preliminary toxicology (Table 5-3, steps 4→7) on 25 compounds would involve rejection of several candidates because of serious toxicity, as well as rejection based on phase I clinical data (steps 7→8). The estimate of 6 to 18 months for the time required for the initial toxicological studies leading to the selection of the final compound is, in fact, very optimistic because it assumes that work on 25 compounds will be initiated essentially simultaneously, which is certainly not the case now.

The third comment refers to the cost estimates. There are major uncertainties about the ultimate cost of toxicological studies, since this figure could vary enormously depending on the choice and cost of the animals used for testing as well as on whether the FDA would require the same kinds of toxicological studies required for current oral contraceptives (which are taken on an almost daily basis as compared to the intermittent one for our hypothetical once-a-month pill). A further and greater uncertainty is the estimate for phase III clinical studies (Fig. 5-1, steps 8→9). In response to demands by consumers that virtually all actual and potential side effects of such a drug be known prior to government approval for marketing, the FDA might require that women be studied for much longer periods of time than the four years hypothesized in the critical path map; this may in fact be the single greatest uncertainty involved in the planning of any new contraceptive development.

Irrespective of the final cost figure—somewhere between $15 million and $46 million—allocation of such a sum by a government or private agency in the form of grants to various *nonindustrial* laboratories would be insufficient to accomplish the desired goal of producing an agent ready for wide public use; cost and time estimates here are based on the availability in *one existing organization* (that is, in the research divisions of a large pharmaceutical company) of all the manpower, facilities, and logistic support required for the type of sophisticated technical schedule and activity outlined in Fig. 5-1. If these facilities had to be created de novo and the required infrastructure had to be supported exclusively from funds allocated to such a project, then the final cost would have to be multiplied several times.

Finally, whatever the overall cost estimate, one has to realize that, as has happened several times in the past, the drug might be rejected for various safety or efficacy reasons by the FDA or by the developer

TABLE 5-3

Cost and time data for the development of a luteolytic "once-a-month" pill

Step Identity No.	Function	Duration of function (years)	Cost ($)
1	Start of project.		
1 to 2	Laboratory chemical synthesis of compounds for biological screening program (four chemists at $81,000 per chemist per year).	4	1,300,000
1 to 3	Development of biological models to test luteolytic or abortifacient compounds. Use of synthesized compounds in test systems in rodents and monkeys to determine mechanism of action.	1.5	550,000
2 to 4	Synthesis of larger amounts of active compounds selected in biological test systems to be used in preformulation, formulation, and phase I toxicological and clinical studies.	2	360,000
2 to 5	Synthesis of radioactive material of the most active compound in biological tests for use in biochemical metabolism.	0.25	18,000
3 to 4	Continued biological studies on mechanism of action of active compounds.	1.5	415,000
3 to 6	In vitro and in vivo studies of stability, solubility, and absorption of active compounds to assist formulation and tableting.	0.75	180,000
4 to 7	Toxicological studies for phase I clinical studies. It is assumed that, since only short-term therapy is envisaged, FDA will not require toxicological studies such as are required for current oral contraceptives. It will be sufficient to study LD_{50} (dose lethal to 50 percent of animals) in 60 rats and 16 dogs per compound, using 25 compounds; 15 compounds are expected to be found satisfactory for phase I clinical studies.	0.15-1.5	340,000
	If usual phase I contraceptive toxicological studies are required (see Table 5-1), the following numbers of animals will be needed for 25 compounds: 12,000 rats, 2,400 rabbits, 800 dogs, and 5,400 primates for LD_{50} 90-day toxicological, teratological, and abortifacient studies.	(4)	(38,500,000)
6 to 7	Formulation and tableting for phase I clinical studies.	0.75	180,000
5 to 7	Metabolic studies in rodent or primate and human with synthetic radioactive material already prepared. Both oral and intravenous administration may be studied.	0.75	70,000

		Years	Cost
7 to 8 to 9	Toxicological and teratological studies for phase II and phase III clinical studies. Although FDA may require very limited studies for clinical phase I because of short-term dosing, it has been assumed that toxicological studies required for later clinical work will be as stringent as in current oral contraceptive development, involving long-term teratological and repetitive-abortion studies of five compounds for 1 year, in 160 rats, 32 dogs, and 32 primates (phase II) and, for the best of the five compounds, 2-year studies in 240 rats, 7-year studies in 64 dogs, and 10-year studies in 80 primates (phase III).	7 to completion of all toxicology[a]	1,100,000
	If usual phase II contraceptive toxicological studies are required, the following numbers of animals will be required for study of one compound: 800 rats, 160 dogs, 160 primates, for 1 year.	(3)	(900,000)
	If usual phase III contraceptive toxicological studies are required, the following numbers of animals are required for study of one compound: 240 rats for 2 years, 64 dogs for 7 years, and 80 primates for 10 years.	(7)	(1,100,000)
7 to 8	Phase I clinical studies. It is assumed that 15 compounds will have proved satisfactory in the toxicological studies. A single dose will be administered to a small number of women to cause abortion in the 1st or 2nd month of pregnancy. The best compound will be selected for phase II and phase III clinical studies. With a one-dose level and costs of $1,190 per woman per menstrual cycle, for 3-cycle studies the total cost for 15 compounds is $540,000. Therefore, costs for developing 2 different doses are:	0.75	1,080,000
8 to 10	Formulation, tableting, and cost of material for phase III clinical studies, including cost of material for long-term toxicity.	0.25	550,000
8 to 9	Phase II and phase III clinical studies of the best compound will be combined. A requirement of 1,000 women studied for 10,000 cycles is assumed.	4	900,000
	Total time and cost to time prior to FDA application	10 to 17	14,533,000
	Preparation of FDA registration file	0.5	110,000
	Grand Total (toxicity studies of Table 5-1 not included)	10.5 to 17.5[b]	14,643,000
	Grand Total (toxicity studies of Table 5-1 included)	17.5	46,303,000

[a] Two-year studies in rats, dogs, and primates are necessary for NDA application, but ongoing 7-year studies in dogs and 10-year studies in monkeys are required (see Table 5-1). When certain FDA toxicological study requirements for contraceptives are given as a possible alternative, the duration of the study and its associated extra cost are given in ( ). All cost estimates for primates are based on the use of $200 monkeys; major upward revisions would have to be made if higher apes such as chimpanzees were employed.
[b] The development time is calculated, not by summing all times in the time breakdown, but from the Critical Path Map (Fig. 5-1), following the longest course of development.

SOURCE: Adapted and updated from C. Djerassi. "Birth Control After 1984." Science, vol. 169, 1970, pp. 941-51.

himself at a very late stage of the phase III clinical trials. Thus, to increase the chances of developing a successful new female contraceptive agent it would be best to launch at least two efforts simultaneously of the type described here, which of course would double the cost.

Time and Cost Estimates for a New Male Contraceptive Agent

Currently no counterpart to the female oral contraceptive pill is available for the male. The critical path for such a male agent is very similar to that outlined for the female once-a-month pill, except that a longer time estimate is required for the beginning stages—that is, to discover suitable leads giving rise to compounds that warrant clinical investigation. To expedite such a development, it would be highly desirable if several programs—each costing about $5 million—of the type outlined in Fig. 5-2, steps 1→2→4→8 and 1→3→7, were instituted simultaneously in several pharmaceutical laboratories.

FIGURE 5-2

Critical path map for development of a male antifertility agent

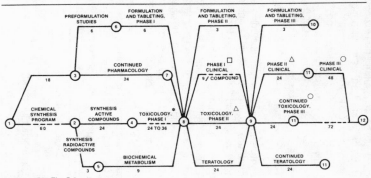

see legend to Fig. 5-1
* 25 compounds into toxicology for phase I clinical
□ 15 compounds into phase I clinical (assumes 10 lost from results of toxicology)
△ 5 compounds into phase II toxicology and clinical studies
○ 1 compound into phase III toxicology and clinical

SOURCE: C. Djerassi. "Birth Control After 1984." *Science*, vol. 169, 1970, pp. 941-51.

Nothing will stimulate future research on a practical male contraceptive agent more than the discovery of viable and significant chemical leads—a typical example being the recently announced Chinese male pill (discussed in Chapter 10) which is based on the cottonseed constituent gossypol. However, even with such chemical leads we encounter three additional difficulties associated with the development of a chemical contraceptive drug for the male.

First, our basic knowledge of the reproductive biology of the male is even less advanced than our knowledge of the reproductive biology of the female, and a great deal of fundamental work needs to be done, much of it probably in subhuman primates.

Second, actual clinical contraceptive work with men has so far not drawn the same degree of attention as has birth control work with women. Furthermore, there are special features associated with such clinical studies in the male that make the process more time consuming. The human spermatogenic cycle lasts approximately 12 weeks. Therefore, it is likely that preliminary testing alone—including initial drug treatment, control, post-treatment recovery observations, and evaluation of the data—would take nine months per compound (compared with two to three months for females), depending on the point where the drug in question attacks the spermatogenic sequence. For each agent such pilot testing (Fig. 5-2, steps 8→9) would have to be carried out in groups of at least five males, at each of three widely spaced dose levels, in order to get some idea of the effective human dose. Observations should combine evaluation of the effect on sperm formation or sperm motility, or both, with observations of organ toxicity and other side effects, including libido. At present in the U.S. there seem to be available clinical facilities for evaluating only a few male contraceptive drugs at a time. The complications associated with such limited facilities would be even greater in phase II and phase III clinical studies. Women can easily be assembled for clinical studies through their association with Planned Parenthood clinics and individual obstetricians or gynecologists, but there is no simple mechanism for assembling similar groups of males for clinical experimentation. The prisons and armed forces are theoretically the most convenient sources, and results would have to be based largely on examination of masturbation sperm samples rather than on an evaluation of fertility control in an average population, as can be done with the female. However, predicting definite infertility solely on the basis of sperm count is notoriously unreliable.

This leads to the third difficulty—namely, men are, generally speaking, less interested in, and have greater reservations about, procedures that are aimed at decreasing their fertility. If a fertility control drug were to be taken orally, men would probably be even less reliable about taking a tablet regularly than women have proved to be, and use efficacy (as opposed to theoretical efficacy) could be determined on a large scale only through long-term studies of married couples, the failure rate being the number of unwanted pregnancies. Thus, women would have to participate in these large-scale phase III trials, be willing to run the risk of becoming pregnant, and be assured an abortion in case of failure.

Given the hurdles associated with the development of a male Pill enumerated above, I estimate that it would require 12 to 20 years and at least $15 million before such an agent would be available to the U.S. consumer. What this agent might actually be and how it might exert its effect will be discussed in detail in Chapter 7.

The Role of the Pharmaceutical Industry

At the beginning of this chapter I stated that we should find means of encouraging the pharmaceutical industry to become more involved in contraceptive research. Why is this involvement so critical?

Except for a few special vaccines, essentially all modern prescription drugs have been developed by pharmaceutical companies. I know of no case in which all of the work (chemistry, biology, toxicology, formulation, analytical studies, and clinical studies through phase III) leading to governmental approval of a drug was performed by a government laboratory, a medical school, or a nonprofit research institute. This does not mean that many of the basic discoveries leading to the development of a drug ultimately used by the public are not discovered in such nonindustrial laboratories, or that certain important steps (for example, much of the clinical work) are not performed outside of industry. Nevertheless, it is a simple fact that in modern industrial nations pharmaceutical firms play an indispensable role in the development of any drug. Socialist countries have developed counterparts to the pharmaceutical industry, but these counterparts to date have had practically no impact on drug innovation in general and new contraceptive development in particular (with the possible exception of the Chinese male pill).

The public is frequently unaware of this key constructive function of the pharmaceutical industry—a function not directly related to the marketing role of these firms but rather to their unique ability to organize, stimulate, and finance multidisciplinary research covering the entire gamut of the scientific disciplines required to convert a laboratory discovery into a practical drug. In addition, the organizational efforts involved in preparing a complete New Drug Application (NDA) in the United States are completely outside the capabilities of nonprofit institutions and are not undertaken by government agencies, although the latter could presumably mobilize the requisite manpower and funds for such purposes.

At present in the U.S., all of the expenses associated with the development of a new prescription drug are borne by private industry, eventually to be recovered from sales. The ever-increasing cost of drug development is certainly responsible in part for the progressively decreasing number of new drugs introduced in this country.

Some of the special FDA requirements that have been imposed on drugs used for fertility control are understandable and justified; similar requirements would undoubtedly be imposed on any other drug (for example, preventive medication in atherosclerosis) administered for long periods (usually years) to healthy people. These requirements are a response to the rapid acceptance by so many women of these new birth control agents as well as to our increasing knowledge of human reproductive physiology in general and our accumulated experience with oral contraceptives in particular.

Unfortunately, neither the public nor the government is facing realistically the following facts. The costs of developing contraceptive agents have escalated to such an extent that it is unlikely that the traditional course of drug development will lead rapidly, or possibly even eventually, to the introduction of fundamentally new contraceptive drugs. The financial return for such long-term, high-risk endeavors is simply not attractive. If the present research climate and regulatory requirements had prevailed in 1955, steroid oral contraceptives would without doubt still be a laboratory curiosity today.

Yet in all likelihood toxicity and testing requirements will in the future become more stringent and time consuming, not less so. Further criteria (e.g., testing for potential mutagenesis, ever-more diverse metabolic effects, etc.) are being added in response to accumulated new knowledge. Costs will continue to escalate enormously. No decision maker in industry can ignore the concept of return on investment. (And on the whole, costs are calculated much more realistically in the industrial than in the governmental sector, where many hidden costs are simply paid unknowingly by the taxpayer and profit need not be considered.) In any calculation of return on investment, time, particularly in an inflationary climate, is an overriding factor. Other reasons why time is so expensive were well summarized by Dr. John H. Abeles, one of the most able drug security analysts, in a speech he made in 1978 to a group of financial security analysts. His points are important because in a capitalist system sooner or later management must take into consideration the attitudes of actual or potential stockholders.

> [When evaluating the price of a stock], do not pay for a drug that is not due on a sophisticated market within five years. There is too much uncertainty and vicissitude surrounding drug development to invest in drugs further out. Certainly, distant promising drugs or technologies need to be monitored but investors should not allow themselves to be "prostaglandinized" as they were in the early 1970s by the publicity on Upjohn's early efforts in this [prostaglandin] field. We hesitate to pay "on faith" for the vague "quality" of research and, recognizing the elements of serendipity and adversity that permeate drug research, recommend that the contribution of the aggregate number of drugs on the market within five years be the research premium accorded the current valuation of the stock.
>
> Even if a drug is likely to arrive in five years, do not pay for it until the appropriate animal toxicology has been completed. . . .
>
> Do not pay for a drug unless some human efficacy has been demonstrated, even if it is expected to reach the market in five years' time. . . .
>
> In calculating contributions by individual drugs to long-term growth rates, do not go beyond five years after marketing. Too much can happen in the way of adverse effects, unexpected competition, or general marketing considerations to be at all confident of projections of more than five years.

In 1970, I estimated that the cumulative five-year expenditure for contraceptive research during the period 1965-69 by just five American pharmaceutical companies amounted to about $68 million. My survey did not include all of the major American pharmaceutical companies active in the birth control field, nor did it include any European firms. Thus it is likely that the pharmaceutical industry worldwide contributed over $100 million for contraceptive research and development during these five years. This was an enormous sum by any standards and it was spent almost entirely on work dealing with contraceptive hardware (whereas a substantial portion of government funds was devoted to ancillary activities—for example, sociological and demographic studies). I wrote then that it was unrealistic to expect that larger sums or, in fact, even the same sums will be spent by the private sector in the future when the eventual recovery of such expenditures becomes more and more distant and problematical. Since 1970 several pharmaceutical companies have completely dropped out of the contraceptive field (including Eli Lilly & Co., the largest of them all), almost all of the active ones have scaled down their efforts, and no newcomers have entered. Neither this lack of competition nor the pharmaceutical industry's overall reduction in financial and manpower allocation works to society's benefit.

In 1976 the Ford Foundation sponsored a major study, known as the Greep Report (after the project director Dr. Roy O. Greep), on contraceptive developments. Included in the study was a rather detailed survey of the financial expenditures in this field by the pharmaceutical industry, government, and private foundations. Some of the results are summarized in Table 5-4 and demonstrate dramatically the decrease in the relative contribution of the pharmaceutical industry to contraceptive research and development and the increase in government funding.

TABLE 5-4

Total Expenditures (U.S.) for Reproductive Research (1965-74)

	1965	1970	1974
Total Sum	$32,000,000	$55,000,000	$62,000,000
Contribution (%)			
Pharmaceutical Industry	39	24	19
Government	36	46	61
Private Foundations	25	30	20

SOURCE: Modified from R.O. Greep, M.A. Koblinsky, and F.S. Jaffe. *Reproduction and Human Welfare: A Challenge to Research.* Cambridge: MIT Press, 1976.

It is clear that taxpayers are spending more money on birth control research and development, but are they also getting more for their money? I do not believe so. Dr. Oscar Harkavy of the Ford Foundation ended his formal testimony at the March 1978 hearings of the House Select Committee on Population with the following statement: "Given the increased costs of meeting appropriately stringent regulatory requirements, and the increasing difficulty of obtaining adequate product liability insurance, contraceptive development is an increasingly unattractive way for private industry to allocate its funds and scientific effort. Contraceptive development is

Monkey. Mixtec, postclassic, *ca.* A.D. 900–1100.

of social benefit, however, and government should seek ways of encouraging industry to keep active in the field."

Irrespective of who stays active in the field and how we encourage the involvement of private industry, for all practical purposes the rules of the game for everyone—in both private and public sectors—have changed irrevocably. Now that we understand those rules, we shall see, in Chapters 7 and 8, how they affect the development of new male and female contraceptives. But first we need to examine some of the sources of public pressure that generated the rules and that continue to shape developments in the birth control field.

Questioning figure. Quimbaya, Colombia, *ca.* A.D. 400–700.

The Public's Right to Know

DR. ALAN S. GUTTMACHER: I am not attacking the hearings. I believe in free speech. I believe everybody has a right to be heard. But unfortunately, when it comes to medical matters, the negative is so often more clearly understood than the positive by lay people. This is just the nature of the problem, sir. I have not the solution to it.

SENATOR GAYLORD NELSON: Well, my own view is that [holding these hearings] is about the only solution that there is. My own view, furthermore, is that you will conclude, yourself, after a couple of years that the greatest benefit to the pill and the development of more effective devices, or one of the great benefits, is the effect of these hearings.

> Testimony from hearings of the Senate Subcommittee on Monopoly of the Select Committee on Small Business, 91st Congress, February 25, 1970.

THE PUBLIC'S RIGHT TO KNOW is fundamental in a free society. It is invariably associated with freedom of the press, but much less frequently with the quality of press coverage. Just as freedom of speech does not license one to shout "fire" jokingly in a crowded theater, so freedom of the press does not license the media to disseminate important information—especially that of a complex, technical nature—irresponsibly and with little appreciation of the consequences. Nevertheless, those whose job it is to keep the public informed are frequently inclined to shout "fire" at the top of their voices without knowing whether anything is burning or how to put out the flames if there are any.

Congress, too, plays a vital role in influencing the quality of information the public receives. Often stimulated into inquiry by a newspaper story or press release, Congress becomes a forum for generating further media coverage. Unfortunately, the quality of congressional inquiry, especially in technical fields, is itself often low, and because of this, along with uncritical coverage of congressional hearings, the public's right to know is sometimes fulfilled in a manner that is both superficial and misleading, and even irresponsible.

Unrestricted open disclosure is an issue of public policy often raised in the context of health. The field of birth control is no exception, and in this chapter I shall address both the benefits and the costs of this legislative/press interplay, which serves as the principal source of public information about birth control.

The Nelson Hearings

Between January and March of 1970, Senator Gaylord Nelson's Senate Subcommittee on Monopoly of the Select Committee on Small Business held a series of hearings, known as the Nelson hearings, which were convened, according to the committee's press statement, "to explore the question whether users of birth control pills are being adequately informed concerning the Pill's known health hazards." At first sight a subcommittee on monopoly of the Select Committee on Small Business is a peculiar forum for holding hearings not on prices, monopoly, or small business, but on the side effects of oral contraceptives. However, chairmen of congressional committees are powerful men and Senator Nelson has for many years used his position as subcommittee chairman to investigate the American pharmaceutical industry—not because it is small business, but because in his opinion it is too profitable.

Politically a liberal, Nelson in his Senate work has shown compassion and concern for public welfare, including increased and improved family planning in America and elsewhere. However, science and technology are not his forte and some of his proposals over the years to reform the pharmaceutical industry have been extraordinarily naive and have not led to any significant new legislation. Not surprisingly, the U.S. pharmaceutical industry considers the Senator from Wisconsin to be a major antagonist, and little love has been lost over the years between the Senator and that industry.

In the specific context of oral contraceptives, Senator Nelson felt that physicians frequently kept women uninformed about the potential side effects of the Pill and that the pharmaceutical companies were directly or indirectly responsible for this state of affairs. His complaint was not without merit, but his approach to the problem proved to be far from productive.

On the first day of the 1970 hearings on the safety of the Pill, Nelson stated, "I hope that these hearings will be regarded as a major incentive to the researchers, physicians, biologists, chemists, drug companies, and government agencies to find answers to the many questions which have been and are being raised by oral and other contraceptives. It is urgently necessary that solutions be found as quickly as possible which are compatible with the health, welfare, and the dignity of human beings here and throughout the world." In the end, the record of the Nelson hearings filled three volumes totaling 1,402 pages. Not only does this record provide an interesting window into the American political process in operation, it also raises the question whether so much verbiage and paper is justified by the results. Though few laymen today may remember the Nelson hearings, they are worth examining in detail because their impact on the future of fertility control research has been enormous. Were the benefits worth the costs?

In spite of repeated claims by Senator Nelson about the "balanced" nature of these hearings, most of the vocal Pill antagonists were scheduled to testify during the earlier part of the hearings, which received maximum newspaper publicity. Though Nelson stated that the witness stand was open to any representative from any pharmaceutical company, not one testified. In my opinion this was an important tactical mistake, but one that reflected the industry's suspicion of both the adversary character of the forum and the Senator himself. (I do know that one pharmaceutical company official who wrote to Nelson volunteering to testify was never contacted by Nelson or his staff in reply.)

Press coverage of the Nelson hearings was intense; it started weeks before they began and involved almost daily headlines in even as serious a newspaper as the *New York Times*. The headlines in mid-

January 1970 were alarming, to say the least. Consider the following headline and opening paragraph from the January 18, 1970, edition of the *San Francisco Sunday Examiner & Chronicle,* the second largest paper in California: "Wave of Alarm Over the Pill—Alarmed women across the nation are calling their doctors after learning of testimony before a Senate subcommittee about possible hazards of birth control pills."

The sensational nature of much of the Senate testimony and the even more sensational press coverage were at times astounding. That both so often lacked any critical evaluation was even more disturbing. Consider this testimony by Dr. Herbert Ratner, a public health official, on January 22, 1970:

> DR. RATNER: Incidentally, leaving the pill out in the open so as not to forget it has led to numerous child poisonings.
>
> SENATOR DOLE: Do we have some evidence on how many cases you know of?
>
> DR. RATNER: Of accidental poisoning, child poisoning, it [accidental ingestion of oral contraceptives] was the number two cause two years ago in Missouri, and it has a high incidence in the United States.
>
> SENATOR DOLE: From the pill?
>
> DR. RATNER: Yes—child poisoning. Now, remember, the problem is that the woman does not want to forget to take the pill. And there are underlying psychological reasons why she has ambivalence about taking the pill, so she always keeps it where she can see it, which means the child can see it, and so this became the number two cause of child poisoning reported in the Government literature and reported in the newspapers and it came as a cause—
>
> SENATOR DOLE: Not to hold you up, but have there been numerous child poisonings because of the pill? If you will just insert some evidence on that, it would be helpful.

The record then states that Dr. Ratner subsequently supplied the following bibliography: "Contraceptive pills have become a major . . . source of childhood poisoning, the Public Health Service reports. There were 962 reported childhood poisonings due to the Pill during 1962 to 1965, according to Mr. Henry L. Verhulst, chief of the Poison Control Branch of the P.H.S. *Modern Medicine,* May 9, 1966, p. 28." In checking the original reference in *Modern Medicine,* I found that Dr. Ratner skipped only three words in the above quote that contraceptive pills have become a "major... source of childhood poisoning," namely, "although relatively benign." This omission sheds a rather different light on "Pill poisoning."

But there is more. The *Modern Medicine* article was in fact only a news comment on the original article by H.L. Verhulst and J.J. Crotty which appeared in the *Journal of Clinical Pharmacology* (1967). The authors cited in a table that in 1965, 450 cases of accidental oral contraceptive ingestion by children under the age of five were reported; they then concluded: "A recent analysis of oral contraceptive reports showed that where the symptoms were indicated on the form, 99 percent of the ingestions had checked signs and symptoms—none."

This should be contrasted with the annual incidence of approximately 200 deaths of children attributable to aspirin poisoning. Though I am not suggesting that aspirin be banned, I do not know of a single reported case of accidental death in children resulting from the intake of oral contraceptives. In fact, there seems to be no "poisoning" of children at all—only inadvertent ingestion. I emphasize this point because as a result of Dr. Ratner's testimony, which was critically evaluated neither by Senator Nelson's staff nor by the press, scare headlines again appeared. One dramatic example from Jack Anderson's widely syndicated column "Merry-Go-Round" (*San Francisco Chronicle*, April 29, 1970) was headlined "New Frightening Dangers of 'The Pill.'"

The following excerpt is typical of the contents of Anderson's article: "For the 8 million American women taking birth control pills, who already face an increased risk of heart attack and blood clots, this column has uncovered a new and frightening danger. ... In most cases, the youngsters took their mother's pills thinking they were candy. The reports don't specify how serious the effects were, but the poisonings increased rapidly at the end of the data period. ... All too typically, most drug companies are more interested in profits than in protecting children." When you compare the contents of the Anderson column with the concluding quotation "signs and symptoms—none" in 99 percent of the cases from the scientific article upon which his "evidence" was largely based, you will appreciate why I am concerned about the quality of press coverage and the impact of such distortions on the public.

Having gotten a taste of the caliber of some of the testimony at the Nelson hearings and the way such testimony was sensationalized in the press, it is instructive to read in detail a portion of the testimony of Dr. Elizabeth B. Connell, at that time associate professor of obstetrics and gynecology at Columbia University. Unfortunately, her testimony was not heard until February 24, well over a month after the initial negative reports and scare headlines had appeared in the newspapers. Her solid, unsensational testimony did not garner the headlines or coverage that the January witnesses received, but its eloquence speaks for itself:

I happen to have been born a female and have five sons and a daughter. Thus I realize that I represent a group not previously heard by this committee and I certainly cannot in any sense be considered to be opposed to the perpetuation of the species. I shrink from approaching my testimony in such a highly personal manner, but after carefully reviewing the situation, it seemed to me that only in this way might my combined areas of experience be of some value to you.

In looking at a subject with as many ramifications as the oral contraceptive, all of us who deal with individual patients as well as major programs face many difficulties. On the one hand, we appreciate the obvious necessity for finding contraceptive methods which are 100 percent effective and 100 percent safe—this is not entirely the province of the academic purist. The thought that any method which we currently employ may fall short of this ideal is intensely disturbing to doctors.

At the other end of the scale, we see the tragic results of unwanted pregnancies and the growing twin horrors of overpopulation and pollution. Those of us who live and work between these two extremes understandably find ourselves in a somewhat schizoid situation. To date, these hearings have not made our lives any easier. It seems to me that much of the previous testimony has been rather like a bikini; what it has uncovered has been interesting, but what it has left concealed is vital.

To my mind, one major misfortune has been the artifical and totally erroneous creation of two camps of doctors, the pro-pill and the anti-pill. Except for a few extremists among us, such an arbitrary division is not only totally unrealistic but also most regrettable. I believe that I speak for the overwhelming majority of physicians when I state most emphatically that I do not belong to either group.

I firmly believe that no thinking objective doctor can be

totally pro-pill or totally anti-pill. We all recognize the tremendous contribution made by these agents to medicine and society, and we use them with the same judgment and the same respect we pay to any powerful drug. In this respect, we are pro-pill.

We also recognize that there is an element of risk in all potent medications, and so for particular patients, we are anti-pill. However, to be forced daily by current pressures to declare ourselves as belonging to either the far left or the far right on this question is not only increasingly annoying but is actually incredibly destructive. Segregation of doctors into opposing camps is of value to no one, least of all the women we are all dedicated to serving.

I would like to look first at what has come out of the preceding days of testimony, as viewed by a self-styled moderate. First of all, virtually nothing has been presented in these hearings that those of us working in this field have not heard many times over. When I examined the vintage of the testimony to date, I discovered that some is relatively new, much is several years old, and a few pearls of information were in print long before I started in medical school.

It has been frequently asserted that the hearings, thus far, have been slanted, one-sided, and unfair. Objective consideration suggests that in one sense, this criticism may indeed be valid. The bias which I feel has been noticeable on previous days has been the bias of positive results. No scientist of experience would question the capability and integrity of almost all the previous witnesses. Their work has been meticulous and their results are not in question. What is disturbing is the fact that such a great percentage of time has been devoted to two areas—first, experimental work carried out by competent men in excellent laboratories, but far removed from patient care and its implications; and second, to side effects which occur in a very small percentage of the patient population. *What has been missing to date and what I think is needed to maintain an overall proper balance and perspective is a better look at the vast majority of women who can and are taking oral contraceptives safely and effectively* [my italics].

As a physician who began to practice before the advent of the pill, I am constantly aware of the immense difference it has made to the lives of women, to their families, and to society as a whole. The look of horror on the face of a 12-year-old girl when you confirm her fears of pregnancy; the sound of a woman's voice cursing her newborn and unwanted child as she lies on the delivery table; the absolutely helpless feeling that comes over you as you watch a woman die following criminal abortion; the hideous responsibility of informing a husband and children that their wife and mother has just died in childbirth—all these situations are deeply engraved in our memories, never to be forgotten. Since we have had more effective means of contraception, the recurrence of these nightmares has blessedly become less frequent. The thought that we may once again be forced to face these disasters on an increasing scale because of the panic induced by these hearings strikes horror into the hearts of all of us who have lived through this era once before.

A great deal of very positive information was presented here last month. Aside from the obvious personal, social, and economic advantages of planned pregnancy, we were told of lowered prenatal loss, fewer abnormal babies, and lessened maternal risks.

Unfortunately, the general public was not always made aware of this type of information to the same degree that they were made painfully aware of the frightening speculations and the diversity of professional opinion.

One month later, the voluminous hearing record ended with the following exchange between Senator Dole and Senator Nelson:

SENATOR DOLE: [Since this is the final day of the pill hearings] perhaps some reflection is in order. There is some difficulty in my mind in trying to place the hearings within the subcommittee's jurisdiction. The chairman has expressed his idea of the hearings' purpose. The desire to know whether the American public has been properly informed is admirable, but it lacks germaneness to the subcommittee's mandate.

Regardless of the authority under which we are pursuing this investigation, we must recognize that the impact has been substantial. We have at least belatedly seen some elements of balance established for the record, if not in the publicity surrounding the hearings. Headlines such as "Pill

Takers Held More Cancer Prone" were the hallmarks of January's hearings. Testimony raising questions casting doubt dominated the hearings and the headlines. Risks predominated over benefits. Fears were emphasized over effectiveness.

The interval between the January and February hearings began to show the dimensions of the reaction. It is accurate to say that these hearings may not have originated the fear evidenced the past few months. Nonetheless, these hearings have amplified the doubts and uncertainties the American woman has had about oral contraceptives. Another unfortunate aspect of these hearings is that no new knowledge has been disclosed. Several witnesses have related that all the "disclosures" made are well known by the medical profession.

SENATOR NELSON: I will not take the time to respond, except to say that although very little of the information presented here or perhaps none of it was new to the experts in the field, quite obviously a lot of it was not known to the practicing physician who prescribes the pill and the public which consumes it. *And the fact that the Commissioner [of the FDA] himself recognized the necessity for producing a package insert which I announced as one of the purposes of the hearings last year, I think amply justifies the hearings* [my italics].

The people of the country are entitled to know the facts about the pill, and since two-thirds of the doctors were not informing the user, this package insert will perform that function. I happen to be one of those who believes that the public is intelligent enough to receive and evaluate and make decisions on information that the Government has. And this was all Government information, unpublicized previously.

SENATOR DOLE: Mr. Chairman, *I certainly do not have any quarrel with the public's right to know, but they could have known without sensational publicity had we held executive hearings. We would not have frightened 3 or 4 million women. There would not be a group described yesterday as "unwanted Nelson babies" down the pike about 7 or 8 months from now* [my italics].

Although the Nelson hearings produced no legislation, at least one administrative act can be related directly to them, namely, the requirement instituted subsequently by the FDA that detailed package inserts specifying the Pill's side effects accompany every oral contraceptive container. Since most men never see these inserts and even many Pill-taking women do not read them, I reproduce one in full on pages 101-3. Take a look.

The pros and cons of the Pill package insert have been debated extensively. In principle, I am in favor of package inserts for *all* drugs, from over-the-counter items like aspirin to prescription drugs. Nevertheless, I seriously question whether the legalistic manner in which the negative side effects of the Pill are described in order to protect the manufacturer against possible liability suits is a helpful way to convey important information. This package insert can be frightening to the nonspecialist, if not overwhelming.

It is interesting that a rather similar document could be constructed for aspirin by listing the occasional side effects, which include allergies, asthma, hives, edema, nausea, vomiting, disturbances of hearing and vision, anemia, mental confusion, sweating, thirst, diarrhea, and gastrointestinal bleeding. Every substance that a person ingests (from a natural foodstuff to a synthetic drug) has actual or potential side effects. But just listing them is not enough. In preparing such a package insert the character of the overall target population for the drug, the manner in which the drug is being distributed (i.e., over-the-counter or prescription), and the individual's risk/benefit analysis should also be considered. I am convinced that although the Pill package insert in its current format may convey meaningful and constructive information to some women, to the majority it is likely to be counterproductive. I wonder how many abortions and unwanted pregnancies it has caused indirectly among women who, out of fear, abandoned the Pill without using other contraceptive methods.

The indirect consequences of the Nelson hearings on future developments in contraception have been tremendous: the FDA became even more cautious than it had been previously, and the pharmaceutical industry responded with decreased expenditures and efforts in the contraceptive field just as the lag times and costs associated with contraceptive developments were escalating. In my opinion, these hearings, more than any other single factor, have slowed down the development clock of new contraceptive methods.

The Press

The uncritical and sensational reportage of so-called dire conse-

NORINYL® 1 + 50 21-DAY Tablets
(norethindrone 1 mg. with mestranol 0.05 mg.)

NORINYL® 1 + 80 21-DAY Tablets
(norethindrone 1 mg. with mestranol 0.08 mg.)

NORINYL® 1 + 50 28-DAY Tablets
(21 norethindrone 0.05 mg. tablets followed by 7 inert tablets)

NORINYL® 1 + 80 28-DAY Tablets
(21 norethindrone 0.08 mg. tablets followed by 7 inert tablets)

NORINYL® 2 mg. Tablets
(norethindrone 2 mg. with mestranol 0.1 mg.)

NOR-Q.D.®
(norethindrone Tablets 0.35 mg.)

BREVICON® 21-DAY Tablets
(norethindrone 0.5 mg. with ethinyl estradiol 0.035 mg.)

BREVICON® 28-DAY Tablets
(21 norethindrone 0.5 mg. with ethinyl estradiol 0.035 mg. tablets followed by 7 inert tablets)

DETAILED PATIENT LABELING

Oral contraceptives ("the pill") are the most effective way (except for sterilization) to prevent pregnancy. They are also convenient and, for most women, free of serious or unpleasant side effects. Oral contraceptives must always be taken under the continuous supervision of a physician.

It is important that any woman who considers using an oral contraceptive understand the risks involved. Although the oral contraceptives have important advantages over other methods of contraception, they have certain risks that no other method has. Only you can decide whether the advantages are worth these risks. This leaflet will tell you about the most important risks. It will explain how you can decide whether the pill as safely as possible by telling him/her about yourself and being alert for the earliest signs of trouble. And it will tell you how to use the pill properly, so that it will be as effective as possible. There is more detailed information available in the leaflet prepared for doctors. If you need further help, ask your physician or pharmacist.

WHO SHOULD NOT USE ORAL CONTRACEPTIVES

A. If you have any of the following conditions you should not use the pill:
1. Unusual vaginal bleeding that has not yet been diagnosed.
2. Known or suspected pregnancy.

B. If you have or have had any of the following conditions you should not use the pill:
1. Heart attack or stroke.
2. Clots in the legs, lungs, brain, heart or elsewhere.
3. Chest pain (angina pectoris).
4. Known or suspected cancer of the breast or sex organs.
5. Severe liver disease.

C. Cigarette smoking increases the risk of serious adverse effects on the heart and blood vessels from oral contraceptive use. This risk increases with age and with heavy smoking (15 or more cigarettes per day) and is quite marked in women over 35 years of age. Women who use oral contraceptives should not smoke.

D. If you have scanty or irregular periods or are a young woman without a regular cycle, you should use another method of contraception because, if you use the pill, you may have difficulty becoming pregnant or may fail to have menstrual periods after discontinuing the pill.

WHAT YOU SHOULD KNOW ABOUT ORAL CONTRACEPTIVES

This leaflet describes the advantages and risks of oral contraceptives. Except for sterilization, the IUD and abortion, which have their own exclusive risks, the only risks of other methods of contraception are those due to pregnancy should the method fail or not be used conscientiously. Your doctor can answer those questions you may have with respect to methods of contraception.

1. What Oral Contraceptives Are and How They Work. Oral contraceptives are of two types. The most common, often simply called "the pill", is a combination of an estrogen and a progestogen. This kind of female hormones. The amount of estrogen and progestogen can vary, but the amount of estrogen is most important because both the effectiveness and some of the dangers of oral contraceptives are related to the amount of estrogen. This kind of oral contraceptive works principally by preventing release of an egg from the ovary. When the amount of estrogen is 0.05 milligrams or more, and the pill is taken exactly as directed, oral contraceptives are more than 99% effective (i.e., there would be less than one pregnancy if 100 women used the pill for 1 year). Pills that contain 0.02 to 0.035 milligrams of estrogen vary slightly in effectiveness, ranging from 98% to more than 99% effective.

The second type of oral contraceptive, often called the "mini-pill", contains only a progestogen. It works in part by making the uterus (womb) less receptive to any fertilized egg that reaches it. The mini-pill is less effective than the combination oral contraceptive, about 97% effective, because it preventing release of an egg from the ovary. In addition, the progestogen-only pill has a tendency to cause irregular bleeding which may be quite inconvenient. The progestogen-only pill is used despite its lower effectiveness in the or cessation of bleeding entirely. The progestogen-only pill has a

discussion below, while based mainly on information about the combination pills, should be considered to apply as well as to the mini-pill.

2. Other Nonsurgical Ways to Prevent Pregnancy. As this leaflet will explain, oral contraceptives have several serious risks. Some other methods of contraception have lesser risks. They are usually less effective than oral contraceptives, but, used properly, may be effective enough for many women. The following table gives reported pregnancy rates (the number of women out of 100 who would become pregnant in 1 year) for these methods:

PREGNANCIES PER 100 WOMEN PER YEAR

Intrauterine device (IUD), less than 1-6;
Diaphragm with spermicidal products (creams or jellies), 2-20;
Condom (rubber), 3-36;
Aerosol foams, 2-29;
Jellies and creams, 4-36;
Periodic abstinence (rhythm), all types, less than 1-47;
 —Calendar method, 14-47;
 —Temperature method, 1-20;
 —Temperature method.—intercourse only in post-ovulatory phase, less than 1-7;
 —Mucus method, 1-25;
No contraception, 60-80.

The figures (except for the IUD) vary widely because people differ in how well they use each method. Very faithful users of the various methods, with the exception of the calendar method of periodic abstinence (rhythm), may achieve lower pregnancy rates than those given above, which are the average results for large groups of women. Excluding the single pill every evening, but it is an effort that many couples undertake successfully. Your doctor can tell you a great deal more about these methods of contraception.

3. The Dangers of Oral Contraceptives

a. *Circulatory disorders (abnormal blood clots, strokes, and heart attacks).* Blood clots (in various blood vessels of the body) are the most common of the serious side effects of oral contraceptives. A clot can result in a stroke (if the clot is in the brain), a heart attack (if the clot is in a blood vessel of the heart), a pulmonary embolism (a clot which forms in the legs or pelvis, then breaks off and travels to the lungs), or loss of a limb (a clot in a blood vessel in an arm or leg). Any of these can cause death or disability. Clots also occur rarely in the blood vessels of the eye, resulting in blindness or impairment of vision in that eye.

The risk of this kind of disease increases with higher estrogen doses. It is therefore important to keep the dose of estrogen as low as possible, so long as the oral contraceptive works. The risk of abnormal clotting increases with age in both users and nonusers of oral contraceptives. The risk of abnormal clotting increases with age in both users and nonusers of oral contraceptives, but the increased risk from the contraceptive appears to be present at all ages.

The risk may be greater if your blood type is A, B, or AB rather than O.

In addition to blood-clotting disorders, it has been estimated that women taking oral contraceptives are twice as likely as nonusers to have a stroke due to rupture of a blood vessel in the brain.

Furthermore, cigarette smoking, by oral contraceptive users increases the risk of serious adverse effects on the heart and blood vessels. This risk increases with age and with heavy smoking (15 or more cigarettes per day) and becomes quite marked in women over 35 years of age. For this reason, women who use oral contraceptives should not smoke.

For oral contraceptive users in general, it has been estimated that the risk of having a heart attack due to a circulatory disorder is about 1 in 12,000 per year, whereas for nonusers the risk is about 1 in 50,000 per year. In the age group 30 to 44, the risk is estimated to be about 1 in 2,500 per year for oral contraceptive users and about 1 in 10,000 per year for nonusers. The risk is concentrated in older women, in those with a long duration of use, and in cigarette smokers. The effects on the circulatory system may persist after oral contraceptives are discontinued.

Even without the pill the risk of having a heart attack increases with age and is also increased by such heart attack risk factors as high blood pressure, high cholesterol, obesity, diabetes, and cigarette smoking. Without any risk factors present, the use of oral contraceptives alone may double the risk of heart attack. However, the combination of cigarette smoking, especially heavy smoking, and oral contraceptive use greatly increases the risk of heart attack. Oral contraceptive users who smoke are about 5 times more likely to have a heart attack than users who do not smoke and about 10 times more likely to have a heart attack than nonusers who do not smoke. It has been estimated that users between the ages of 30 and 39 who smoke have about a 1 in 10,000 chance each year of having a fatal heart attack compared to about a 1 in 50,000 chance in users who do not smoke, and about a 1 in 100,000 chance in nonusers who do not smoke. In the age group 40 to 44, the risk is about 1 in 1,700 per year for users who smoke compared to about 1 in 10,000 for users who do not smoke and to about 1 in 14,000 per year for nonusers who do not smoke. These are average figures for Great Britain; comparable estimates for the U.S. may be higher. Heavy smoking (about 15 cigarettes or more a day) further increases the risk. If you do not smoke and have none of the other heart attack risk factors described above, you will have a smaller risk than listed. If you have several heart attack risk factors, the risk may be considerably greater than listed.

b. Formation of tumors. Studies have found that when certain animals are given the female sex hormone estrogen, which is an ingredient of oral contraceptives, continuously for long periods, cancers may develop in the breast, cervix, vagina, uterus, ovary, pituitary and liver.

These findings suggest that oral contraceptives may cause cancer in humans. However, studies to date in women taking currently marketed oral contraceptives have not confirmed that oral contraceptives cause cancer in humans. Several studies have found no increase in breast cancer in users, although one study suggested oral contraceptives might cause an increase in breast cancer in women who already have benign breast disease (e.g. cysts).

Women with a strong family history of breast cancer or who have breast nodules, fibrocystic disease, or abnormal mammograms or who weren't exposed to DES (diethylstilbestrol), an estrogen, during their lives in a pregnancy must be followed very closely by their physician if they choose to use oral contraceptives, rather than another method of contraception. Many studies have shown that women taking oral contraceptives. Strong evidence has emerged that estrogens (one component of oral contraceptives), when given alone (unaccompanied by progestogen) for periods of more than one year to women after the menopause, increase the risk of cancer of the uterus (womb). There is also some evidence that a kind of oral contraceptive which is no longer marketed, the sequential oral contraceptive, may increase the risk of cancer of the uterus. There remains now evidence, however, that the oral contraceptives now available (containing estrogen and progestogen in combination, or progestogen alone) increase the risk of this cancer. Cancer of the cervix may develop more readily in long-term (3-4 years) users of the pill who had preexisting abnormal Pap smears.

Benign or malignant liver tumors have been associated with short-term as well as long-term oral contraceptive use. The benign (non-malignant) tumors do not spread, but they may rupture and produce internal bleeding, which may cause death.

c. Dangers to a developing child if oral contraceptives are used in or immediately preceding pregnancy. Oral contraceptives should not be taken by pregnant women because they may damage the developing child. An increased risk of birth defects, including heart defects and limb defects, has been associated with use of sex hormones, including oral contraceptives, in pregnancy. In addition, the developing female child whose mother has received DES (diethylstilbestrol), an estrogen, during pregnancy has a risk of getting cancer of the vagina or cervix in her teens or young adulthood. This risk is estimated to be about 1 in 1,000 exposures or less. Abnormalities of the urinary and sex organs have been reported in male offspring so exposed. It is possible that other estrogens, such as the estrogens in oral contraceptives, could have the same effect in the child if the mother takes them during pregnancy.

If you stop taking oral contraceptives to become pregnant, your doctor may recommend that you use another method of contraception for a short while. The reason for this is that the lost fetuses are more likely to be abnormal. Whether there is an overall increase in "miscarriages" in women who have stopped the pill as compared with women who do not use the pill is not known, but it is possible that there may be. If, however, you do become pregnant soon after stopping oral contraceptives, and do not have a miscarriage, there is no evidence that the baby has an increased risk of being abnormal.

d. Gallbladder disease. Women who use oral contraceptives have a greater risk than nonusers of having gallbladder disease requiring surgery. The increased risk may first appear within 1 year of use and may double after 4 or 5 years of use.

e. Other side effects of oral contraceptives. Some women using oral contraceptives experience unpleasant side effects that are not dangerous and are not likely to damage their health. Some of these may be temporary. Your breasts may feel tender and your ankles may swell. Some of the face, is possible weight, and your ankles may swell. Many of these effects are seen more frequently with combination oral contraceptives containing 0.05 milligram or more of estrogen. You may notice unexpected vaginal bleeding or spotting of the skin, particularly of the face, is possible changes in your menstrual period. Irregular bleeding is frequently seen when using the mini-pill or combination oral contraceptives containing less than 0.05 milligram of estrogen.

More serious side effects include worsening of migraine, asthma, epilepsy, and kidney or heart disease because of a tendency for water to be retained in the body when using oral contraceptives are used. Other side effects are growth of preexisting fibroid tumors of the uterus, mental depression; and liver problems with jaundice (yellowing of the skin). Your doctor may find that level of sugar and fatty substances in your blood are elevated; the long-term effects of these changes are not known. Some women develop high blood pressure while taking oral contraceptives, which may persist after discontinuation. High blood pressure may lead to serious disease of the kidney and circulatory system. Your physician may wish to check your blood pressure more frequently if you have a history of toxemia of pregnancy, kidney disease or increased blood pressure.

Other reactions have been reported occasionally. These include more frequent urination and some discomfort when urinating, kidney disease, nervousness, dizziness, an increase in or loss of hair, an increase or decrease in sex drive, appetite changes, cataracts, and a need for a change in contact lens prescription or inability to use contact lenses.

After you stop using oral contraceptives

As discussed previously, you should wait a few months after stopping the pill before you try to become pregnant. During these few months, use another form of contraception. You should consult your physician before resuming use of oral contraceptives after childbirth, especially if you plan to nurse your baby. Drugs in oral contraceptives are known to appear in the milk, and the long-range effect on infants is not known. Furthermore, oral contraceptives may cause a decrease in your milk supply as well as in the quality of the milk.

4. Comparison of the Risks of Oral Contraceptives and Other Contraceptive Methods. The many studies on the risks and effectiveness of oral contraceptives and other methods of contraception have been analyzed to estimate the risk of death associated with various methods of contraception. This risk has two parts: (a) the risk associated with the method itself (e.g., the risk that an oral contraceptive user will die due to abnormal clotting), and (b) the risk associated with failure of the method (death due to pregnancy or abortion). The results of this analysis are shown in the bar graph below. The height of the bars is the estimated number of deaths per 100,000 women each year. There are six sets of bars, each set referring to a specific age group of women. Within each set of bars, there are two bars for oral contraceptive users, one referring to users who smoke and one referring to users who do not smoke, and five bars for other contraceptive methods including one bar representing no method of contraception. ("Traditional contraception" means diaphragm or condom.)

This analysis is based on present knowledge and new information could, of course, alter it. The analysis shows that the risk of death from all methods of birth control is low compared to the risks of childbirth, except for oral contraceptives in women over 40 who smoke. It shows that the lowest risk of death is associated with the condom or diaphragm (traditional contraception) backed up by early abortion in the case of failure of the condom or diaphragm to prevent pregnancy. Also, at any age the risk of death associated with use of traditional contraception even without a backup method of abortion is generally the same as, or less than, that from use of oral contraceptives.

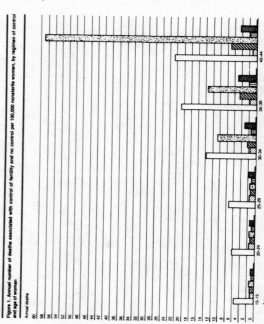

Figure 1. Annual number of deaths associated with control of fertility and no control per 100,000 nonsterile women, by regimen of control and age of woman

a. Present or past conditions that mean you should not use oral contraceptives:

Clots in the legs, lungs or elsewhere
A stroke, heart attack, or chest pain (angina pectoris)
Known or suspected cancer of the breast or sex organs
Severe liver disease
Irregular or scanty menstrual periods before starting to take the pill

b. Present conditions that mean you should use oral contraceptives:

Unusual vaginal bleeding that has not yet been diagnosed.
Known or suspected pregnancy.

c. Conditions that your doctor will want to watch closely or which might cause him to suggest another method of contraception:

A family history of breast cancer	Epilepsy
Breast nodules, fibrocystic disease of the breast, or an abnormal mammogram	Mental depression
	Fibroid tumors of the uterus
Diabetes	Gallbladder disease
High blood pressure	Asthma
High cholesterol	Problems during a
Cigarette smoking	prior pregnancy
Migraine headaches	Plans for elective surgery
Heart or kidney disease	History of jaundice

d. Use of any of the following kinds of drugs, which might interact with the pill: antibiotics, sulfa drugs, drugs for epilepsy or migraine, pain killers, tranquilizers, sedatives or sleeping pills, blood thinning drugs, vitamins, drugs being used for the treatment of depression, high blood pressure, or high blood sugar (diabetes).

e. Once you are using oral contraceptives, you should be alert for signs of a serious adverse effect and call your doctor if they occur.

Sharp pain in the chest, coughing blood, or sudden shortness of breath (indicating possible clots in the lungs)
Pain in the calf (possible clot in the leg)
Crushing chest pain or heaviness (indicating possible heart attack)
Sudden severe headache or vomiting, dizziness or fainting, disturbance of vision or speech, or weakness or numbness in an arm or leg (indicating a possible stroke)
Sudden partial or complete loss of vision (indicating a possible blood clot in the eye)
Breast lumps (you should ask your doctor to show you how to examine your own breasts)
Severe pain or mass in the abdomen (indicating a possible tumor of the liver)
Severe depression
Yellowing of the skin (jaundice)
Unusual swelling

2. How to Take the Pill So That It Is Most Effective

Your physician has prescribed one of the following dosage schedules. Please follow the instructions appropriate for your schedule.

20-Day Schedule: Counting the onset of flow as day 1, take the first pill on day 5 of the menstrual cycle whether or not the flow has stopped. Take another pill the same time each day, preferably at bedtime, for 20 days. Then wait for 7 days, during which time a menstrual period usually occurs, and begin taking 1 pill every day on the 8th day after you took your last pill, whether or not the menstrual flow has stopped. This cycle is repeated 20 days on pills and 7 days off pills. Tablets for the control of excessive bleeding (hypermenorrhea): If you are taking NORINYL 2 mg Tablets for the control of excessive bleeding (hypermenorrhea), your physician may examine you and determine whether you should stop taking the pills after 3 cycles to determine the need for further treatment. The information contained in this leaflet regarding who should not use the pill, the dangers of the pill and safe use of the pill applies to the use of the pill for hypermenorrhea, as well as for contraception.

21-Day Schedule: Counting the onset of flow as day 1, take the first pill on day 5 of the menstrual cycle whether or not the flow has stopped. Take another pill the same time each day, preferably at bedtime, for 21 days. Then wait for 7 days, during which time a menstrual period usually occurs, and begin taking 1 pill every day on the 8th day after you took your last pill, whether or not the menstrual flow has stopped. This cycle is repeated 21 days on pills and 7 days off pills until time for the physician's examination and pill refill.

28-Day Schedule: Counting the onset of flow as day 1, take the first pill on day 5 of the menstrual cycle whether or not the flow has stopped. Take another pill the same time each day, preferably at bedtime, for 21 days. Then take pills 22 through 28 (which are a different color) and expect a menstrual period during this week. Pills 22 through 28 contain no active drug and are included simply for your convenience—to eliminate the need for counting days. After all 28 pills have been taken, whether bleeding has stopped or not, take the first pill of the next cycle without any interruption. With the 28-day package, pills are taken every day of the year with no gap between cycles.

with each pill missed. If you miss one pill, you should take it as soon as you remember and also take your next pill at the regular time, which means you will be taking two pills on that day. If you miss two pills in a row, you should take one of the missed pills as soon as you remember, discard the other missed pill, and take your regular pill for that day at the proper time. Furthermore, you should use an additional method of contraception in addition to taking your pills for the remainder of the cycle. If more than 2 pills in a row have been missed, discontinue taking your pills immediately and use an additional method of contraception until you have a period or your doctor determines that you are not pregnant. Missing pills numbered 22-28 (orange pills) in the 28-day schedule does not increase your chances of becoming pregnant.

At times there may be no menstrual period after a cycle of pills. Therefore, if you miss one menstrual period but have taken the pills exactly as you were supposed to, continue as usual into the next cycle. If you have not taken the pills correctly, and have missed a menstrual period, you may be pregnant and should stop taking oral contraceptives until your doctor determines whether or not you are pregnant. Until you can get to your doctor, use another form of contraception. If two consecutive menstrual periods are missed, you should stop taking pills until it is determined whether you are pregnant. If you do become pregnant while using oral contraceptives, you should discuss the risks to the developing child with your doctor.

Even if spotting or breakthrough bleeding should occur, continue the medication according to the schedule. Should spotting or breakthrough bleeding persist you should notify your physician.

NOR-Q.D.* (norethindrone) Tablets 0.35 mg. Schedule: Take the first pill on the first day of the menstrual flow, and take another pill each day, every day of the year. The pill should be taken at the same time of day, preferably at bedtime, without interruption, whether bleeding occurs or not. If prolonged bleeding occurs, you should consult your physician.

The chance of becoming pregnant increases with each pill missed. If you miss one pill, you should take it as soon as you remember and also take your next pill at the regular time, which means you will be taking two pills on that day. If you miss two pills in a row you should take one of the missed pills as soon as you remember, discard the other missed pill, and take your regular pill for that day at the proper time. Furthermore, you should use an additional method of contraception in addition to taking NOR-Q.D.* until you have a period or your doctor determines you are not pregnant. If more than 2 pills in a row have been missed, NOR-Q.D. should be discontinued immediately and an additional method of contraception should be used until you have a period or your doctor determines that you are not pregnant.

Whether or not you have missed a period within 45 days of your last period, you may be pregnant. You should stop taking NOR-Q.D. until your doctor determines whether or not you are pregnant. If you can get to your doctor, use another form of contraception. If you do become pregnant while using NOR-Q.D., you should discuss the risks to the developing child with your doctor.

3. Periodic Examination

Your doctor will take a complete medical and family history before prescribing oral contraceptives. At that time and once a year thereafter, he will generally examine your blood pressure, breasts, abdomen, and pelvic organs (including a Papanicolaou smear).

SUMMARY

Oral contraceptives are the most effective method, except, sterilization, for preventing pregnancy. Other methods, when used conscientiously, are also very effective and have fewer risks. The serious risks of oral contraceptives are uncommon and the "pill" is a very convenient method of preventing pregnancy

If you have certain conditions or have had these conditions in the past, you should not use oral contraceptives because the risk is too great. These conditions are listed in this leaflet. If you do not have these conditions, and decide to use the "pill", please read this leaflet carefully so that you can use the "pill" most safely and effectively.

Based on his or her assessment of your medical needs, your doctor has prescribed this drug for you. Do not give the drug to anyone else.

DETAILED PATIENT LABELING

SYNTEX (F.P.) INC.
HUMACAO, PUERTO RICO 00661

17-101-15-2

FEBRUARY 1978

quences of the Pill has its mirror image in equally uncritical and sensational reporting of supposed technological breakthroughs on the horizon in the birth control field. In my view, the public is just as ill-served by distorted positive news as it is by negative news. On December 2, 1978, for example, the *San Francisco Chronicle* carried on its front page the headline "New Method of Birth Control" (see facing page) with the accompanying story on an inside page:

> An injectable, time-release contraceptive for women that could replace birth control pills and is effective for six months has been successfully developed and tested in baboons at the University of Alabama in Birmingham, medical researchers reported yesterday.
>
> Researchers also said the technique could be used in the future for administering other drugs needed every day, such as insulin for diabetics.
>
> Clinical trials for human use of the contraceptive will be conducted in Mexico by the same Mexico City investigators who first tested oral contraceptives.
>
> Dr. Lee R. Beck of the university's department of obstetrics and gynecology said researchers successfully combined a contraceptive steroid and a biodegradable plastic to form microscopic beads that release the steroid over a period of time.
>
> The beads, which are harmlessly absorbed by the body, are suspended in a sterile saline fluid that can be injected over a determined period of time. Beck said the system offers advantages over the pill and could replace it in the future.
>
> "We are particularly pleased that the injectable contraceptive does not contain estrogen, an element in the pill which has been linked to such side effects as thrombophlebitis (blood clots) and hypertension (high blood pressure)," Beck said.

Let us examine this story briefly. What does "new" mean? The reader obviously expects something novel, but work on injectable, sustained-release contraceptives has in fact been under way since the 1960s in a number of laboratories around the world. The active ingredient of the steroid contraceptive mentioned in the article is exactly the same as that used in many conventional oral contraceptives, and its side effects are not very different from those of the Pill, especially with regard to potential long-term consequences. The

New Method Of Birth Control

See Page 3

San Francisco Chronicle

The Largest Daily Circulation in Northern California

114th Year No. 270 ★ ★ ★   SATURDAY, DECEMBER 2, 1978   777-1111 🕮 20 CENTS

Inside

Despite a previous denial, the State Department admitted it had been warned of abuses at Georgetown. Page 2.

A noontime memorial service for Mayor Moscone and Supervisor Milk was held at San Francisco State. Page 2.

Jim Jones left clues to his impending dementia in an anti-suicide rally at the Golden Gate Bridge. Page 2.

A judge ruled a stewardess can be fired for being fat, but the same standards must be applied to males. Page 3.

A talent scout from Las Vegas hired one dancer and liked a couple more at auditions in Redwood City. Page 4.

A fleet of U.S. and Soviet spacecraft will begin reaching Venus Monday in a triumph of the space age. Page 4.

Governor Brown will skip the midterm Democratic convention in Memphis to concentrate on his budget. Page 6.

Sixty-six U.S. companies, including big ones, were threatened by a judge for withholding information. Page 6.

President Carter designated 56 million acres of land in Alaska as national monuments. Page 7.

The Romanian president renewed his battle with his Warsaw Pact allies in a wildly cheered speech. Page 9.

TOP OF THE NEWS

Pushy Russians have replaced Ugly Americans in Vietnam, according to a Canadian journalist. Page 10.

President Carter met with a top Egyptian in an effort to get Mideast negotiations going again. Page 11.

PLO leader Yasser Arafat said he would be willing to renounce violence in exchange for a Palestinian state. Page 11.

The Prime Minister designate of Japan said he was like a "flourescent lamp" that will "take time to light up." Page 12.

The Voice of America said China is not jamming its broad-

casts — but rather is encouraging listeners. Page 12.

Alfred Eisenstaedt, who took photos for Life magazine since 1936, is at 79 part of the repaginated Life. Page 15.

Patricia Harmsworth leads a life as Lady Rothmere that some consider "somewhat untraditional." Page 15.

The stock market had its strongest gain in a month with the Dow Jones average up more than 12 points. Page 49.

The U.S. dollar climbed above the 200 yen level in Tokyo for the first time since July. Page 49.

Weather

Bay Area: Mainly fog Saturday, with patchy fog or clouds in the evening. Lows, 30s to 40s; highs, upper 50s. Page 18.

advantage of a sustained-release contraceptive is that it eliminates the need for daily Pill taking. Conversely, its disadvantage is that a woman cannot negate its action on short notice if she is bothered by side effects; she must wait for months for its effects to wear off.

The last paragraph of the article extols the fact that the contraceptive "does not contain estrogen," as if this were something out of the ordinary, when in fact virtually all work that has been going on with injectable steroid contraceptives since the early 1960s has dealt with estrogen-free progestational compounds. In addition, three different preparations of the so-called minipill, which is estrogen-free, are now on the market. These preparations, however, command only 1 to 2 percent of the total U.S. oral contraceptive market. Why? Because bleeding irregularities unavoidably associated with progestogen-only preparations do not appear to be acceptable to the vast majority of American women who take the Pill (though they seem to be more acceptable to women in some of the lesser-developed countries). Thus, estrogens are added to most oral contraceptives, in spite of some of their side effects, to overcome these menstrual irregularities.

The curious reporter might at least have questioned why the clinical trials have to be "conducted in Mexico." Is it because there are not enough data available so that clinical studies can be carried out in the U.S. with FDA approval? The answer to this is very likely "yes." Is it also because such an agent would be unattractive to American women? Again, the answer is very likely "yes."

Why do I belabor the inaccuracies and superficiality of this article? I do so because it is typical of the vast majority of stories published in the American and foreign press on so-called new advances in birth control. No wonder the average woman is unhappy with her current mode of contraception and expects prompt relief via some new breakthrough, which according to her favorite newspaper is just around the corner.

Even my favorite newspaper, the *New York Times,* is not innocent of uncritical demands or unrealistic expectations in the field of fertility control. For example, on July 6, 1969, in an editorial about the need to curb world population growth, the *Times* stated, "If significant reductions in population growth are to be achieved, there must be a technological breakthrough in contraception similar to that in food production." This statement is symptomatic of the public's desire to believe that so-called revolutionary technological developments can solve all of our problems. The reference to a "technological breakthrough in contraception similar to that in food production" alludes to the "green revolution," which involved the combined use of improved strains of wheat with fertilizers and irrigation. A counterpart to this breakthrough in the contraceptive field would be a new and cheaper chemical process for manufacturing contraceptive pills—such a development would reduce the price of the Pill but certainly not its side effects. The counterpart in the food production field to a *real* technological breakthrough in contraception would be the development of a completely new food—for example, a synthetic one—whose acceptability in different populations would first have to be established, following many years of toxicology, teratology, and mutagenicity testing, and whose mode of ingestion (for example, in pill form) would be quite novel. If solving the world's food problem depended on such a fundamental breakthrough, the prospects for achieving that goal in the twentieth century would be minimal.

It is almost self-evident that the press usually mirrors society's prevailing value judgments. Consider the following article (which appeared on February 4, 1976, in the *New York Times* and other newspapers carrying Associated Press releases) describing possible deleterious effects of caffeine on pregnant women:

> Citing tests that show the offspring of animals fed caffeine suffer higher rates of birth defects, a consumer group has urged the government to warn pregnant women "vigorously but with delicacy" to lower their coffee consumption. The Center for Science in the Public Interest said yesterday that some animals fed equivalents of caffeine present in 11 cups of coffee had given birth to offspring with cleft palates, missing digits and malformed skulls.
>
> It is clear that caffeine causes birth defects when animals are exposed to moderately high levels of the drug, the Center said in a letter to Dr. Theodore Cooper, Assistant Secretary for Health in the Department of Health, Education, and Welfare.
>
> Although the animal and human studies do not prove conclusively that caffeine causes birth defects, miscarriages, or infertility in humans, the evidence is suggestive enough to require a public education campaign and more extensive research, said Michael Jacobson, co-director of the private, non-profit organization based in Washington. Mr. Jacobson said that the government warning he proposed "should be pursued vigorously, but with delicacy, so

as not to frighten women or induce guilt feelings in mothers of children with birth defects."

I ask you to reread this article and substitute the words "the Pill" for "caffeine." In the second paragraph for the words "11 cups of coffee" substitute "a two-day dose of the Pill." Then ask yourself whether the Center for Science in the Public Interest—or in fact most consumers—would be prepared to tell the government that such a warning about the Pill "should be pursued vigorously, but with delicacy." Does this not say something about our priorities? When it comes to risk taking, we are willing to say "yes" to coffee or tobacco, but "no" to birth control drugs.

The interplay between the public, the press, legislators, and the FDA is full of feedback mechanisms, each of which stimulates as well as restricts the other. Legislators and the press mirror the public's almost pathetic desire to grasp at opportunities to escape from the tremendous ambiguities surrounding important issues facing us. Birth control is only one example. The public's right to know *is* fundamental, but legislators and the press must exercise their influence more responsibly. Even more importantly, we as individuals must accept the responsibility to evaluate critically the information we receive. We cannot expect, and should not seek, black-and-white answers to essentially grey questions.

Critically Evaluating a Scientific Article

Critically evaluating a newspaper article is not enough. We should look at the original source behind such media coverage, and in technological areas this is usually found in technical articles. Often these can be incomprehensible and boring to the layman and journalist, but there are clear exceptions. One such exception is an article reproduced below, announcing a remarkably novel, even provocative approach to contraception—one that acts by the olfactory route—which appeared in December 1965 in the *Canadian Medical Association Journal*. Since the article contains a minimum of technical jargon and is fascinating as well, I include it here without further comment:

Studies on a New, Peerless Contraceptive Agent:
A Preliminary Final Report
Julius S. Greenstein, AB, MS, PhD, Pittsburgh, Pa., U.S.A.

In reviewing the vast literature on drugs that interfere with the reproductive process, it becomes relatively simple to categorize them into several main classes: (1) drugs administered to the male to control spermatogenesis, (2) vaginal spermicidal agents to inhibit released spermatozoa, (3) drugs administered to females to suppress ovulation, (4) drugs administered to females to inhibit corpus luteum formation, and (5) drugs administered to females to inhibit implantation or to destroy blastocysts. In addition, there are indications that drugs may eventually be perfected that will bring about destruction of epididymal spermatozoa or operate effectively at the levels of the ovary or ovum.

Experience with such agents has shown the necessity for concern over the problems of safety following long-term usage. Side effects are a continuing hazard with many of the drugs now in use, and in some cases the inhibition of reproductive potential is unalterable. Moreover, there is the very important factor of cost to the user. Finally, there is the recognition that the relative merit of any drug is measured by consumer acceptance and the ability of the user to follow instructions: unfortunately, educational and economic levels are lowest in the very areas of the world where population control is most urgent.[1]

Aside from continuing research into intravaginal contraceptive agents, there is a striking absence of any effort to develop an agent which when applied to the female would directly affect the reproductive potential of the *male* partner. This report will describe a new contraceptive agent which (1) is applied to the female, (2) is perfectly safe to both sexes without regard to dosage or duration, (3) has no physiological effect on the female's reproductive capacity or endocrinology, (4) renders the male infertile, both temporarily and *ad libitum*, (5) has only the most desirable side effects, (6) is very inexpensive, (7) is extremely simple to apply, and (8) will find eager acceptance in any population regardless of educational, social or economic status.

Developmental Background

The story of the development of this new agent as a chemical contraceptive is an eloquent testimonial to the virtues of pursuing research tangential to one's original undertaking, and to the ever-present factor of serendipity. One must also admit to a measure of inspiration that can only be described as heaven-sent.[2]

The tale begins with our initial interests and investigations relative to (of all things) an odour problem that prevailed in our animal research facilities. We had installed a highly recommended commercial deodorant dispenser but none of a variety of available deodorant fluids was satisfactory. We, therefore, set about to concoct a deodorant fluid that would satsify our own stringent requirements. After much toil and error, we produced a fluid which was not only perfectly safe and effectively killed offensive and obnoxious odours on contact, but also was completely nonirritating and yet had a most pleasant, yea compelling, aroma.

Almost immediately after the new deodorant fluid was installed, we noticed some rather startling phenomena. For one thing, the noise level in the animal rooms rose sharply. It soon became apparent that the animals (mice, rats, guinea pigs, hamsters, dogs and monkeys) had greatly increased their copulatory frequency and vigour irrespective of their inherent biological rhythms. Moreover, we found that the married employees working in the animal rooms as animal caretakers and research personnel no longer brought their lunches to work, but with singular unanimity went home at the noon hour. Tardiness and absenteeism among them became a problem. Concurrently, it became obvious that a ban on the mixing of attendants of the two sexes in the same animal room was both prudent and necessary.

These developments, while disturbing to some degree, were negligible when contrasted to the astonishing events that followed. Within a matter of days or weeks (depending on the species) we realized that none—absolutely none—of the females of any species was becoming pregnant. Of course, this had catastrophic implications for our various research programs, but fortunately these losses were overshadowed by the brilliant discovery of the contraceptive agent that forms the basis of this report.

Animal Studies

Our first logical undertaking was to test experimentally the simple hypothesis that emerged from our empirical experience, namely, that something in the deodorant influenced fertility to an astonishing degree. Accordingly, the affected animals were randomized into three equal groups per species, one group remaining in the deodorized rooms, the second group transferred to identical quarters without deodorizers, and the third group placed in new quarters with deodorizers filled only with commercial fluid. The results were clear and emphatic: Group I animals remained infertile; Group II and Group III animals immediately resumed their normal fertility and fecundity. The conclusion that our deodorant concoction was responsible for the observed infertility was unequivocal.

With typical male self-assurance, we undertook to examine the *females* for the causative factors leading to their infertility. We employed every known gross anatomical, histological, histochemical, biochemical, endocrinological, physiological and psychological test of reproductive capacity and could find no evidence of malfunctioning of the female reproductive systems and accessory structures. We could only conclude, reluctantly, after months of exhaustive investigation, that the females were normal in all respects, and that we should turn our attention to the males.

Because fewer parameters of male reproductive capacity are available for study, the task of working up the males was completed in a shorter time. However, we seemed to be up against a blank wall. In all cases of allegedly infertile males, testicular spermatogenesis was

normal, the accessory glands were in good working order, and copulatory behaviour was normal (to say the least). Ejaculates were being successfully deposited. Yet, as so often happens in these times of sophisticated scientific technology, we had overlooked the obvious. For when we took the trouble to examine the ejaculates obtained by masturbation, artificial vagina, or by post-coital recovery from the site of deposition, the answer to the enigma stared back at us through the narrow barrel of the microscope tube: THERE WERE NO SPERMATOZOA IN ANY OF THE SEMEN SAMPLES.

The next steps were obvious. We undertook a systematic study of the male tracts before, during, and immediately after copulation. Since testicular studies had established that spermatogenesis was normal, and the ejaculation process was also normal, the difficulty was apparently related to a failure of spermatozoa to negotiate their usual route. Males were sacrificed at appropriate intervals, the reproductive tracts excised *in toto* and then quick-frozen to prevent dislocation of their contents. The tracts were extended to a standard length and sectioned into equal segments with an egg slicer.[3] This simple procedure enabled us to examine the contents of the resultant segments upon thawing.

With the amazing consistency that has characterized all of our observations, spermatozoa were found in all segments representing the vasa efferentia, epididymis, and vas deferens but never distal to the ampullary outlet of the vas deferens and the ejaculatory duct. Where present, the spermatozoa retained every indication of normal viability and motility. We, therefore, had presumptive evidence for the existence of a functional "tube-locking mechanism" responsible for the retention of spermatozoa in the ampulla of the vas deferens.

Repeated attempts to demonstrate this occlusive mechanism by histologic techniques failed. Accordingly, we instituted a series of *in vitro* studies, the details of which have been published elsewhere. . . .[4]

Drug Chemistry and Application

The details relative to the synthesis and structure of the drug are protected by patent considerations (since we intend to make a fortune) but we can disclose the pertinent essentials. The synthesis begins with the reduction of nitrobenzene in alkaline solution to bring about the necessary coupling. Because of the proprietary nature of the reducing agent employed, the product is not azoxybenzene, azobenzene or hydrazobenzene as might be expected, but a new compound whose molecular configuration can be revealed to the extent shown in Fig. 2.

Fig. 2.—(ARMPITIN-4) Chemical configuration of the reactive portion of the Armpitin molecule.

It is immediately apparent that the molecule has a dumb-bell shape and this is quite fortuitous, since the very shape of the compound has mass appeal to the users. (There is a very strong personal identification between a woman and her toiletries.) In addition, the layman can quickly identify the —NO— groups and relate these to the obvious contraceptive connotation. What is even more remarkable, the synthesis can be readily controlled so that the number of —NO— groups may be regulated from one to infinity. This in itself would not be so extraordinary were it not for the fact that both extensive animal and clinical trials have clearly demonstrated that for each additional —NO— group in the backbone of the structure there is a corresponding one-day effectiveness of the drug! Thus, if there are four —NO— groups (as illustrated) the drug is absolutely effective for four days and no longer. This has limitless commercial and therapeutic possibilities which we will exploit fully.

We have chosen to designate the drug "Armpitin" since in our clinical experience its effectiveness is most pronounced when it is applied to the female axillary regions. The drug can readily be incorporated into a roll-on, spray, cream or any other convenient form of applicator currently used by commercial deodorant manufacturers. The user will be able to purchase the preparation in a variety of dispensers appropriately designated Armpitin-1, Armpitin-3, Armpitin-7, Armpitin-10, etc., depending upon the desired therapeutic duration of effect and the patient's customary personal habits; the arabic number signifying the precise number of days of guaranteed effectiveness. We are even considering the possibility of a placebo preparation, called "Armpitin-Jr.," as an educational toy aimed at the "pre-teens" market.

Clinical Studies

Volunteers were recruited using professionally approved persuasive tactics.[5] After appropriate screening to eliminate organic disease and subjective bias, 345 patients were instructed in the use of Armpitin and the results analyzed for a total of 2415 cycles. No pregnancies resulted during the time of cyclic administration. Twenty-one of the subjects stopped application of the drug to conceive and all attained pregnancy on the first cycle. Two subjects discontinued the medication (at the husbands' request) because of their own increased libido, and one suburban housewife ceased to cooperate because of guilt feelings associated with improved marital relations. All were totally free of any side effects (Table I).

TABLE I.—Incidence of Side Effects in 345 Patients Using Armpitin

Symptoms*	No. of subjects affected
Nausea	0
Vaginal spotting	0
Weight gain	0
Breast fullness and tenderness	0
Swelling of ankles	0
Superficial phlebitis	0
Cramps	0
Premenstrual tension	0

* Increased libido was frequently noted and invariably accepted happily.

A. Effect of Armpitin on Female Libido

The apparent enhancement of libido observed in these studies warranted further inquiry. Before proper assessment of the effect of Armpitin on libido in women can be made, it must be acknowledged that the literature on the existence of variations in libido during the normal menstrual cycle is contradictory.[6-8] Part of the wide differences in viewpoint can be attributed to the reluctance of investigators to question women directly on this subject. Accordingly, having no such qualms, we conducted an inquiry among the successive women who volunteered for these trials, the only stipulation being that they be married for at least one day prior to interrogation. After determining the patient's willingness to co-operate, she was asked for the usual dull particulars concerning frequency of sexual intercourse and frequency of orgasm, followed by these specific questions: (1) "Does intercourse appeal to you more at certain times during your menstrual cycle?" and (2) "Is the optimum time related to your menstrual period?" There were 300 patients who qualified under the criteria established for the study, ranging in age from 13 to 66 years. The same questions were asked of these patients in a follow-up study after employing Armpitin for a period of not less than six months. The results are presented in Table II.

TABLE II.—Libido Distribution in the Normal Menstrual Cycle and After Armpitin Medication

Distribution	Before Armpitin		After Armpitin	
Time of maximum libido	No.	Percentage	No.	Percentage
Just prior to menstruation	50	16.66	0	00.00
Just after menstruation ..	50	16.66	0	00.00
Just prior to and just after menses	50	16.66	0	00.00
During menstruation ..	50	16.66	2**	00.67
At midcycle ..	50	16.66	0	00.00
Anytime	50*	16.66	298	99.33
Totals ...	300	100.00	300	100.00

*Seventeen of these patients reported that they were too busy to notice.

**Both patients had periods of menstrual flow averaging 24-28 days.

Analysis of the results suggests that prior to Armpitin medication, this random sample of the female population showed a fairly random distribution of libido with no particular part of the menstrual cycle being favoured. On the other hand, the data offer reasonable support for the premise that Armpitin enhances sexual desire without regard to stage of the reproductive cycle. Admittedly, the sample is small but the differences between the data before and after Armpitin use are statistically significant at an absurd level of confidence.[9]

B. Effect of Armpitin on Male Libido

In questioning the male partners of our patient sample, we uncovered no evidence that Armpitin exerts any direct effect on the male libido. However, a significant degree of sexual hyperexcitability was common among these males as a natural response to the behaviour of their mates. As reported earlier, only two husbands were forced to admit that the attentions required of them were beyond their capacities.

Discussion

It seems superfluous to enumerate the advantages, ramifications, and potentialities of Armpitin as a contraceptive agent. The data speak for themselves with resounding clarity and persuasiveness. It remains only to place in proper perspective some of the clinical and pharmacological implications of these findings.

We can safely add Armpitin to that small group of therapeutic agents, notably the androgens, that are effective in enhancing libido in women. Androgens are usually administered to women for the treatment of dysmenorrhea or breast carcinoma, and the libidinous result is frequently unwanted and at best only secondary to the purpose of the therapy. Admittedly, androgen therapy may be used for the primary purpose of increasing female libido, but we suggest that in such circumstances Armpitin is obviously superior in that it does nothing to upset the normal endocrinologic relationships. On the basis of extensive personal observations as well as patient interviews "in depth," it appears that Armpitin exerts its influence on libido by significant vasocongestive changes in the female organs of primary or secondary response.

Armpitin, like cocaine and possibly amphetamine,[10] seems to produce a degree of sexual hyperexcitability (without the disagreeable intoxication) upon inhalation that leads to increased overt sexual behaviour but without reduced sexual performance.

The role of olfactory stimuli in mammalian reproduction is well established.[11] Sex attraction and aggressive sexual behaviour is, after all, the underlying basis for the popularity of perfumes down through the ages. Similar direct neural effects of natural odours on the opposite sex are well known in the ungulates, rodents and primates, to cite a few examples. More significantly, recent evidence has accumulated that odour can constitute an exteroceptive factor acting through neurohumoral mechanisms analogous to those evoked by visual stimuli and light. The most familiar of these are the Lee-Boot, Whitten, and Bruce effect in mice. Readers familiar with the Bruce effect will appreciate that the action of Armpitin can be described superficially as the *reverse* of the Bruce effect. In all modesty, rather than submit to the temptation of coining a new eponym bearing the name of the present author, we offer the suggestion that the action be termed the *Ecurb effect* for two reasons: (1) *E-c-u-r-b* is Bruce spelled backwards, and (2) *E-curb* would at the same time denote *E*(ejaculation)-*curb*(inhibition).

It is interesting to note, parenthetically, that the odoriferous glands of mammals differ remarkably in anatomical position, i.e. being occipital in the Arabian camel, suborbital in the antelope, scapular in the fruit bat, sternal in the opossum, suprascapular in the guinea pig, and (most germane to this discussion) axillary in man.[12] In any case, we are beginning to recognize that certain odours acting as externally secreted chemical messengers can either serve to enhance sex attraction and sexual behaviour by directly evoking instantaneous responses *via* the central nervous system, or bring about a neurohumoral chain of events as a consequence of continuous olfactory stimulation. Armpitin, under the conditions described, both from experimental and clinical viewpoints, has properties that combine to give the best of both possible worlds.

The precise mechanism of action of Armpitin on the male must await further elucidation, but a degree of speculation at this point is justified. As any schoolboy knows,[13] ejaculation is the result of a reflex mechanism. Afferent impulses arise in the glans and are transmitted to the fifth lumbar and first sacral segments of the spinal cord. Here motor impulses originate and are carried by reflex action to the musculature of the vasa deferentia, ejaculatory ducts and prostate glands, moving the combined secretions into the urethra. The orgasmic culmination of the reflex is the result of recurring contractions of the constrictor urethrae, bulbo and ischiocavernosi and transverse peronei musculature causing the forcible expulsion of the seminal fluid from the prostatic and membranous portions of the urethra to and through the urethral meatus.

While ejaculation may be purely a reflex action, it usually involves activity of the highest cortical levels.[14] It has been established that the total male orgasmic experience develops in two stages.[15] Stage I consists of movement of seminal constituents into the prostatic urethra. Stage II includes the movement of seminal fluid from the prostatic urethra through the membranous and penile urethrae to the urethral meatus.

In spite of the lack of comparable human data, our animal studies support our belief that Armpitin has a quiescent effect on the myoneural junctions controlling the flow patterns within the vasa efferentia, epididymis and the vas deferens and a concomitant "tube-locking" effect on the ampullary outlet of the vas deferens and the ejaculatory duct. Fortunately, the sensation of ejaculation is not lost even during Stage I, since the drug has no effect on the contractions of the accessory gland organs. Thus the fluid (seminal plasma) which progresses to the second stage consists of the combined contributions of the prostate, seminal vesicles and bulbourethral glands but is completely devoid of spermatozoa. In substance, Armpitin achieves a unique physiological separation of spermatozoa from seminal fluid, depriving the ejaculate of its reproductive potential without detracting from the male's total sexual experience or in any way contributing to a "castration complex" or other deep sense of inferiority which would certainly otherwise obtain if the orgasm lacked an appreciable emission. This is a remarkable pharmacological phenomenon when one realizes that the basic sympathetic and somatic nerve pathways necessary for emission and ejaculation are left intact, the drug inhibition acting selectively only on the neuromuscular portions of the tract required for the forward progression of the germ cells.[16]

Summary

Data from animal experimentation and clincial findings relative to a new, *ne plus ultra* contraceptive drug are presented with exceptional thoroughness and invincibility. The agent, a non-steroidal, synthetic derivative of coupled nitrobenzene, the active portion of which has the configuration

$$\langle\!\!\!\!\!\bigcirc\!\!\!\!\!\rangle-NO-NO-NO-NO----\langle\!\!\!\!\!\bigcirc\!\!\!\!\!\rangle$$

when applied to the axillary regions of the female causes a temporary and reversible infertility in the male partner upon inhalation. The drug, appropriately named Armpitin, is entirely safe at all levels of dosage and duration of medication, is completely innocuous to the female, is applied like any commercial deodorant, has the sole side effect of increasing female libido, and effects a specific but temporary male sterilization of controlled duration by instigating an occlusive mechanism in the region of the ampullary ejaculatory duct junction that completely excludes spermatozoa from the ejaculate without detriment to the male's sexual experience. With exemplary humility and grace, the therapeutic and pharmacologic implications of this fantastic addition to the physician's armamentarium are discussed.

REFERENCES

1. STURM, A. AND DRANG, B.: Population control and human sexuality, Harder & Harder Press, New York, 1961.

2. GABRIEL, A.: Personal communication.

3. YOLK, A., AND WHITE, B.: On slicing a hard-boiled egg, *Popular Mechanics*, 39: 251, 1948.

4. AUGER, D. *et al.*: The analysis and treatment of stoppages in pipes of all descriptions, Proceedings Vth International Congress of Plumbers and Pipefitters, Milan, 7: 233, 1965.

5. MESMER, F. A.: The power of positive persuasion, *Suggestive Quart.*, 2: 15, 1807.

6. BONVIVANT, B.: Unmarried love, 23rd ed., Peyton Publications, N.H., 1947.

7. HAIRSPLITTER, B. A.: Differences in the libidinous organization of man and woman, Lurid Press, London, 1891.

8. LOVE, O.: Ideal divorce, 12th ed., Holiday Press, Reno, 1951.

9. ROULETTE, R.: Statistics and what you can do with them, Confound Press, New York, 1959.

10. SNIFF, I.: Inhalers and impotence, *J. Armenian Med. Ass.*, 135: 909, 1957.

11. MUSK, A., CIVET, B. and CASTOREUM, C.: Neurohumoral responses to odours and stenches, *Arch. Intern. Disorders*, 28: 108, 1961.

12. SCHMECKEN, Z.: Die Hautdrüsenorgane der Säugetiere, *Unnaturwissenschaften*, 46: 63, 1960.

13. GOOSE, M.: A child's guide to erotica, Golden Days, Garden City, 1963.

14. RELIEF, P.: Physiology of micturition and ejaculation, *No. African Med. J.*, 14: 502, 1950.

15. MEN, C.: A contribution to the neurophysiology of orgasm, *Chinese J. Urol.*, 48: 821, 1957.

16. Apologies are extended to those sincere and dedicated scientists who may recognize not entirely coincidental resemblances to their authentic and valued contributions to the literature on reproduction.

When did you realize that this article was a spoof? If you did not catch on at first—or at all—do not feel too bad, because among the ranks of those who did not realize the tongue-in-cheek character of this masterpiece were a number of scientists and other professionals who should have known better. For instance, in 1966, a few months after the appearance of this article, I had occasion to talk to a group of security analysts who were evaluating the investment prospects of pharmaceutical companies active in the oral contraceptive field. I briefly showed one of them Dr. Greenstein's article and pointed out the summary and Table I. Sophisticated as this analyst was, he nearly jumped out of his chair and was ready to write a "sell" recommendation for the stock of Syntex and Searle—the two pharmaceutical companies whose earnings at that time most heavily depended on oral contraceptive sales; it took some time for me to convince him that the article was not real.

Dr. Edward T. Tyler of the UCLA School of Medicine—one of the best-known clinicians in the field of oral contraceptives and the first person to have carried out clinical experiments with norethindrone, the active chemical ingredient of over half of all birth control pills—reviewed the entire scientific literature on antifertility agents in the 1967 *Annual Review of Pharmacology*. He perpetuated Greenstein's spoof by ending his review in the following manner:

> One interesting recent development related to a new preparation described by Greenstein, who reported on a new contraceptive drug, Armpitin, which when applied to the axillary regions of the female causes a temporary and reversible sterilization in the male partner upon inhalation. Easily applied, like any commercial deodorant, Armpitin is said to have the sole side effect of increasing female libido. The author reported that the active portion of the molecule has the following configuration:

> Armpitin was synthesized in the search for a deodorant to solve an odor problem in animal research facilities. After the drug was installed in the dispenser, it was soon apparent that (a) all the animals species had greatly increased their copulatory frequency and vigor; (b) married employees working in the animal rooms no longer brought their lunches but went home at the noon hour; (c) a ban on mixing of attendants of the two sexes in the same animal

room was required; and (d) absolutely none of the females of any species was becoming pregnant. A total of 345 human volunteers used Armpitin for 2415 cycles and there were no pregnancies.

Scientists, like journalists, do not always read the original literature, and if you are not a chemist (who would be enormously surprised by the chemical structure of Armpitin), then Tyler's matter-of-fact summary might throw you off guard. Indeed, until recently, when I was informed otherwise by the article's author, I like many others had assumed that Dr. Tyler had actually accepted the article as gospel truth since reviewers of scientific fields are notorious for skimming the literature superficially. In the years since the article was written, Dr. Greenstein has received an amazing number of serious inquiries from around the world about this mysterious substance. An example of a letter written by a foreign investigator as late as July 1978 follows:

> In 1967 Tyler published a review of "Ann. Rev. Pharmacology" in which he stated that following the appearance of Armpitin there are many investigators concentrating their attention on some of other related substances free of such side effects as Armpitin. Since then we have not found any further article about Armpitin. I wonder if there are any investigators now engaged in the searching of Armpitin-like substances in America or other countries.
>
> I am very interested in the theoretical aspect of the pharmacological phenomenon of Armpitin, could you give me any references about it? I would be much obligated if you could let me have the patent number of Armpitin and its reprint, and I also hope to get some samples of Armpitin.

Executives of various pharmaceutical companies in the U.S. and abroad have contacted the author to inquire about licensing rights (e.g., "Nous avons lu avec intérêt votre article relatif à un 'nouvel et incomparable agent contraceptif', l'ARMPITIN. Nous aimerions avoir plus de renseignements sur ce produit pour une éventuelle commercialisation, en particulier sur les formes de présentation."). Even editors of some medical journals were apparently misled, because one such editor, after reprinting Greenstein's article on Armpitin, was prompted to write to the editor of the *Canadian Medical Association Journal* expressing some concern that the paper may not have been a serious one after all. The Canadian editor in his reply had to call attention to the fact that he had written a lengthy editorial entitled "Humouring the Physician," which contained the following two paragraphs that apparently had been overlooked by many:

> Some readers may protest that in describing this contribution as an elegant, indeed, an incomparable spoof, the editors are spoiling the fun. However, no matter what is said here, it is a safe bet that a few readers will take it as "gospel" and will phone Dr. Greenstein or the Journal inquiring for further details or seeking a supply of *Armpitin* for research purposes.
>
> The *Armpitin* account should be recognized for what it is—a masterpiece. A spoof is a difficult enough matter to carry off *in vivo* when nothing is recorded but fleeting impressions, but to bring it off faultlessly in cold print, in a deadpan burlesque of scientific journalism with all its trappings of structural formulas, tracings and voluminous references, is a feat which compels admiration.

The flood of inquiries addressed to Dr. Greenstein has slowed down during the intervening 14 years, but it has not stopped.

Under the circumstances we should not be surprised that laymen also were misled by Greenstein's article, but some of their comments seem more intelligent than those of some physicians. The following brief extract from a 1970 letter to Dr. Greenstein speaks for itself:

> Assuming that such a deodorant contraceptive as Armpitin does exist, many interesting questions arise. It would be a great boon to the couple who did not wish to have any children at a particular time. However, if Armpitin were worn like a deodorant, would not every man who came within smelling distance of the woman wearing Armpitin also become sterile? Or is Armpitin applied immediately before intercourse and washed off a short time thereafter?
>
> Why must it be worn by the woman? Wouldn't it be at least as effective if worn by the man, since the physical change occurs in him?
>
> Is one whiff of the odor enough to cause sterility for a certain number of days depending on the number of NO groups as discussed in the article? If this were the case, then why wouldn't an inhalator be just as effective as an axillary deodorant?

Dr. Greenstein had actually anticipated this question; in an earlier letter to one of his many fans he had written: "You may be interested

Smiling head. Veracruz, classic, *ca.* A.D. 500–700.

to know that I have now developed 'Anti-Armpitin' nosedrops that protect innocent males seated in crowded public conveyances from strap-hanging female users. This development became necessary after repeated reports of unexplained infertility in male commuters on city buses and trolley cars."

Any journalist or layman who tells me that scientists living in glass houses should not throw rocks is absolutely correct. However, when it comes to birth control on a global scale, we all really live in one glass house, and none of us should throw rocks. Dr. Greenstein's article is the only amusing aspect of an otherwise deadly serious double-edged problem—the manner in which public opinion is formed, not only in the birth control field but in other technical areas as well, and the importance of critically evaluating what we read and hear regarding complex technical issues. It is almost invariably lay persons, be they journalists or legislators, who are responsible for shaping the general public's perception of problems in technical areas. Public opinion in turn is sometimes translated into legislation that affects the future of such research and development. In a democratic society the creation of public policy and its implementation are inherently political. Unfortunately, the politicization of complicated technical scientific issues often invites superficiality (both from the press and legislators) as people seek simplified, black-and-white answers to complex, grey questions. Still, despite the inefficiency and pitfalls, most of us accept the political resolution of societally important technical issues as an unavoidable feature of democratic decision making. Given this fact of life, today's public opinion climate will have a profound effect on the future of contraception—what improvements in existing methods might be made, what new methods might be developed, and when. For it is the politics of contraception, rather than science, that now plays the dominant role in shaping that future.

Male figure. Colima, archaic, *ca.* 200 B.C.–A.D. 100.

7

Future Prospects
in Male Contraception

> [*The Pill*] *is entirely the invention of men. And why did they
> do it? . . . Because they are extraordinarily unwilling to ex-
> periment with their own bodies. . . . It would be much safer
> to monkey with men than monkey with women. . . . The ideal
> contraceptive undoubtedly would be a pill that a man and a
> woman would have to take simultaneously. . . .*
>
> Margaret Mead, *Chemical and Engineering News,*
> October 25, 1971

EVEN AS WISE A WOMAN as the late Margaret Mead can be drawn
into making emotional statements when the discussion turns to birth
control in women. How justified are her comments?

That the female oral contraceptive pill was "entirely the invention
of men" is indeed correct, but that unfortunately is a reflection of
a cultural phenomenon that is long overdue for major change—the
lack of women in many scientific fields, including contraceptive research. (Even here the situation is rapidly changing. For instance,
at a major international symposium held in 1978 in Norway on the
topic of male contraception, nearly 20 percent of the scientifiic
participants were women. I would suspect that a decade or two ago
only 1 or 2 percent of the participants would have been women.)

The early history of the Pill shows clearly that so-called male reluctance to experiment with their own bodies never even entered into the equation. The original work to develop orally effective progestational steroids was prompted by concerns about the treatment of menstrual disorders, infertility, and possibly cervical cancer; the contraceptive applications of these drugs followed only later (see Author's Postscript). It is certainly true that much more contraceptive research has been and is being conducted with females than with males. And most of the decisions about this research have been and are being made by men, although this situation will change in the not-too-distant future. But I am convinced that if women were in charge of all relevant decisions in contraceptive research, they too would concentrate on improvements in female fertility control. Judith Norsigian of the Boston Women's Health Book Collective—hardly a male chauvinistic enterprise—summarized the situation succinctly in her testimony before the 1978 hearings of the House Select Committee on Population: "In 1976 in particular, there was considerable funding in the area of male contraception. However, the majority of research, especially now, is still focused on women. I am not sure that this is inappropriate, since women are the ones who ultimately become pregnant and give birth. I do think that far more women must be involved in the research process."

Male or female, research scientists in the birth control field would agree that Mead's statement that "it would be much safer to monkey with men than monkey with women" is simply incorrect, except with regard to male sterilization. Still, this is a common misperception, one which is best rebutted through the words of another woman author, Ann Banks, writing in *Boston Magazine:* "Such gnashing of teeth is understandable, given that comparable caution did not prevail in the early phase of research into the birth control pill for women. Still, the object is safe, reliable contraception, not revenge."

Mead's final comment that "the ideal contraceptive undoubtedly would be a pill that a man and a woman would have to take simultaneously" is from a technical standpoint unrealistic. She may have thought that a higher degree of safety with fewer side effects would be obtained if each partner used a contraceptive pill that is of sufficiently low dosage to be only moderately effective alone. Though it is true that the cumulative effectiveness of two such less-than-ideal contraceptives would be much higher if each partner took it, this presupposes that a low-efficacy contraceptive agent would be intrinsically safer than one of high efficacy. Yet there is no reason to believe that this is so. Furthermore, most barriers to contraceptive development today are related to *safety* rather than *efficacy;* thus, there is no reason to believe that a low-efficacy drug would necessarily be any easier to develop than one that is more effective.

However, if the point is that the "ideal" birth control method would be for a man and a woman to be able to *share* the contraceptive burden, then we come to one of the justifications for developing a male contraceptive pill. If such a pill were available, partners could alternate periodically in the use of their respective Pill (e.g., every year or two; shorter periods would be pointless since complete inhibition of *spermatogenesis,* sperm production, alone takes over two months) and thus eliminate one of the greatest disadvantages of the oral contraceptives currently available—namely, continued exposure of one person to a single powerful agent for long periods of time. Actually, I can think of a much more compelling reason for having available more and better male contraceptive methods: it is not unreasonable to ask the man to carry more than an equal share of the contraceptive burden since the woman bears all of the reproductive load.

It is unfortunate that interest in a male equivalent of the Pill is growing during a period when the regulatory and public opinion climate is not conducive to such fundamental new developments. Ironically, women are largely responsible for the current restrictive climate; their understandable complaints about side effects and clinical experimentation have made safety and caution today's watchwords. As pointed out correctly by Ann Banks, unless revenge is the motive one cannot apply the criteria for clinical research in the 1950s to research conducted today. In fact, research on the Pill during those early days was at least as extensive as and, most likely, far more extensive than research carried out on most other comparable drugs used by men or women.

The Male Reproductive Process

In order to understand the vulnerable links in the male reproductive process that might offer novel approaches to male birth control, we need to have at least a simplified view of the complex sequence of events that governs the 82-day life cycle of a human sperm (74 days for spermatogenesis and 7 to 8 days for maturation) and its habitat before the sperm enters the female in its search for an unfertilized egg.

FIGURE 7-1

Male Reproductive Organs

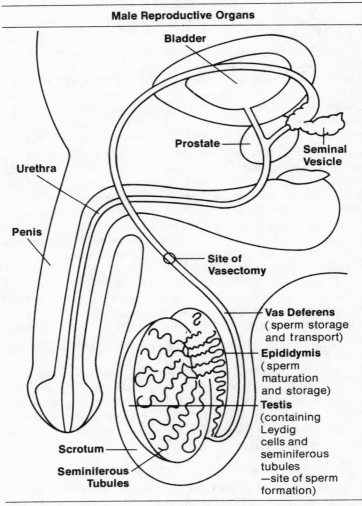

Spermatogenesis occurs in the seminiferous tubules contained within the testes (Fig. 7-1). These tubules are over 700 feet long and produce in excess of 30 million sperm per day. Once formed, the sperm passes into the epididymis, a 20-foot-long duct, where it matures and is stored. During this maturation process, the sperm acquires its fertilizing capacity as well as its capacity for independent movement. Subsequently, the sperm is stored and transported in

FIGURE 7-2

Hormones Involved in Male Reproduction

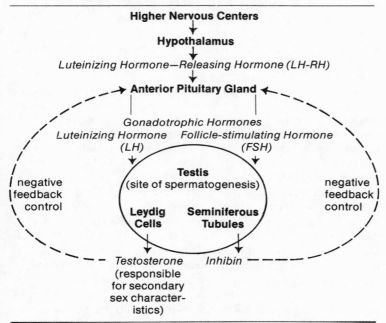

Higher Nervous Centers
↓
Hypothalamus
↓
Luteinizing Hormone—Releasing Hormone (LH-RH)
↓
Anterior Pituitary Gland

Gonadotrophic Hormones
Luteinizing Hormone   Follicle-stimulating Hormone
(LH)   *(FSH)*

Testis
(site of spermatogenesis)

**Leydig   Seminiferous
Cells   Tubules**

negative
feedback
control

negative
feedback
control

Testosterone   Inhibin
(responsible
for secondary
sex character-
istics)

the vas deferens, a duct nearly one foot long where the sperm is diluted by the secretions of the seminal vesicle and the prostate gland to comprise the seminal fluid that is eventually ejaculated through the urethra in the penis into the female genital tract.

Another important constituent of the testes are the Leydig cells, which produce the male sex hormone *testosterone* —responsible for the male's secondary sexual characteristics as well as his libido. Testosterone production in the testes is governed by complex hormonal mechanisms (depicted in Fig. 7-2). The hypothalamic gland is stimulated by the central nervous system to secrete several hormones called the releasing factors or releasing hormones, RH. (The isolation, purification, and chemical structure elucidation of these hypothalamic releasing hormones was accomplished in the early 1970s by two groups headed by R. Guillemin and A.V. Schally, who shared the Nobel Prize in medicine in 1977 for this fundamental discovery.) The key releasing hormone regulating male as well as female reproduction is the luteinizing hormone-releasing hormone, LH-RH, whose chemical nature is relatively simple; it is a decapeptide, that is, it is composed of ten amino acids. This hypothalamic hormone, in turn, stimulates the anterior pituitary gland to secrete two other hormones, known as gonadotrophins, which are usually referred to simply as LH (luteinizing hormone) and FSH (follicle-stimulating hormone). In contrast to RH, the gonadotrophins are very complex glycoproteins (i.e., they contain sugars and amino acids) and, given the current state of the art, they are beyond the scope of feasible laboratory synthesis.

In the male, LH stimulates the Leydig cells in the testes to produce the male sex hormone testosterone. A complex negative feedback mechanism governs the male hormonal system. For example, if too much testosterone is produced, the concentration of LH drops so as not to overload the body with testosterone; conversely, if the concentration of testosterone falls below a certain level, then the concentration of LH rises.

The biological role of FSH, the other pituitary gonadotrophic hormone, is much less obvious in the male than in the female. In the male, FSH apparently exerts its effect upon the seminiferous tubules in the testes to produce a substance called inhibin, to which testosterone is bound. Through another negative feedback mechanism, inhibin can lower the circulating level of FSH if it gets too high.

In contrast to the female, who is born with her life's supply of eggs, the male continually produces sperm and thus offers an almost lifelong target for potential genetic damage to the next generation. This is important for contraceptive strategy in that chemical interference with the early stages of sperm production is accompanied by the greatest genetic risk, while manipulations of later stages in sperm maturation are potentially less dangerous. It is for this reason that I discuss the most obvious male contraceptive strategies in the order of increasing risk. They are 1. interference with the transport of the sperm before it reaches the seminal vesicle and prostate gland so that ejaculated seminal fluid will not contain sperm; 2. interference with the processes occurring during maturation and storage of the sperm in the epididymis; 3. interference with sperm production in the testes; and 4. interference with the hormonal mechanisms at the anterior pituitary or hypothalamic levels, which would disturb both testosterone production and the production of sperm.

One: Interference with Sperm Transport

The simplest way of interfering with the transport of mature sperm prior to ejaculation is to rupture or block the vas deferens (see Fig. 7-1). This is accomplished by vasectomy, which involves a simple incision into the scrotum, severance of the vas deferens, and tying off of the two ends, after which the scrotal incision is closed with a few stitches. The procedure is performed under a local anesthetic and can be completed in less than 30 minutes. (Mass vasectomies in India have shown the operational feasibility of this procedure in lesser-developed countries.) Minor variations in the cutting and ligation steps have been reported and though these are of no consequence for men who are not concerned with the possibility of reversibility, the actual operational technique does affect greatly the chances of eventual microsurgical repair. For example, if too long a segment of the vas deferens is removed (the usual segment is 1-5 cm.), the success of future attempts to recombine the ruptured ends surgically is greatly reduced.

Other than coitus interruptus and the condom, vasectomy is the only method of fertility control currently practiced by males. Unfortunately, because reversibility is so difficult, it is for all practical purposes considered only by fathers or middle-aged and post-middle-aged men who are not interested in having more children. The number of men in this category is not negligible; currently over 600,000 men per year undergo this simple operation in the U.S.

Except for occasional minor side effects shortly following the operation, the longer-term effects of vasectomy appear minimal or are not yet documented. A possible long-term effect meriting concern is that in an appreciable number of men, reabsorption by the body of the sperm, which after vasectomy does not get removed through ejaculation, may lead to the production of circulating antibodies specific to sperm. The potential consequences of this immunological reaction in the *infertile* man seem to be low, but reestablishing fertility in the presence of sperm-specific antibodies is a major concern.

This brings us to the more difficult question of psychological side effects of vasectomy in terms of sexual performance. One study based on interviews of 42 couples for four years following vasectomy and comparisons with a similar number of couples using oral contraceptives suggests some changes in sexual satisfaction among the former. In several instances, coital frequency initially increased in the vasectomized group but was then followed by temporary impotence. This was attributed to an overreaching of sexual capacity by some men who were apparently concerned about demasculinizing effects of vasectomy and were consequently trying to demonstrate their masculinity. Studies of the long-term psychological and physiological side effects of vasectomy in large population groups are now under way. It is likely that the fear of loss of potency rather than apprehension about the simple operation itself has stopped many men from undergoing vasectomy.

From a technical standpoint, only minor improvements in the surgical procedure are to be anticipated or indeed even required. One possible improvement in male sterilization would be to replace the surgical intervention in vasectomy by a chemical one; for instance, injecting a mixture of ethyl alcohol and formaldehyde into the vas has worked in a limited number of males. Chemical sterilization has the advantage of eliminating potential complications from surgery or fear of surgery, and on a mass scale it may be both more economical and easier to administer. But care would have to be taken not to inject such a solution into the bloodstream, which could have extremely serious consequences.

Reversibility of Vasectomy

This is an area where a large amount of work still needs to be done and where success could have a major impact, since younger men and those who have not yet decided whether they wish to have children could be sterilized. Given the current state of the art, no man should undergo a vasectomy assuming that it can be successfully reversed. Even without the threat of malpractice suits, no surgeon would guarantee success. Reversal of a vasectomy is a complicated, time-consuming, and expensive microsurgical operation (essentially a "resewing" of the ruptured vas under a surgical microscope) that requires a great deal of experience. Since the late 1940s, the surgical literature (notably in the United States and India) has recorded various incidences of success ranging from 50 to 90 percent in terms of sperm reappearance in the ejaculate, but only from 10 to 60 percent success in terms of subsequent pregnancies; 30 percent is probably a more realistic expectation. This disappointing success rate may in part be related to the immunological inhibition of sperm activity resulting from the antibodies that are created in the immunological reaction following vasectomy, thus making a man infertile for the as-yet-undetermined lifetime of such circulating antibodies.

Many bioengineering attempts have been made to reverse vasectomy mechanically (these have involved experiments in dogs as well as humans). Such efforts have included insertion of a plastic plug or clip—either of which can be removed during a subsequent surgical operation—and even fancier devices with valves that may be activated from outside the human body. As a superfancy example, I quote from a description of U.S. Patent No. 3,731,670 issued on May 8, 1973, to James M. Loe, whose invention is entitled "Corporeal Fluid Control Using Bistable Magnetic Duct Valve." The device is shown in Fig. 7-3 on page 130, though it may terrify some men just to read about its mode of action:

> When used to provide contraception by selective male fertility control, valve 2 is surgically implanted in both of the vasa deferentia through a scrotal incision. (The valve can be implanted in only one vas if the remaining vas is resected as in ordinary vasectomy.) The valve is implanted so that occludable seat 8 is the distal end with respect to the testicle. Thus seminal fluid pressure, generated in the testes, will act to improve the seal of closure member 6 when it sits on the occludable seat 8.
>
> If tubular extensions . . . are used with valve 2, each should be about 0.4 inch in length. These extensions improve the fluid seal between the outer periphery of the valve and the inner surface of the vas, and also retain the valve more stably in the vas.
>
> The size of valve 2 is determined by the inner diameter of the vas in which it is installed. For the adult human male this size is typically about 0.045 inch in diameter. The length of said valve is about 0.070 inch.
>
> As previously noted, long term blockage of a vas deferens can lead to permanent sterility due to damage to the epididymal tubules from buildup of spermatic fluid pressure. Since the valve of this invention can be opened temporarily (e.g., at six month intervals), to provide periodic reestablishment of continuity of the vas deferens to release this pressure, it is extremely advantageous in that it can be used to effect long term blockage o the vasa deferentia without imparting permanent sterility [Note that such periodic "flushing" offers no remedy to infertility caused by immunological reactions associated with vasectomy.]

Such devices caused a flurry of excitement during the mid 1970s, but the current consensus of opinion is that their potential failure rate (e.g., lack of effective operating control via the externally applied magnet) would make them impractical for use on a wide scale. I can even imagine amusing bedroom scenes with the man discovering that his female partner's gentle caresses really included a hidden

FIGURE 7-3

Magnetic Duct Valve for Reversible Vasectomy

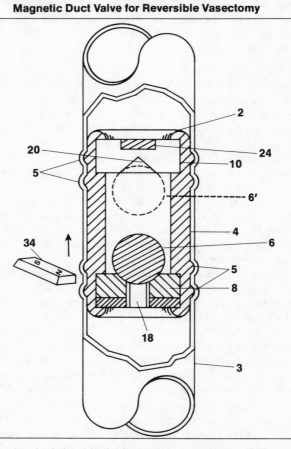

magnet with which his blocked vas deferens was opened surreptitiously. Research and financial support for such mechanical devices are currently at a very low level.

Human Semen Storage

Because vasectomies are for all intents and purposes irreversible at present, the collection of an adequate amount of semen prior to vasectomy, and its preservation for eventual use in artificial insemination, is frequently mentioned as an alternative.

An extensive literature exists on bull semen storage because artificial insemination in cattle has been going on for many years. However, bull semen is not human semen; indeed, many of the techniques used in artificial insemination of cattle have not been transferable even to sheep. Experiments in which human semen is mixed with glycerol and then cooled to the temperature of liquid nitrogen (−196°C) have proven effective in preserving motility of human spermatozoa for several years. This determination of efficacy is based not only on microscopic examination of the semen but also on successful artificial insemination of women with frozen semen stored up to four years. However, the actual numbers involved are small, and there are many questions still unanswered. Can semen be preserved from 10 to 30 years (not unreasonable if a 20-year-old man undergoes vasectomy)? What is the success rate in artificial insemination with such stored semen? Will offspring be normal? These are not trivial technical questions and, though in principle the storage of semen sounds both possible and simple, I can think of no way whereby essential data can be accumulated in less than a decade or two.

Lack of such data, however, has not prevented some venturesome entrepreneurs from appearing on the scene. As early as 1972, even before much was known about the viability of human sperm, a commercial sperm bank opened in Maryland. For an initial payment of $80, the customer received a pleasant setting for masturbation, and for an additional $18 a year he was guaranteed (?) storage of his semen. As reported in *Science* in April 1972:

> The customer need only have observed at least 48 hours of prior continence—to ensure a high sperm count—to qualify as a depositor. He strolls into Idant's small laboratory, which is manned only by a secretary and a laboratory biologist, fills out a form, and plunks down the $80 fee required for the processing and freezing of three semen specimens. He then retreats to a tiny room furnished with a comfortable armchair, two pornographic magazines, and an ashtray. (He may also drop off his sample on the way to work, providing it is less than 2 hours old at the time of deposit.) The ejaculate is examined, diluted with a glycerol preservative, and stored in 12 or 15 little plastic vials resembling ball-point pen refills. The vials are stored in three metal cannisters and submerged in stainless steel barrels filled with liquid nitrogen, which bubbles away at its boiling point of.−196°C.

It seems, however, that customers of this Maryland laboratory had simply paid the rather stiff price of $80 for being permitted to masturbate once. Six years later Dr. R. Ansbacher of San Francisco reported in the journal *Fertility and Sterility:* "The early enthusiasm for using frozen semen has been tempered in the past two years, mainly as a result of the lowered conception rates achieved as compared with those achieved with fresh donor semen. The ideal method for freezing gametes has not yet been found, and the commercialization of sperm banking has not been developed as previously publicized. . . . Sperm banks are not reliable fertility insurance for men who elect to undergo vasectomy, since there is no assurance that an individual's semen sample can tolerate the freezing procedure and subsequent thaw."

In a similar vein, Dr. A.M. Karow—whose extensive experience with artificial insemination in the treatment of human infertility prompted a January 14, 1979, *New York Times* headline, "Sperm Banks Win New Acceptance"—wrote to me that "I would think that the average person would not choose to use the storage of semen as a dependable means of 'reversing' the effects of vasectomy."

Assume, however, that sufficient positive experience has finally been accumulated and that we in the U.S. are now prepared to promote semen preservation in hundreds of thousands of men. For only when we reach such numbers can a new fertility control method be considered to have a meaningful impact on either human fertility control or sexual practice. Consider the logistical problems of storing semen samples over decades in a highly mobile society and the possibilities of mismatch ("This can't be my baby!"), loss ("You can't *remember* where you put the cannister?"), human error (the technician forgets to refill the liquid nitrogen containers), and "acts of God" (a blizzard causes a sudden interruption of electricity)—each resulting in the ever-more-typical American reflex action of a multi-million-dollar liability suit. By this I do not mean to suggest that we should abandon further work in the field of human semen preservation, but because of the magnitude of such seemingly trivial problems, I doubt whether this technique will have any large-scale impact on the practice of fertility control in this century.

Two: Interference with Sperm Maturation

In principle, interfering with the process of sperm maturation is to be greatly preferred to interfering with the actual production of sperm because there is little chance of genetic alteration at this stage in the sperm's long life cycle; all of the genetic decisions essentially have been made already within the seminiferous tubules of the testes.

Unfortunately, a great deal of basic research still needs to be done to determine how sperm actually mature in the epididymis. Basically all we know now about sperm maturation is that immature sperm enter the epididymis and mature sperm with the capacity for independent movement leave the epididymal duct. Thus, in the absence of detailed knowledge of the intimate processes affecting sperm maturation, we must depend on empirical observations and even serendipitous discoveries.

One of the these discoveries involves a very simple organic compound known for decades, α-chlorohydrin, which inhibits sperm maturation in rats without affecting either sexual activity or the ability to reestablish fertility after discontinuance of the drug. Unfortunately, experiments with α-chlorohydrin in monkeys indicated that death ensued at the doses anticipated to be effective for antifertility purposes; consequently work with humans has not been pursued. Another group of compounds—synthetic halogenated sugars—has caused sterility in monkeys but not in mice, where high doses simply displayed serious neurotoxic effects.

It is worth noting that DBCP (1,2-dibromo-3-chloropropane), a chemical closely related to α-chlorohydrin and used widely as a soil nematocide for the protection of many crops, has recently received publicity because a number of male chemical workers exposed to DBCP for prolonged periods of time have proved to be sterile. It is quite conceivable that DBCP may interfere in some way with sperm development in the epididymis, though it is also conceivable that α-chlorohydrin, present in some samples of DBCP, may be the responsible agent.

In sum, though we have leads in the laboratory about how to interfere with sperm maturation, in the context of the critical path of a drug's development from the laboratory to the consumer (as discussed in Chapter 5), we are at the early steps of chemical synthesis and biological evaluation. Before these laboratory leads are introduced into millions of bedrooms, at least 12 to 18 years will pass, along with an expenditure of at least $30 million (ignoring inflation).

Three: Inhibition of Spermatogenesis

Interference with the early stages of sperm production is much riskier because of the increased likelihood of genetic mutations. While this caveat does not totally preclude working in the field, the chances of failure are much greater here and much more caution in long-term clinical work—notably in terms of searching for offspring resulting from failure of the method—must be instituted. In fact, how would one carry out such clinical work? Experiments in this area would ultimately require clinical use by thousands of couples of a compound that inhibits sperm formation, followed by careful analysis, in case of method failure, of either the offspring produced or the aborted fetus. Unfortunately, the more dangerous second-trimester abortion would be necessary for fetal studies since only at this stage of pregnancy would fetal malformations become noticeable.

Actually a surprisingly large amount of work has already been done in the area of inhibiting sperm formation, primarily by hormonal methods which will be discussed later. In addition, direct pharmacological interference with sperm production in the testes has been observed using several different types of synthetic organic molecules such as the dinitropyrroles and nitrofurans. These compounds have been studied in animals, and some even in humans, but a variety of toxicological effects at the early preclinical stages eliminated these substances from further consideration.

Perhaps most interesting is a group of compounds known as the bis-dichloroacetyl diamines. These substances were synthesized at the Sterling Winthrop Research Institute as potential amoebacides but later were found also to inhibit sperm formation. They were promptly tested for this effect in prison volunteers; semen samples showed that within two to three months of continuous administration of the drug, sperm counts had dropped to insignificant levels yet returned to normal concentrations upon discontinuance of the drug. The speed with which this clinical trial was conducted 18 years ago would simply be impossible today in the U.S. Moreover, it is very unlikely that such experiments could now be conducted with prison volunteers. The work on these compounds was discontinued around 1961, not for ethical considerations—such prison studies being considered routine at that time—but rather because the compounds were found to have major Antabuse effects; in other words, they could not be tolerated in the presence of alcohol without causing nausea, vomiting, and other unpleasant side effects. Considering that, at least in the Western world, sex and alcohol often go together, Shakespeare's words about alcohol in Macbeth—"It provokes the desire, but it takes away the performance"—would be true with a vengeance if this type of male contraceptive were employed.

We in the U.S. and the Western world are still at the very beginning stages of the critical path in our search for a chemical male contraceptive agent that would inhibit sperm formation. However, in early 1979, newspaper articles appeared in the Western press describing experiments conducted in the People's Republic of China with a natural constituent of cottonseed oil that reportedly interferes with sperm formation in human males. This work is described in detail in Chapter 10 and may turn out to be the most interesting lead we have in the field of male contraception.

Four: Interference with Hormonal Balance

More work has been done on interference with the hormonal balance at the pituitary and testicular levels than on any other potential approach to male contraception because, just as with the work leading to the female oral contraceptive pill, there is available a body of fundamental knowledge about the hormonal control mechanisms (see Fig. 7-2) which offers specific points of attack in the male's reproductive process. Unfortunately, hormonal interference in the male has exactly the same inherent disadvantages as it does in the female: it tampers with a very complex interplay of various hormones and thus is likely to lead to a variety of actual or potential negative side effects. Moreover, given the present regulatory climate and society's attitude toward safety and risk taking, together with what we have learned about potential side effects from 20 years of clinical experience in the female, the development of hormonal contraceptives for males is now likely to take very much longer than did comparable work with female hormonal contraceptives. Nevertheless, there is an interesting operational contradiction: although it will take a very long time (perhaps 12 to 18 years) to bring a male hormonal contraceptive pill to the public, initial clinical experiments with humans can actually be conducted much earlier than might ordinarily be expected.

To understand this apparent contradiction, it is necessary to remember the generalized critical path map for the development of a male antifertility agent outlined in Fig. 5-2. If one followed the traditional path of starting with the chemical synthesis of a *new* substance, one would not reach the stage of small-scale phase I clinical trials for determining toxicity in humans until a minimum of five to six years had elapsed. However, most of the experiments with male hormonal contraceptives have *started* with such clinical trials because the active ingredient in this instance has not been a new substance but a known hormone previously used for other therapeutic applications either in the male or female. Thus, initial animal toxicology experiments have not been required since major acute toxic effects in humans are not expected in short-term therapy. If such phase I clinical research is successful, meaning that no serious toxicity is noted in a few human volunteers given a thera-peutically effective dose of the drug, one must then return to the earli-er steps of longer-term animal toxicology and formulation studies.

The theory behind attempts to develop a male hormonal con-traceptive is relatively simple, but the development process itself is complicated. Briefly, what most clinicians have tried to do—in many cases successfully—is inhibit the secretion of the gonadotrophic hormones LH or FSH through the administration of steroid hor-mones. Because of the negative feedback loop (see dotted arrow in Fig. 7-2) between testosterone and LH, excess testosterone secretion inhibits gonadotrophin production, which in turn prevents en-dogenous production of testosterone in the Leydig cells within the testes. Testosterone is needed not only for the secondary sex charac-teristics but also for spermatogenesis. Thus, ironically, the adminis-tration of high doses of testosterone actually *inhibits* sper-matogenesis because the circulating testosterone inhibits the secre-tion of LH which, in turn, inhibits production of testosterone *within* the testes, and it is this endogenous testosterone that is needed for spermatogenesis. The exogenously administered circulating testos-terone, however, is sufficient to maintain libido and other secondary sexual characteristics.

Such experiments have actually been conducted in humans, primarily with injectable testosterone preparations because orally effective androgens (male sex hormones) cause substantial liver func-tion impairment if given for long periods of time. Although these preliminary experiments have shown that it is possible to lower the sperm count to levels that lead frequently, though not invariably, to infertility (it is often forgotten that abnormally low sperm count is no absolute guarantee of infertility), the dosages required are so high that there are very serious questions whether such levels of testos-terone can be given for long periods of time to males without danger of major side effects—including prostatic cancer and a variety of cardiovascular and metabolic disorders. Females would incur equiv-alent risks if their contraceptive method were based on the continu-ous administration of high dosages of estrogen.

Testosterone, however, is not the only steroid that inhibits LH secretion from the anterior pituitary gland. The two types of female sex hormones—the estrogens and the progestational hormones (both natural progesterone or the synthetic progestational agents present in current female oral contraceptives)—will also do the job. Administration of both types of female hormones has been studied in men, but in order to offset the total elimination of the male sex drive, testosterone has had to be given concurrently (either by long-lasting injection or implants). In principle these methods work, but as yet no really satisfactory combination regimen has been discovered that overcomes one of the most serious side effects of such therapy— gynaecomastia, or breast growth.

The World Health Organization currently has under way a number of trials with groups of five to ten men in Korea, Chile, Thailand, Mexico, and India to determine effective doses (by injection) of mixtures of progestational steroids and androgens. Ironically, these *human* clinical trials are required to establish the efficacious dose before one can do adequate *animal* toxicology needed to determine safety and long-term side effects. The vexing problem of finding a suitable animal model for such studies has not been solved, and it is indeed unlikely that any single animal species will do. The rabbit has been identified as a potential animal model in which the reduction of spermatogenesis by such steroid combinations can be studied and any significant teratogenic (birth defects in offspring) effects can be examined.

When selecting animal models for research related to reproduction and sexual performance in humans, certain special criteria—in addition to those conventionally used, such as mode of excretion, plasma half-life, etc.—must also be taken into consideration. Thus, in 1978 Dr. Roger Short called specific attention to what many persons may have felt intuitively, namely, that man is the sexiest of all animals, and that this fact should not be ignored when animal models are selected for reproductive research. Man is probably the only animal in whom estrus has nothing to do with sexual attractiveness: the female is always attractive to the male since sexual arousal and intercourse among humans are not related to reproduction, as is the case in virtually all other species. Particularly noteworthy is the fact that the human male has an enormous penis (when erect) relative to his body size (the gorilla's erect penis is smaller than a human's thumb). This is probably a reflection of evolutionary adaptation to man's sex life: it permits many more sexual positions, and the human penis's abnormally large size may be a result of genetic selection for producing pleasure rather than just delivering semen.

Short also called attention to the enormous differences in absolute and relative testis size between species. The gorilla, which has an extremely low copulatory frequency, has only minute testes (0.018 percent of total body weight), whereas in the chimpanzee, with his frequent copulations in the wild, the comparable figure is 0.269 percent. Man falls in between (0.079 percent), perhaps reflecting our comparatively low but sustained frequency of intercourse, and Short points out that selecting the macaque monkey as an animal model for contraceptive research, for instance, may be totally inappropriate since in this primate the weight of the testes may range from 0.46 to 0.92 percent of the total body weight. He concludes that "considerable thought needs to be given to this problem [selecting appropriate animal models] if we are to obtain results that are in any way meaningful to a human situation."

In addition to studies with the natural sex hormones, work has also been carried out with synthetic steroids that are "antiandrogens," meaning that they inhibit the biological functions of the male sex hormone. Such compounds again resemble progestational compounds in terms of biological activity and it is probably desirable to administer them together with some male sex hormone, although in several clinical experiments with anti-androgens no other hormone supplement was given.

Another potential area of investigation in the search for a male hormonal contraceptive is the possible role of inhibin (see Fig. 7-2), a substance that apparently is produced by the seminiferous tubules in the testes and exerts a negative feedback upon the gonadotrophic hormone FSH. The role of FSH in the human male is not yet completely understood, but it may be involved in some aspect of spermatogenesis, and to that extent inhibin may affect spermatogenesis as well. (It was only in 1977 that it was actually demonstrated unequivocally that inhibin exists and that it is a polypetide, i.e., made up of amino acids.) If a male contraceptive approach is to be based on inhibin, then it is fair to say that it is at least 20 years away from reality and only then if it satisfies the following two criteria: First, it must be shown that inhibin suppresses FSH levels to a degree sufficient to interfere with spermatogenesis and yet not cause a similar LH suppression. Second, the complete chemical structure of inhibin must be elucidated and found to be of a type synthesizable in the laboratory in order to provide adequate quantities, since isolation from natural (animal) sources is out of the question as a large-scale supply route.

There is one other basic hormonal approach that should be discussed, at least briefly. We can move upward (see Fig. 7-2) from the testes and anterior pituitary gland to the hypothalamus since inhibition of the appropriate releasing hormone (e.g., LH-RH) secreted by the hypothalamus would presumably have the same effect as inhibition of the gonadotrophic hormones by administration of steroids (e.g., testosterone). The chances of chemically synthesizing effective

LH-RH antagonists are good (see Chapter 8), but suppression of spermatogenesis by this route is again very likely to be associated with loss of libido and potency because of inhibition of testosterone production in the testes.

All of these experiments, although theoretically interesting, are still at the very earliest stages of the critical path for developing a male hormonal contraceptive pill. Just as the overriding concern today regarding female hormonal contraceptives is the possible link to cancer, notably of the breast and uterine cervix, an analogous concern has been expressed for the male with respect to the possible link between the long-term administration of male hormones and benign prostatic tumors and prostatic cancer. Prostatic cancer risk increases with age, and because of this only relatively young volunteers should be selected for studies of such drugs. Techniques recently have been developed that permit the monitoring of prostatic function, which has not been done in the past.

The actual and potential psychological problems associated with male contraceptives cannot be ignored. So far I have only mentioned the psychological problems with respect to libido in the context of vasectomy. However, loss of libido is much more likely to become a real problem in any hormonal contraceptive method, in spite of assurances to the contrary, because of the enormous psychological component associated with sexual potency in the male. Drs. Marian C. Diamond and Carol C. Korenbrot, editors of a recent book entitled *Hormonal Contraceptives, Estrogens and Human Welfare,* wrote, apparently with some irritation but also with justification: "Development of male contraceptives involving the sex steroid hormones testosterone and estrogen are considered 'no-no's' because they are purported to reduce male libido. However, women using oral contraceptives report a variety of effects on libido and often a general mental depression, and yet oral contraceptives are widely prescribed. The documentation that allows use of the one contraceptive, but not the development of the other, is not clear. The need to know more about the effects of oral contraceptives on human sexuality and behavior is critical."

One must, of course, agree with the impeccable logic of Drs. Diamond and Korenbrot, but I must point out that a woman with reduced libido can still participate in sexual intercourse, while a man unable to get an erection is unquestionably in worse shape. The best solution to this problem would be a combination of a male contraceptive and a libido enhancer. Indeed, a libido enhancer per se would be an important contribution, not only commercially but also in terms of alleviating a fair amount of human misery in males. Unfortunately, developing such an agent and, especially, establishing double-blind clinical protocols (in which neither the subject nor the researcher knows the identity of the experimental drug or the placebo) that would lead to FDA clearance for initial clinical research, let alone final marketing approval, is quite another matter. I realize that there would be no dearth of volunteers, but what precisely should one measure?

Physiologist Julian Davidson at Stanford University has examined the effect of testosterone in some hypogonadal (underdeveloped testes resulting in impaired testosterone secretion) males and among other parameters of sexuality determined the number of erections from whatever source per unit time. While he has found some correlation between erections and the amount of testosterone in the blood, he points out that no such correlation exists in the general male population. Given the fact that men were primarily responsible for developing the female contraceptive pill, perhaps it is only fair to wait for women scientists to develop the first male libido enhancer. My own feeling is that such a development would expedite male contraception more than any other factor.

The present state of affairs with respect to hormonal approaches to male contraception is well summarized by Bruce Schearer of the Population Council: "As the first chapter of extensive clinical research into the development of a hormonal male contraceptive draws to a close, it must be concluded that—in spite of nearly six years of vigorous research and development—effective new contraceptive products for men are not yet imminent." I would rephrase Schearer's prognosis more brutally by predicting that every postpubescent American female reading this chapter in 1979 will be past the menopause before she can depend on her male sexual partner to use his Pill.

Given my pessimistic prognosis, who am I to argue with Barbara Seaman's advice to the House Select Committee on Population:

> There have long been reports of temporary sterilization for men accomplished through heat. Dr. John Rock had some of his Harvard students try an insulated jock strap, and he said it worked. (We took his word about the Pill, didn't we?) Dr. Martha Voegli, a Swiss physician working in India, has long advocated the following technique: For three weeks, a man takes a daily forty-five minute bath in water of 116 degrees Fahrenheit. This procedure, she says, should then render him sterile for six months, after which

his normal fertility will return. We don't know whether such methods are entirely safe, but certainly they are economical. Let's find out if they might be safe and effective for some men, at least, so that men also might have the option of practicing drug- and device-free birth control.

Considering the current craze for hot tubs in California, perhaps an epidemiological study for temporary sterility among such male aficionados is in order.

Male figure. Colima, classic, *ca.* A.D. 100–400.

Woman giving birth on stool. Nayarit, classic, *ca.* A.D. 100-400.

8

Future Prospects in Female Contraception

ALTHOUGH WE CAN EXPECT only minimal improvements in male contraceptive hardware over the next decade, in that same time frame there are several existing female contraceptive methods that could at least be improved and even a few new ones that could be developed. Why is there such a difference—both qualitatively and quantitatively—between male and female methods? The answer is simple. First, intensive work on new contraceptive methods has a head start of at least two decades in the female, and it will take a long time before this gulf is narrowed; second, our repertoire of basic information is much more complete concerning the female reproductive process than it is concerning that of the male; third, there are more stages in the female reproductive time sequence—from ovulation to birth of a baby—in which this process can be interrupted than there are in the male, where we have only one target, the sperm.

In order to understand the rationale behind the various approaches to female contraception, let us look—as we did in the discussion of male contraception—at the female reproductive system (Fig. 8-1) and at the interplay of the various hormones that govern many of the female reproductive processes (Fig. 8-2).

The Female Reproductive Process

The female hormonal mechanisms are almost analogous to those

FIGURE 8-1

Female Reproductive Organs

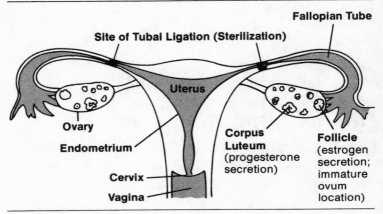

in the male (see Fig. 7-2), the main difference occurring at the gonadal level. At different times during the menstrual cycle of the female, two sex hormones are generated in the ovaries: the estrogen estradiol (responsible for female secondary sex characteristics) and the progestational hormone progesterone (responsible for the maintenance of pregnancy). In contrast to the male, who continuously produces sperm throughout his lifetime as long as he has functioning testes, the female at birth has her total complement of eggs, numbering at least half a million, of which only about 400 mature during her reproductive life.

The ovaries contain the Graafian follicles, one of which matures about every four weeks during a woman's active reproductive years. The follicle plays a dual role in the female reproductive process. First, it functions as an endocrine organ and when stimulated by the gonadotrophic hormone FSH (follicle-stimulating hormone) secreted by the anterior pituitary gland, the follicle itself secretes the female estrogenic hormone estradiol. The second, nonendocrine role of the follicle is that it contains the immature egg. Estrogen secretion by the follicle, which reaches its height toward the end of the second week of the menstrual cycle, leads to maturation of the egg. At this point, ovulation (i.e., departure of the mature egg from the follicle) is stimulated by the production of a second gonadotrophic hormone, LH (luteinizing hormone), also secreted by the anterior pituitary gland. The empty follicle is then converted into another temporary endocrine organ—the corpus luteum ("yellow body")—which se-

FIGURE 8-2

Hormones Involved in Female Reproduction

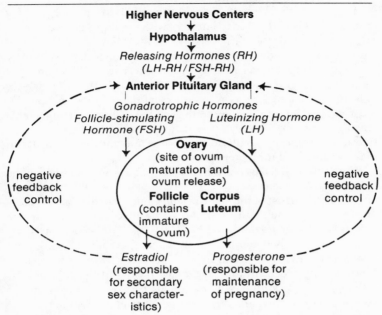

Higher Nervous Centers

Hypothalamus

Releasing Hormones (RH)
(LH-RH / FSH-RH)

Anterior Pituitary Gland

Gonadrotrophic Hormones
Follicle-stimulating   *Luteinizing Hormone*
Hormone (FSH)   *(LH)*

Ovary
(site of ovum
maturation and
ovum release)
Follicle   **Corpus**
(contains   **Luteum**
immature
ovum)

negative
feedback
control

negative
feedback
control

Estradiol
(responsible
for secondary
sex character-
istics)

Progesterone
(responsible for
maintenance
of pregnancy)

cretes the second female sex hormone, progesterone, as well as additional estrogen during the second half of the menstrual cycle. If fertilization does not occur, the corpus luteum deteriorates and is shed during menstruation.

Each of the two female steroid sex hormones is involved in a negative feedback loop to the anterior pituitary gland which governs the secretion of the gonadotrophic hormones FSH and LH in the same manner as does the sex hormone testosterone in the male. It is progesterone that inhibits further ovulation once pregnancy has occurred, and for this reason progesterone can be called "nature's contraceptive." However, since estrogens also affect the anterior pituitary gland, continuous administration of doses of estrogen higher than those secreted normally by the woman would also interfere with the hormonal balance that controls fertility and thus can be used for contraceptive purposes. (Dr. Robert B. Greenblatt of the Medical College of Georgia, for instance, reported in a 1977 issue of the *American Journal of Obstetrics and Gynecology* that implantation of pellets of crystalline estradiol subcutaneously into the abdominal wall of women offered high contraceptive protection for six-month intervals.)

Just as with the male, when devising methods of contraception for the female it is preferable to interfere with the reproductive process at the most local level rather than with the complicated hormonal system. Barrier methods, such as the diaphragm, which prevent entry of a sperm into the uterus through the cervix from the vagina, fall into that category. An intermediate approach is the IUD, which, when inserted into the uterus, produces a foreign-body reaction that does not prevent fertilization of the egg but creates an inhospitable environment in the uterus (especially the endometrial lining of the uterus into which a fertilized egg has to implant itself in order to develop further during pregnancy).

With this material as background, let us now proceed to examine some of the female contraceptive options of the future. A very appreciable portion of the financial and clinical manpower resources in the field of female contraception are devoted to the study of side effects of existing methods—the Pill, IUDs, abortion, and sterilization. This trend will continue in the coming decade. However, my intent here is to deal primarily with work on *improved or novel contraceptive procedures* rather than with work of an epidemiological character. Accordingly, I shall focus first on improvements of existing methods that are likely to become available within the next decade before turning to the prospects of fundamentally new alternatives which, in my opinion, cannot possibly be available to women before the close of the century.

Modification of Nonhormonal Methods of Birth Control

Abortion

On a world scale, abortion is one of the most important and widely practiced methods of fertility control among women and, whether we like it or not, it will remain so for a long time. Improvements in surgical procedures such as the extensive use of menstrual extraction (see Chapter 2) have progressed rapidly during the last few years, largely because at the present time surgical procedures do not fall within the formal control of government regulatory agencies but are primarily controlled by peer review groups. However, further major advances in surgical procedures are unlikely to occur, primarily because the existing methods for first-trimester abortions are on the whole quick and safe.

Nevertheless, the number and types of practical issues associated with surgical abortion that still require evaluation are formidable. As an example I cite almost verbatim a rather forbidding table (8-1, pages 148-49) enumerating some of the experiments currently in progress under the auspices of just a single organization (WHO) to provide a glimpse at the geographical range and the numbers of women that are needed to answer some of the obvious questions pertaining to safety.

What is needed in this area are methods that do not involve complicated medical institutional structures (i.e., surgical intervention or hospitalization). Thus, there is continuing interest in chemical methods of abortion, of which the prostaglandins are a typical example. These nonsteroidal fatty acid derivatives, which function largely by stimulating contractions of the uterus, are already being used in therapeutic second-trimester abortions (to replace more dangerous alternatives), but they must be administered in a hospital setting by instillation, either intravenously or directly into the amniotic fluid, over a period of several hours. Intravaginal administration has also been used successfully. A major advance would be the development of an orally effective prostaglandin that could be self-administered by the woman during the very early stages of pregnancy.

Even better would be a "luteolytic agent," a substance that destroys the corpus luteum (see Fig. 8-2), thereby preventing further secretion of progesterone, essential for the maintenance of pregnancy. (Although nature destroys the corpus luteum every month during menstruation, as soon as a fertilized egg is present an impressive stimulating effect is exerted on the corpus luteum which makes its destruction difficult.) A luteolytic agent, if found, could be taken by the woman on a specified day each month to start her menstrual period irrespective of whether fertilization had occurred during the preceding couple of weeks. The chances of developing such agents are reasonable. Indeed, the hypothetical "once-a-month" luteolytic agent described in detail in Chapter 5 is typical—but the development time for such an agent would be on the order of a decade or more.

Sterilization

Ligation or rupture of the Fallopian tubes (see Fig. 8-1) is equivalent to rupturing the male's vas deferens in vasectomy and similarly results in sterility, since the sperm cannot approach the egg and fertilize it, nor can the egg move down into the uterus. Rapid ad-

TABLE 8-1

WHO-Sponsored Abortion Research Under Investigation

Study Designation	Issues Under Investigation	Site, Subjects to be Recruited
Early abortion (45 days)		
Cannula study	Are rigid metal cannulae [tubes] of 4 and 5 mm. diameter as safe and effective as plastic disposable cannulae?	Bombay, Chandigarh, Delhi, Havana, Los Angeles, Ljubljana, Montreal, Seoul, Singapore
	Are one-holed cannulae as good as two-holed cannulae?	
Abortion at 5-6 versus 7-8 weeks	What is the relative safety and effectiveness of the early procedure performed without cervical dilatation compared to the procedure with dilatation at 7-8 weeks?	Computer-based study using data from the cannula study and from the complete study of inpatient/outpatient abortion in Ljubljana and Singapore
First-trimester abortion		
(7-12 weeks)		
Controlled study of anesthesia and inpatient vs. outpatient facilities	Compare local vs. general anesthesia; necessity of overnight hospitalization, etc.	Ljubljana and Singapore
Descriptive comparison of abortion procedures (includes second-trimester and also concurrent sterilization)	What is the relative safety of different abortion techniques among women in a developing country?	17,628 women 13 Indian centers
	What factors affect the risk of complications (including age, parity, anemia, concurrent procedures, etc.)?	
Controlled study of D&C vs. vacuum aspiration (VA)	Are D&C and vacuum aspiration equally safe in terminations of 7-12 weeks gestation?	Hungary 5 centers 5,000 women
Controlled study of D&C vs. VA-mechanical suction pump vs. VA-	Are D&C, mechanical and electrical vacuum pumps equally effective in	Havana 6,000 women

Study	Question	Location/Sample
Electrical vs. mechanical vacuum pumps	Are mechanical pumps as effective as electrical pumps in terminations of 7-12 weeks gestation?	11 centers 4,000 women
Controlled study of concurrent vs. interval abortion/sterilization	Are concurrent abortion with sterilization and interval abortion/sterilization equally safe?	Singapore 400 women randomly allocated to two groups
Second-trimester abortion		
13-15 week descriptive study	Which 13-15 week procedure has the lowest complication rate?	Stockholm—11 hospitals, record-linked study 3,000 women
13-16 week controlled study	Are the use of catheters, rivanol (antiseptic) and rivanol plus prostaglandins equally effective in terminations of 13-16 weeks gestation?	9 centers 1,500 women
Long-term consequences		
Outcome of pregnancy	Are there increased risks of low birth weight, pre-term delivery, or spontaneous abortion following an induced abortion?	Copenhagen, Debrecen, Helsinki, Ljubljana, Lodz, Newcastle-on-Tyne, Seoul, Stockholm, and Warsaw 39,000 women
	Following repeated abortions?	
	Are there different risks associated with the different abortion procedures?	
Prostaglandin and other second-trimester procedures	Ibid, particularly as related to second-trimester abortion.	Stockholm—11 hospitals, record-linked study
Infertility and induced abortion	Is there an increased risk of secondary infertility following induced abortion?	Debrecen and Seoul 2,000 women

SOURCE: World Health Organization. *Special Programme of Research, Development and Research Training in Human Reproduction, 7th Annual Report, November 1978.* Geneva.

vances have been made during the past decade in surgical sterilization procedures for precisely the same reasons as in the case of surgical abortion, namely, lack of a formal regulatory control mechanism. Laparoscopy (tubal ligation by entry through a small incision at the navel rather than through the vagina) has been a major advance and it is not clear how much more scope exists for dramatic improvements in *surgical* sterilization.

Theoretically, *chemical* sterilization (with, for example, mixtures of ethyl alcohol and formaldehyde, or methyl cyanoacrylate—a polymerizing glue), which occludes the Fallopian tubes by means of intrauterine instillation or even direct delivery (with a special device to the Fallopian tube through the uterine cervix), would be more desirable since the inherent disadvantage of female sterilization—penetration of the body wall—invariably carries with it a degree of risk or discomfort that should be eliminated if possible. A modest amount of work has been done in this field and is continuing, one of the pioneers being Dr. Jaime Zipper of Chile, who introduced the first copper-containing IUD. Still, such work is minimal compared to the efforts that are going into improvements in abortion, especially in those countries where conventional abortion is practiced widely and where more immediate public health issues need to be addressed. Because of unexpected complications associated with chemically induced occlusion of the Fallopian tubes, this method has not been investigated extensively. In oversimplified terms, the chemical produces a scar that suffices to block the path of any egg into the uterine cavity but that has some tiny holes through which a few sperm can penetrate. As a result, occasional tubal (ectopic) pregnancies have occurred, and these are life threatening.

Although chemical sterilization offers certain theoretical advantages over surgery, reversibility is practically impossible because the chemicals currently being used cause too much damage to the Fallopian tubes. If eventual reversal is a serious consideration, then one of the more standard surgical techniques should be employed. The success rate of surgical reversal in females in terms of subsequent pregnancies is definitely higher than in males—on the order of 60 to 70 percent—possibly because immunological complications do not arise in the female.

Of indirect relevance to the prospects of greater acceptability of female sterilization may be the recent work in England by Drs. Patrick Steptoe and Robert Edwards in which an egg is removed surgically from the woman, fertilized *ex utero* with the man's semen, and then implanted into her uterus. If this currently controversial procedure ever becomes a routine, widely used method of conception, it could have a major impact on the acceptability of sterilization among young women. Here again we are dealing with a method that depends largely on scrutiny by peer review groups and acceptability by surgeons and patients and is essentially outside the standard regulatory control mechanism of agencies such as the FDA.

IUDs

The other major nonhormonal method of contraception under continuing scrutiny is the intrauterine device. The main emphasis in current IUD research is on reducing the side effects, especially the most common one, excessive bleeding. Recent studies have taught us a great deal about the mechanism whereby IUDs cause such bleeding. Consequently, offsetting approaches have been devised, which primarily involve the administration of anti-inflammatory drugs and substances aiding in coagulation. Medicated IUDs, which contain progesterone (or, eventually, one of the synthetic progestational agents present in oral contraceptives), reduce bleeding and are currently available (see Chapter 2), but they must be replaced every year. Efforts are under way both to extend the lifetime of such medicated IUDs to several years and to learn more about a potentially serious side effect of these devices—an increased incidence of ectopic pregnancies in the event of failure.

The other important area of IUD research that is attracting considerable attention and that could have a major impact in lesser-developed countries is the creation of a satisfactory postplacental IUD which could be inserted immediately after delivery or after an abortion (in some instances the only times when a woman is seen by medical or paramedical personnel) and that will not be ejected or otherwise displaced during the succeeding months as the uterus reestablishes its original size.

Vaginal Microcapsules

Conceptually related to medicated IUDs, but not yet fully developed, are vaginal microcapsules, which contain progestational hormones encapsulated in a biodegradable polymer. Such a capsule is self-inserted into the vagina once a month; it then travels into the uterine cavity where the biodegradation is completed and the progestational hormone is released locally. It is hoped that formulations and dosages can be developed that will release only enough of the progestational hormone to exert a local effect rather than enter the general circulation (thereby affecting the overall hormonal balance).

If such a method is successful, then, strictly speaking, since it does not enter the circulation it need not be classified as a general hormonal contraceptive method even though a steroid hormone is used. Developmental work is still at the baboon level, but it is likely that clinical experiments will be starting within a year or two. Because these experiments involve the use of known agents, long-term toxicology (i.e., longer than two years) may not be necessary; thus, it is conceivable that such a method could become available in the middle to late 1980s.

Ovulation Detection

Considerable interest is now being expressed in improved procedures for determining the woman's fertile period. There are at least two simple methods—frequently used together—that can help a woman predict her time of ovulation. First, the preovulatory period can be determined by marked changes in the quality and quantity of the cervical mucus (usually thick and viscous, but becoming thin and fluid) which a woman can be taught to recognize. Intermenstrual pain (usually referred to by the German term *Mittelschmerz*) is also frequently noted at this time. Second, the end of the fertile phase can be identified by a definite rise in the basal body temperature; women who are not suffering from illnesses that cause elevated temperature may determine the period of ovulation fairly accurately by taking their temperature daily.

Theoretically, accurate detection of the time of ovulation should be the safest method of fertility control and, for sexually disciplined persons, a highly effective one. It has been estimated that the *theoretical effectiveness* of the method, if used correctly and if accompanied by rigorous sexual discipline, is on the order of 98 percent. However, as pointed out most recently in two WHO studies of the rhythm method (see Chapter 2), the *use effectiveness* is quite low.

Attempts are being made to develop ways of determining the period of ovulation even more accurately and I am convinced that, given the extraoradinary advances in analytical biochemical techniques that have been made in recent years, more accurate and more sensitive detection methods will be possible within a few years. Whether these advances—which are based on sensitive measurements of certain biochemical parameters associated with specific hormonal events, such as changes in the urinary excretion of certain estrogens or the sudden rise in concentration of the pituitary hormone LH at mid-cycle—can be converted into simple household detection devices remains an open question. But one can imagine dipsticks or some type of litmus paper that, when placed into urine or saliva, might change color at the onset of ovulation.

Developing simple, accurate methods to detect the onset of ovulation is only the first step in determining the duration of the woman's fertile period. Amazingly little is known about the length of this fertile period, which depends not only on the fertilizable life span of the ovum but also on the fertilizing lifetime of the sperm. Dr. John M. Morris of Yale, in his initial work with postcoital contraceptives, observed motile sperm in cervical mucus up to one week after intercourse. Recent preliminary studies indicate that 85 percent of all conceptions occur from day −5 to day +1, with day +1 being designated arbitrarily as the first day when a rise in basal body temperature is observed. Therefore, simply detecting the actual day of ovulation may well be insufficient.

An accurate method of ovulation detection does not, of course, require sexual abstinence, provided couples are prepared to use barrier methods—such as the diaphragm, foam, or condom—during the fertile period. In terms of contraceptive utility, ovulation detection is most likely to be used by educated and highly motivated populations in technologically advanced countries. The method may be particularly useful in the sexually active American teenage population and among women above the age of 35 who are reluctant to use the Pill or other hormonal contraceptives. However, consider a practical complication that might be encountered in marketing such an analytical kit in the U.S. today. If the package insert for an ovulation detection product is hedged in legalese indicating only *probable* assurance of effectiveness in order to avoid potential liability suits brought by women who become pregnant while claiming to have used the device correctly, then the popularity of the method is likely to be minimal.

Although improved contraception is our primary concern here, we should not forget one very important side benefit of being able to determine accurately the period of ovulation. For those women who have difficulties in conceiving and for whom a successful pregnancy is as important as, or more important than, a prevented one to a woman who wishes no more children, knowledge of the precise time of ovulation can greatly increase the chances for fertilization.

Modification of Existing Hormonal Contraceptive Methods

Aside from relatively minor adjustments in dosage, it is doubtful that any new developments of consequence will occur in the field of standard oral contraceptives. Given current public attitudes and the

regulatory environment in the advanced countries, it is highly unlikely that any pharmaceutical firm would go to the trouble of
developing another Pill, based on a new steroid ingredient, that
combines a progestational agent and an estrogen. The extraordinarily high cost and the long development time associated with such an
endeavor are prohibitive; furthermore, it is not even obvious
whether such efforts would be societally beneficial since such a new
Pill would still suffer from the same fundamental disadvantage as
does the current one—interference with the woman's general hormonal balance. Efforts to convert the daily Pill-taking regimen to a
weekly or a monthly one are continuing at a relatively low level but
will probably have little, if any, impact on future contraceptive
practices. Such regimens still contain the standard progestational
agents and estrogens but in formulations whereby they are deposited
into fatty tissue and subsequently are released slowly from the storage site. There is no reason to believe that any of the systemic side
effects of current daily Pill regimens could be diminished by such an
alternative.

Alternative Delivery Systems

The most likely modifications of the existing hormonal methods
of contraception will be in the area of devising alternative delivery
systems. I am not convinced that such alternatives will have much
impact in the United States or in other Pill-taking countries, but they
are likely to be of considerable importance in many lesser-developed
countries of the world. For instance, the Chinese "paper pill," in
which the steroids are adsorbed on water-soluble paper stamps (see
Chapter 10), offers no real advantages to the user but is cheaper to
manufacture.

The largest research effort that has been carried out during the
past 15 years on an alternative delivery method has focused on
developing sustained-release formulations of steroids that eliminate
daily pill taking. Such work continues today and the formulations
under investigation fall into two major categories: injectable preparations and implants.

Injectable Preparations. The two most widely used steroids in
injectable formulations are depo-medroxyprogesterone acetate
(also known as Depo-Provera or DMPA) and norethindrone enanthate. Norethindrone is the active chemical ingredient used in over
50 percent of all contraceptive pills (see Author's Postscript on the
chemical development of the Pill) and converting it into the enanthate, a 7-carbon fatty acid, makes it more fat soluble. Norethindrone

enanthate is administered in oily solution by intramuscular injection every two to three months. Depo-Provera is injected intramuscularly every three months in the form of a suspension of the crystalline drug in water. Depo-Provera (discussed in Chapter 4 in the context of the beagle experiments) still has not received FDA approval for contraceptive use in the United States, although it *has* been approved by the FDA for use in treating advanced endometrial cancer. However, because there is a considerable demand for an injectable contraceptive in many lesser-developed areas of the world, Depo-Provera has been used as a contraceptive in over 60 countries abroad.

The popularity of injectable contraceptives is attributable not only to convenience (they eliminate the need to take pills) but also to acceptability. In many societies medication by injection is preferred to pill taking ("It must hurt to help!"). Anthropologist J.F. Marshall has hypothesized about these advantages in some detail, using an Indian village population as an example:

> The ideal method of application would be by hypodermic injection, for several reasons. First, because of years of exposure to antibiotics and vaccinations, an injection is an entirely acceptable medical procedure in the village. Indeed, a villager who was not given a shot during a visit to a doctor felt himself somehow cheated. Second, an injection in the arm avoids both the mortifying experience of exposing one's genitals to medical scrutiny, and the necessity of handling one's genitals demanded by the condom, diaphragm, foam, or jelly. Not only is an injection coitus-independent, but like the oral pill, it is genitalia-independent, a highly desirable attribute in a culture in which modesty is imperative and privacy rare. Third, an injection can be given in the village, even in one's home, thus obviating the need to visit a threatening and inconvenient hospital or clinic. Finally, unlike a loop insertion, which requires a female doctor, or a vasectomy, which requires a male doctor, an injection in an arm can be given by either a male or a female.
>
> The injected substance would be a distinctive color— primarily to differentiate it visibly from other kinds of injectable medicines. This anticipates the probability that some villagers, in need of antibiotics but firmly opposed to the idea of contraception, would suspect unscrupulous doctors of trying to enforce population control by sneaking the contraceptive substance into the hypodermic needle.

Such a belief could lead to the avoidance of all injections, as in a neighboring village the belief that vitamin pills were abortifacients led to the shunning of all pills. If it were widely known that the contraceptive liquid—and only the contraceptive liquid—was always blue, a villager could assess for himself that he was, or was not, getting what he wanted.

Moreover, some colors tend to connote certain inherent qualities of substances, and a color should be selected that indicates the injected substance is not dangerously "hot" or "cold." It is likely that the injection would be perceived to be cold, and the contraceptive substance would probably be thought to operate in much the same way as the pill, by decreasing the heat of the genital area below the threshold at which conception can occur. The knowledge that the substance would remain in her body for six months, together with the belief that hot or cold foods and medicines can be dangerous in certain pathological states, might lead a woman to avoid the injection in apprehension of succumbing to one of these states. If a color could be found that connotes warmth but not heat, it would probably lead to a more acceptable contraceptive. Furthermore, to make the substance acceptable to vegetarians, it must not contain any components derived from meat or eggs; therefore a color should be selected, if possible, that does not connote flesh or blood.

Yet, choosing a color can be dangerous. The logo on AID-supplied oral contraceptive packages, for instance, shows a lady in blue. Unfortunately, in certain societies blue seems to be associated with women of ill repute. Considering all the other problems that accompany family planning efforts in lesser-developed countries, indirect association with prostitution is hardly what a contraceptive needs.

The most serious drawback of long-acting injectable contraceptives containing progestational steroids is menstrual irregularities. This is also the drawback of the oral counterpart of estrogen-free progestational therapy, the so-called minipill. So far this problem has not been overcome. These menstrual irregularities include both irregular bleeding and long periods of amenorrhea. According to a recent WHO-sponsored cross-cultural survey, amenorrhea is considered an undesirable side effect by the majority of women (except the young), but considering some of the thought-provoking comments of Roger Short in Chapter 2 concerning lactational amenorrhea, one might well ask whether eliminating menstrual periods for prolonged periods of time might not also have desirable implications. Some of the injectable steroid preparations also contain an estrogen in order to alleviate menstrual irregularities, but this in turn creates other problems associated with the estrogen component of oral contraceptives (e.g., nausea, blood clotting, etc.). Another drawback of an injectable contraceptive is that once it is administered, its effects cannot be reversed; the drug must simply deplete itself naturally.

Relatively little work on injectable contraceptives is taking place in the United States, but the WHO has a large number of projects under way because of pressure from various lesser-developed countries to develop better injectable agents. It is by no means inconceivable that within a decade or so there will be available injectable steroid preparations that lack most of the objectionable side effects. At the very least we will have a body of epidemiological knowledge that will permit a more intelligent utilization of this alternative method of steroid administration.

Steroid Implants. Over the last ten years a great deal of publicity has surrounded sporadic attempts to develop various forms of implants that would release steroids under the skin of the arm or buttocks over periods of one to three years. The active ingredients are similar or identical to those in injectable steroid formulations and the actual and potential side effects, notably irregular bleeding, are the same in both methods. The advantage of sustained-release implants is that they would be longer acting than injections (clinical studies in Brazil with subdermal implants of the steroid norgestrel have shown contraceptive efficacy up to six years), and should the woman wish to become fertile, she has greater flexibility than with an injection in that she could undergo minor surgery to have the implant removed prior to its natural depletion.

Work is currently under way with more sophisticated delivery systems, particularly with polymer networks that break down in the body as a contraceptive steroid is released. Even though the active steroid ingredients are the same as those currently used in oral contraceptives, two-year toxicological testing for carcinogenicity as well as seven-year studies in dogs and ten-year studies in monkeys still have to be carried out on the combination of the steroid and the new delivery system, because regulatory agencies are especially concerned about the potential carcinogenicity of long-acting agents. These concerns, together with the long-term clinical studies needed to provide the necessary epidemiological information, assure that an implantable contraceptive could not possibly be widely distributed until the late 1980s at the earliest.

Vaginal Rings. Still another steroid delivery system, which has been under investigation since the late 1960s, is the vaginal ring, a method concerned not with extraordinarily long steroid delivery but rather with overcoming daily Pill taking. The woman inserts into her vagina a steroid-containing plastic ring that has a contraceptive efficacy ranging from one week to three months. The steroid is absorbed through the vaginal wall and may conceivably produce fewer systemic side effects than does the Pill since a smaller amount of the steroid would enter the general circulation. Still, I doubt whether the vaginal ring will represent a significant improvement in female contraception even if current developmental work leads to FDA approval, though it does have an advantage over other long-acting steroid contraceptives in that the product's effectiveness can be terminated at will by simply removing the ring.

Assuming that sustained-release contraceptives will eventually be widely used, especially in developing countries, then the effect upon lactation and the possible passage of biologically active steroids through the mother's milk to the baby must be monitored. Preliminary work with the injectable steroid Depo-Provera, using radioactive material, showed the presence of small amounts of steroid in the mother's milk for a period of three months after the injection.

Olfactory Delivery. Of the various orifices in the human that have been used for drug delivery, the nose has hitherto not been considered for contraception. During the past few years a group in India working under WHO auspices has investigated intranasal administration of steroids as a possible means of reducing the steroid dosage below levels currently used in oral contraceptives. Such dosage reduction would be feasible if the steroid passes directly into the brain instead of into the general blood circulation. Preliminary experiments in rhesus monkeys looked promising but initial human phase I clinical studies were ambiguous at best in that with the doses employed (which were considerably lower than those used in the Pill) only a few women displayed symptoms of anovulation. A modest effort is still proceeding, but it seems unlikely that women will eventually be found to sniff discreetly from contraceptive nasal spray devices before hopping into bed.

All of the methods of hormonal fertility control discussed thus far have been preventive ones, in the sense that the steroid must be taken prior to intercourse. However, since hormones also affect the subsequent development of the fertilized egg, postcoital methods have also been investigated.

The Postcoital Pill

Chemical interference with embryonic development, particularly in advanced states of gestation, is undesirable. First, there may be moral objections by people who consider such interference equivalent to abortion. Second, if the method fails, the likelihood of producing a malformed offspring is high. Chemical interference shortly after fertilization but before implantation of the ovum in the uterine wall is a much more rational procedure from a scientific standpoint and would also be much less objectionable morally to many individuals.

Ergot alkaloids, vasoconstrictors as well as labor-inducing agents, have been known to be effective in preventing implantation of the ovum in rodents, but their toxicity eliminates their utilization as clinically recommended contraceptives. We have known since the early 1960s that orally administered estrogens such as the steroid ethynylestradiol and the nonsteroid diethylstilbestrol (DES) inhibit implantation of the ovum in the uterine wall. In experiments with rhesus monkeys inhibition of implantation of the ovum was found to occur if an estrogen was administered within a few days after coitus, but pregnancy continued unaffected once implantation of the fertilized ovum had taken place. This effect of estrogens has also been demonstrated in humans, but is markedly different in rodents and rabbits, where pregnancy is interrupted *even after implantation* (albeit with much higher doses of estrogens)—an observation that again illustrates how important it is to select suitable animal models for eventual extrapolation to humans and how misleading information from lower animals at times can be. Based on these monkey experiments, Dr. John M. Morris and Dr. Gertrude Van Wagenen in the mid 1960s carried out a series of studies at Yale University that showed 100 percent success in inhibiting implantation when relatively high dosages of either diethylstilbestrol or ethynylestradiol were administered orally for several days following coitus. This method was used on a limited scale in many university clinics and health services and was eventually approved by the FDA for use in certain instances, such as rape, incest, or where unprotected coitus had occurred and continued pregnancy would be undesirable.

Colloquially this treatment was referred to as the "morning-after pill" and overenthusiastic press reports implied that this was another method that could solve the world's population problem.

However, this approach is hardly desirable for routine contraceptive use in sexually active couples since the so-called minor side effects of high doses of estrogens—including marked nausea and vomiting—are not pleasant. Second, the amount of estrogen consumed would vary greatly depending upon coital frequency, and in sexually active couples the woman could be exposed to potentially hazardous doses of estrogen.

Shortly after completion of the initial successful clinical studies, reports appeared of a rare adenocarcinoma of the vagina in young women who had been exposed *in utero* to DES when their mothers were prescribed this drug in the 1950s (in the mistaken belief that it would prevent miscarriage). Thus, an important reason for restricting the use of DES as a postcoital agent is that a woman may ingest it not knowing she is pregnant, and thus expose an unborn female child to the risks described above. Other estrogens such as ethynylestradiol, which are in their chemical structure totally distinct from DES, are also effective as postcoital agents, but their use under these circumstances may be equally undesirable since we know nothing about the effects of *in utero* exposure to such steroidal estrogens upon the incidence of cancer in the offspring. In view of the fact that highly accurate methods of pregnancy detection that respond within a few days of fertilization are now available, the question must be raised whether such a postcoital agent is really needed at all. (Women who show a positive pregnancy test can undergo menstrual extraction.)

Nevertheless, a postcoital agent may find use in certain cultural settings or societies where intercourse is infrequent, and research in this area is continuing. Progestational steroids have also been considered from time to time as postcoital drugs, though the scientific rationale behind this regimen is unclear. There is no intrinsic reason why a progestational steroid (i.e., an ovulation inhibitor), taken only for a short period of time *after* ovulation and fertilization had occurred, is likely to disrupt pregnancy. A modest amount of work is under way on other drugs that may affect the transport of the egg since transport timing is crucial to fertilization and accelerated or delayed transport is likely to interfere with implantation. Such work is now at a very preliminary stage. Even if a fundamentally new postcoital agent is developed in the future, its use before the late 1980s would be extraordinarily unlikely.

In principle, the Chinese "vacation pill" (see Chapter 10) is essentially a postcoital agent and is recommended in China for those couples who have repeated intercourse for short periods of time followed by long intervals of sexual abstinence. The active ingredient is a synthetic steroid whose mechanism of action is not yet clearly understood. If this steroid is effective because of its intrinsic estrogenicity, then it may operate by mechanisms similar to those of DES and ethynylestradiol. However, there is some indirect evidence that this may not be the case, and further work—notably in China—is likely to shed more light on this matter. In any event, given its specialized use, this postcoital variation is unlikely to be an earth-shaking new contraceptive development that will change fertility control among the masses.

Long-term Prospects in Female Fertility Control

Two methods merit discussion: immunological approaches and hormonal intervention operating at the hypothalamic level. Neither is likely to be introduced until the 1990s at the earliest. (In principle, immunological approaches might work just as well in the male as in the female but the problems and possibilities are more easily exemplified in the context of the female.)

Immunological Approaches

The idea of an antifertility vaccine is attractive to many people. Its potential advantages are simplicity of administration, use of paramedical personnel, and the public's generally positive response to vaccination (although it is not clear whether this attitude would also apply to interference with the reproductive process). A considerable amount of animal experimental work in this area has been carried out in recent years and we now have several leads.

The ideal vaccine would be an antigen that could be synthesized in pure form and that would produce antibodies specific for a particular biologically active substance involved in the reproductive process, rather than being so nonspecific as to interfere with other important hormonal or protein constituents of the body.

By far the greatest progress has been made with antigens derived from human chorionic gonadotrophin (HCG). This hormone is produced by placental cells in very early pregnancy and continues to be secreted until the infant is born. Though the functions of HCG are not well understood, one of them is to trigger the continued secretion of the female sex hormone progesterone, necessary for the maintenance of pregnancy. Thus, sensitization to HCG may be one immunological approach to contraception. One would of course also need to develop a method of terminating such immunization, and we do not yet know how this would be achieved.

One very serious problem encountered in immunological anti-fertility research is selecting and obtaining animal models that are as closely related to the human as possible—the chimpanzee and the gorilla in this instance being the best models. It is very difficult to carry out experiments with such higher primates (see Chapter 5), and experiments with baboons have so far not been especially satisfactory (only low antibody levels are produced in this primate). Another important problem is that HCG is chemically comprised of two large units, called α- and β-subunits. The α-subunit is chemically very similar to that of other polypeptide hormones such as the pituitary growth hormone, the thyroid-stimulating hormone, and the gonadotrophic hormones LH and FSH—all of which are continuously present in the body. Immunization with HCG based on this α-unit, therefore, can cause the production of antibodies that crossreact with all other hormones chemically related to the α-subunit of HCG and can lead to such serious endocrinological disturbances that one would not want to pursue this approach. Fortunately, the β-subunit of HCG is structurally different and work is now under way to synthesize portions of that unit and prepare vaccines based on it.

This is the stage at which much of the work in antifertility immunization currently rests, and although a great deal of basic research is taking place, we are only at the beginning of a long and tortuous path. The safety evaluation of such methods will be crucial and it is unlikely that extensive phase III clinical experiments (see Fig. 5-1) will be under way in the U.S. before the early 1990s (although a few preliminary clinical trials without adequate prior toxicology have been conducted in Brazil, Finland, and Sweden). The possibility of mass vaccination of large segments of the population, even if completely voluntary, is in my opinion left for the twenty-first century. Nevertheless, the immunological route is fundamentally different from all other current approaches to contraception and is clearly worth pursuing.

The degree of eventual acceptability of antifertility immunization will vary among different cultures. Let us consider only one aspect in our own litigious society. Recent attempts to institute swine flu vaccination in the United States could only be put in motion after the federal government agreed to underwrite liability insurance; no pharmaceutical company was willing to even touch the production of swine flu vaccine if the company had to be responsible for possible liability suits. This caution on the part of the frequently burned pharmaceutical industry was well founded. Approximately 3,000 persons sued the U.S. government for side effects (many of them because of the serious but rare Guillain-Barré syndrome) to the tune of over $3 billion. If swine flu vaccine side effects merit $1 million damage per person, what is a likely estimate of damage payments for side effects in immunological birth control?

Methods Based on Hypothalamic Releasing Hormones

The isolation and chemical structure determination of the hypothalamic releasing hormones (RH) by Schally and Guillemin in the early 1970s opened a new chapter in endocrinology and also potentially in human fertility control. As shown in Fig. 8-2, one releasing hormone (usually called LH-RH, but in the female more appropriately referred to as LH-RH/FSH-RH) apparently stimulates the secretion by the anterior pituitary gland of both gonadotrophic hormones, LH and FSH. The structure of LH-RH is relatively simple; it is a decapeptide (made up of ten amino acids) and is usually written in the chemist's shorthand notation (pyro)Glu-His-Trp-Ser-Try-Gly-Leu-Arg-Pro-Gly-NH$_2$. This is meaningless to the layman but its implications are crystal-clear to the chemist: knowing this structure, the chemist can then promptly synthesize dozens of analogs in which one or more of these amino acids is replaced by another amino acid. As a result, a whole series of RH antagonists (which inhibit the effects of RH) as well as agonists (which mimic the effects of RH) have now become available for biological scrutiny.

Initially it was thought that the immediate practical potential of such LH-RH analogs would lie in the treatment of infertility through the stimulation of ovulation in women experiencing difficulty in ovulating, but one could also envisage fertility control applications through carefully timed ovulation promoted by the administration of a releasing hormone—in other words, a chemically induced rhythm method. From an operational standpoint such a method would probably be only marginally acceptable unless the agent could be administered orally, since a woman is unlikely, for purposes of using a rhythm method of contraception, to want to subject herself over a period of many years to monthly injections. However, LH-RH, like all other peptides, is for all practical purposes orally inactive since the enzyme systems in the stomach destroy peptides very rapidly. One would have to ingest huge quantities to swamp the peptide-decomposing enzymes in the stomach in order to have some hormonal material left that would enter the general circulation, and LH-RH's very short duration of action is likely to make accurate timing somewhat dubious. Thus, this method is currently only of theoretical interest.

Still it is worth examining some of the potential applications of synthetic LH-RH analogs to human fertility control, although it is quite conceivable that the first practical applications may actually be found in veterinary medicine (e.g., in artificial insemination of cattle, since bringing all of the cows into estrus at the same time would be economically advantageous). The remarkable lack of species specificity in the chemical structure of these particular releasing hormones (for example, bovine and porcine releasing hormones are equally active in humans) suggests that one might find applications in different animal species with the same substance and thus would not have to repeat all of the toxicological work for each specific application.

Let us now turn to some of the most recent investigations. First, a series of LH-RH antagonists has been synthesized which, as might be expected, blocks rather than stimulates ovulation. In principle, these antagonists have the same action as progesterone and therefore their continuous administration would presumably disrupt the regular menstrual cycle of the female and lead to unpredictable bleeding or amenorrhea. Nevertheless, other side effects may be lower—for instance, steroids increase the metabolic burden on the liver, whereas a decapeptide hardly does so.

Second, LH-RH itself has a paradoxical antifertility effect: its principal biological function is the regulation of fertility, yet when administered to pregnant rats the hormone terminates pregnancy. Apparently both LH-RH and various synthetic mimics exert this antifertility action in rats through luteolysis—destruction of the corpus luteum—a property that has long been sought. However, it remains to be seen whether this luteolytic effect is also observed in humans; other agents, such as prostaglandins, have been found to be luteolytic in many animals, but not in humans.

Even if we are able to develop a biologically useful LH-RH analog, we must still solve the question of how to administer it. The most likely method—in order to overcome gastric decomposition— would be through some type of a sustained-release vehicle, such as an intramuscular injection or an implant. This would mean that a woman would be exposed on a continuous basis to a fixed concentration of RH, which is very different from the natural rhythmic situation. Because such analogs seem to be active percutaneously, another possibility is to apply the compound topically to the skin. But unless an intermittently applied topical regimen can be worked out, this method, too, would entail continuous exposure of the woman to a hormone-like agent that in nature is secreted intermittently.

In sum, work with hypothalamic releasing hormones is clearly an exciting field, but it is roughly at the same developmental stage as was steroid research in the early 1940s. A great deal of basic animal work has to be done before extensive clinical experiments can be undertaken. (A few preliminary clinical studies have been performed in Sweden and Germany with an analog synthesized by the Hoechst pharmaceutical firm in West Germany.) And long-term toxicological experiments would be absolutely indispensable in formulating a contraceptive regimen based on sustained-release administration of such potent hormones. Though by now this must sound like a broken record or a tired refrain, unfortunately we are again at the very early stages of the critical path of the development of a drug from laboratory to consumer.

Where Do We Go From Here?

Where does this leave us? The modern young woman living in an affluent society, who practices contraception but is dissatisfied with currently available methods, was surely not very pleased by my conclusion in the preceding chapter that she "will be past the menopause before she can depend on her male sexual partner to use his Pill." And reading the present chapter, she will have reached the conclusion that she will be past the menopause, or at the very least rapidly approaching it, before major changes in female contraception are likely to occur.

Does this come as a surprise? It does to many people, and I believe that it is primarily the result of unrealistically optimistic reports of breakthroughs on the horizon that are continuously fed to the American public. Take, for instance, the following exchange from the Nelson hearings in the U.S. Senate on February 25, 1970, between Dr. Alan Guttmacher, one of the pillars of the American birth control movement, and Senator Jacob Javits of New York:

> DR. GUTTMACHER: I think we are still in the horse and buggy days of effective contraception. I am optimistic in feeling that in five years, we shall have methods that are infinitely superior and safer than either [the Pill or the IUD].
>
> SENATOR JAVITS: I would like to tell you just by way of confirming your own view that Dr. Guy Iman, who has just

won the Nobel Prize for medicine, addressed the session of trustees of the Salk Biological Institute of La Jolla. I am a trustee and I heard it. His appraisal was precisely yours, that within five years, we should have as marked an advance in this science as we have had up to now. It is very interesting. I thought you might be interested.

DR. GUTTMACHER: I am happy to be confirmed by such a distinguished person.

SENATOR JAVITS: Is he not one of the most distinguished individuals in this field?

DR. GUTTMACHER: Yes, he is.

I am not citing this exchange because of the amusing error in the transcript in referring to the codiscoverer of the hypothalamic releasing hormones, Dr. Roger Guillemin, as Dr. Guy Iman, or because Senator Javits, with inadvertent prescience, awarded him the Nobel Prize seven years before he in fact received it. I am citing this testimony to point out that not five years but even nine years later no "methods that are infinitely superior and safer than either the Pill or the IUD" have appeared.

The prediction for new advances in fertility control "within five years" continues to haunt us. In 1974 a distinguished biomedical scientist, Dr. Sheldon G. Segal, currently director of the Rockefeller Foundation's Population Program, stated in an article and in subsequent congressional testimony that "based on current knowledge and without the need for additional fundamental studies to establish feasibility, the following 'new' or 'modified' contraceptives may be developed within the next three- to five-year period." He then listed 18 contraceptive procedures—"thirteen for use by women, five by men." But the question is, when he talks about new or modified contraceptives that "may be developed within the next three- to five-year period," what do the public or legislators or newspapers understand him to mean? To the public such a statement presumably means that people could use such an agent after three to five years have elapsed. To biomedical scientists making such predictions, the phrase really means only that the results are sufficiently promising that one could apply for further research grants to carry out more investigative work. There is nothing inherently wrong with this type of "grantsmanship," but the public must realize that after a laboratory development is made, the lengthy process to bring the drug to the consumer has just begun. Indeed, many of the hurdles have not even been identified, let alone overcome. Thus, it is no surprise that of the 18 "new" or "modified" methods outlined by Dr. Segal in 1974, none of the five male methods and only one of the 13 female procedures (medicated IUDs, which were already at a very advanced state of clinical development in 1974) has been introduced to the public for contraceptive practice by 1979. How many times will we have to rewind this magic five-year clock before women will actually have at their disposal a fundamentally new contraceptive agent? In the present climate, I fear at least three or four times. There is simply no way of expediting the process if risk avoidance and safety are the overriding objectives.

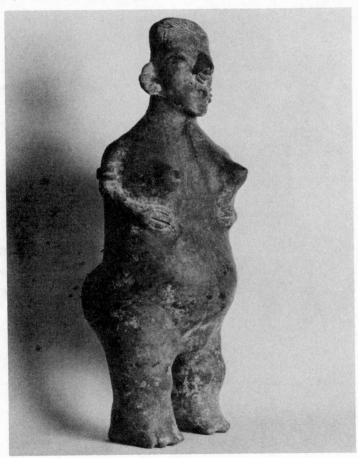

Pregnant woman. Nayarit, classic, *ca.* A.D. 100–400.

Conqueror and captive. Jalisco, classic, *ca.* A.D. 100–400.

9

Birth Control à la 1984

. . . coercion is generally accepted for two of the three factors
that affect population growth, but not the third—accepted, that
is, for mortality and migration but not fertility. . .
Bernard Berelson, *Studies in Family Planning,* 1974

As BERELSON NOTES ABOVE, most citizens do not question the state's
right to implement large vaccination programs or to establish public
health and sanitation services aimed at reducing disease and
mortality—in other words, to introduce compulsory measures
aimed at death control. Similarly, most citizens accept some restrictions on immigration into their country and certain populations even
tolerate, at least tacitly, restrictions on emigration. At the present
time, however, government-imposed birth control is not acceptable
in any nation in the world.

During the mid 1960s various laymen, legislators, and scientists
concerned with the economic and environmental effects of rapid
population growth began to speculate whether drastic government-
imposed birth control procedures might become necessary in some
countries if voluntary use of birth control methods failed to stem the
tide of world population growth. For instance, in 1968 Dr. M.M.
Ketchel of the Oakridge Population Research Institute predicted in

Medical World News that "in a relatively short time—five to 15 years—scientists will discover ways of controlling the fertility of an entire population." His article listed the characteristics that such a fertility control drug would need to possess: "First, it should lend itself to being easily and unobtrusively taken by the entire population. In large cities, such an agent might be added to the water supply, but other methods would be required in less-developed areas. The agent must be completely harmless and its effects easily reversible, lest the fertility of a population be reduced too much. It should also be inexpensive. Finally, it should not interfere with the family planning activities of individual couples or affect their sex lives in any way." Presumably, Dr. Ketchel was thinking of birth control methods that governments could implement nationwide without, however, making it compulsory for the individual to use the method (e.g., if a contraceptive agent were added to the water supply, an individual could drink bottled water).

Speculations by Some Prophets

In an article I wrote in *Science* in 1970 entitled "Birth Control After 1984," I called externally imposed extensions of voluntary fertility control methods "Orwellian," for they conjure up images of the totalitarian state depicted so vividly by George Orwell in *1984*—though in Orwell's novel no conventional birth control methods, voluntary or by government edict, are actually mentioned. In Orwell's nightmare vision of a future society, only the "ultimate solution" is employed—namely, chastity, which in his Newspeak language is called "goodsex." Orwell writes, "The sex instinct would be eradicated. Procreation will be an annual formality like the renewal of a ration card. We shall abolish the orgasm."

By contrast, Aldous Huxley pays considerable attention to birth control in *Brave New World*, the story of another government-controlled futuristic society. Written in 1932, Huxley's novel depicts a world that is basically hedonistic, quite different from the terror-ridden Orwellian universe. Birth control in *Brave New World* is practiced universally in a quasi-voluntary way by making sex very enjoyable and natural procreation and parenthood utterly unappetizing. Promiscuity is encouraged; hormone pregnancy substitutes for the women and sex hormone chewing gum for the men are universally available; "Malthusian belts" containing a variety of contraceptives are worn by all women. "From twelve to seventeen," he writes, "Malthusian [birth control practice] drills three times a week had made the taking of these precautions almost as automatic and inevitable as blinking."

In *Brave New World Revisited,* written in 1958, Huxley, horrified by the world population explosion, sheds the mantle of the novelist and writes directly:

> In the Brave New World of my fable, the problem of human numbers in their relation to natural resources had been effectively solved. An optimum figure for world population had been calculated and numbers were maintained at this figure (a little under two billions, if I remember rightly) generation after generation. In the real contemporary world, the population problem has not been solved. On the contrary it is becoming graver and more formidable with every passing year. It is against this grim biological background that all the political, economic, cultural and psychological dramas of our time are being played out. As the twentieth century wears on, as the new billions are added to the existing billions (there will be more than five and a half billions of us by the time my granddaughter is fifty), this biological background will advance, ever more insistently, ever more menacingly, toward the front and center of the historical stage. The problem of rapidly increasing numbers in relation to natural resources, to social stability and to the well-being of individuals—this is now the central problem of mankind; and it will remain the central problem certainly for another century, and perhaps for several centuries thereafter.

In the final chapter "What Can Be Done?" Huxley becomes the dazzling prophet:

> What is to be done? Obviously we must, with all possible speed, reduce the birth rate to the point where it does not exceed the death rate. At the same time we must, with all possible speed, increase food production, we must institute and implement a worldwide policy for conserving our soils and our forests, we must develop practical substitutes, preferably less dangerous and less rapidly exhaustible than uranium, for our present fuels; and, while husbanding our dwindling resources of easily available minerals, we must work out new and not too costly methods for extracting these minerals from ever poorer and poorer ores—the

poorest ore of all being sea water. But all this, needless to say, is almost infinitely easier said than done. The annual increase of numbers should be reduced. But how? We are given two choices—famine, pestilence and war on the one hand, birth control on the other. Most of us choose birth control—and immediately find ourselves confronted by a problem that is simultaneously a puzzle in physiology, pharmacology, sociology, psychology and even theology. "*The Pill*" [my italics] has not yet been invented. When and if it is invented, how can it be distributed to the many hundreds of millions of potential mothers (or, if it is a pill that works upon the male, potential fathers) who will have to take it if the birth rate of the species is to be reduced? And, given existing social customs and the forces of cultural and psychological inertia, how can those who ought to take the pill, but don't want to, be persuaded to change their minds? And what about the objections on the part of the Roman Catholic Church, to any form of birth control except the so-called Rhythm Method—a method, incidentally, which has proved, hitherto, to be almost completely ineffective in reducing the birth rate of those industrially backward societies where such a reduction is most urgently necessary? And these questions about the future, hypothetical Pill must be asked, with as little prospect of eliciting satisfactory answers, about the chemical and mechanical methods of birth control already available.

Huxley wrote these words two years before the first oral contraceptive was introduced into medical practice. Deliberately or inadvertently, he thus fathered the term "the Pill" in the currently accepted sense—a piece of esoterica that I was delighted to uncover on rereading Huxley's book recently, since I had always assumed that "the Pill" had simply slipped into our vernacular gradually and anonymously.

Huxley's question of how to persuade a populace to use a birth control pill was taken up by one of the most interesting scientists of this century, Leo Szilard. The first physicist to conceive of an atomic chain reaction, Szilard, together with Enrico Fermi, was issued the first patent in America in the field of atomic energy (U.S. Patent No. 2,708,656) and was one of the key persons to convince President Roosevelt to sponsor the Manhattan project, which produced the first atomic bomb. After World War II, Szilard became one of the most vocal and persuasive opponents of atomic weaponery and switched to the field of biology. He founded the Council for a Livable World, a lobbying group that gave financial support to the election campaigns of senators who were sympathetic to the concept of nuclear disarmament, and was one of the founders of the Pugwash Conferences on Science and World Affairs, which in the late 1950s and early 1960s were one of the most important avenues of informal East-West exchange between scientists concerned with disarmament.

As part of his conversion from physicist to biologist, Szilard, along with William Doering, wrote an important letter in 1957, proposing the establishment of two interdependent research institutes (Research Institute for Fundamental Biology and Public Health and Institute for Problem Studies) dedicated to public health problems. Birth control was at the top of his priority list for these institutes, as was the importance of enlisting for them innovative thinkers rather than officially recognized professionals from traditional fields. To quote briefly from this amazing letter:

> Clearly it would be highly desirable to develop some biological method of birth control, adequate for the needs of the underdeveloped areas of the world. . . . It is by no means certain that any of the present developments, aimed at finding a really satisfactory method for birth control, are moving in the right direction. Too few of the men active in this field have the kind of imagination and productivity that one finds among those attracted by fundamental biological problems of intrinsic interest. Too many are inclined to look upon the solution of the problem as a lifetime job. . . . It is conceivable that . . . gynecologists will come up with a really satisfactory method of contraception, but it is more likely that an invasion of "outsiders" may provide the right answers. . . . The attraction of the problem of mammalian reproduction to younger scientists is mainly due to the recognition of its overwhelming importance for population control in the underdeveloped areas of the world. A good solution would be a drug that might be administered once a month to women in the form of a pill. Even better, perhaps, would be a drug that could be mixed in with certain staple foods, such as for instance rice, and made accessible to large families who live in poverty. Such an "infertility brand" of staple food might perhaps be sold—with a government subsidy—at a price below that of the "commercial brand" of the staple. This type of drug administration would demand the use of a

drug that is without any detrimental physiological effect for both women and men.

Szilard also wrote short stories, several of which incorporated some of his scientific prophecies. Thus, in his wise and clever story "The Voice of the Dolphins" (contained in his book of the same name, written in 1961), he envisages that the Cold War ends when the Russians and Americans set up a joint research project that has no bearing on national defense or other security issues. The two governments decide upon Vienna as the site of the project (an amazing prediction considering that this is precisely where, ten years later, the Soviet Academy and the U.S. National Academy of Sciences established the International Institute of Applied Systems Analysis) and on molecular biology as the field of research. The Institute concentrates on learning the language of the dolphins and establishing communication with them in order to take advantage of their extraordinary intelligence. The next five Nobel Prizes for physiology and medicine are awarded to the joint Russian-American Institute for advances made by the dolphins. The dolphins' crowning discovery is a contraceptive food:

> In the fifth year of its operation, the Institute isolated a mutant form of a strain of commonly occurring algae, which excreted a broad-spectrum antibiotic and was able to fix nitrogen. Because of these two characteristics, these algae could be grown in the open, in improvised ditches filled with water, and they did not require the addition of any nitrates as fertilizer. The protein extracted from them had excellent nutritive qualities and a very pleasant taste.
>
> The algae, the process of growing them and the process of extracting their protein content, as well as the protein product itself, were patented by the Institute, and when the product was marketed—under the trade name Amruss— the Institute collected royalties.
>
> If taken as a protein substitute in adequate quantities, Amruss markedly depresses the fertility of women, but it has no effect on the fertility of men. Amruss seemed to be the only answer to the prayer of countries like India. India had a severe immediate problem of food shortage; and she had an equally severe long-term problem, because her population had been increasing at the rate of five million a year.
>
> Amruss sold at about one tenth of the price of soybean

protein, and in the first few years of its production the demand greatly exceeded the supply. It also raised a major problem for the Catholic Church. At first Rome took no official position on the consumption of Amruss by Catholics, but left it to each individual bishop to issue such ruling for his diocese as he deemed advisable. In Puerto Rico the Catholic Church simply chose to close an eye. In a number of South American countries, however, the bishops took the position that partaking of Amruss was a mortal sin, no different from other forms of contraception. . . .

When the decline in the numbers of those who went to confession became conspicuous, it came to the attention of the Pope. As is generally known, in the end the issue was settled by the papal bull "Food Being Essential for Maintaining Life," which stressed that Catholics ought not to be expected to starve when food was available. Thereafter, bishops uniformly took the position that Amruss was primarily a food, rather than a contraceptive.

Insurmountable Difficulties?

From a technical standpoint, developing a practical contraceptive agent that a government could impose forcibly on an entire population is not really very different from developing an agent of the type described by Szilard or Huxley for use in a voluntary or quasi-voluntary setting. These agents only become Orwellian if consumption becomes compulsory.

First, then, let us consider the practical requirements for a population-wide contraceptive agent, or sterilant, that could be added to water or staple foods, after which we will then examine some of the hardware and software problems associated with its development and use.

Although a sterilant need only exert its antifertility action in one sex, it must not have any deleterious effect on the opposite sex or on people not of reproductive age (i.e., infants, children, or the elderly). The compound must be active in a contraceptive sense at a rather low concentration (since some people may ingest very little of the water or food in which the agent is present) and must be harmless over an enormous dose range (consider the tremendous variations in body weight and food intake between infants and adults). The substance ideally should be tasteless and should be specific for humans so that we do not indiscriminately practice birth control on other species that may be exposed to the active ingredient. And in order to prevent *all* births from ceasing, the effects of the sterilant should be reversible through the administration, presumably by government authorization, of a counteracting agent.

Given these requirements, we can now consider some of the monumental technical problems that would have to be surmounted:

1. In order to insure universal use in a compulsory setting, the substance, if added to food, would have to be incorporated by the supplier rather than by the consumer. Even then, unless it were included in a foodstuff that is universally required (e.g., salt), a dissenter could simply eliminate it from his or her diet and thus escape its contraceptive effects. In any event, the contraceptive additive would have to be stable during processing (baking, heating, sterilization) and during exposure to oxidants or light in the course of packaging and shipping.

2. Since everyone must drink water, water might seem to be an ideal vehicle for a contraceptive agent, but even here enormous difficulties would be encountered. Incorporation of a sterilant would be feasible only if water was supplied through a central system and was not obtained directly from wells. This limitation alone would make such a method unworkable for at least half of the world's population. Moreover, regardless of the method of incorporation into the water, the contraceptive agent would have to display chemical stability under the following conditions: on coming in contact with pipes and other metal objects, on exposure to light and oxidants in a holding tank or reservoir, on exposure to extreme temperatures during cooking or refrigeration (i.e., lack of precipitation from solution), and on exposure during cooking to minerals in water or to commonly consumed foodstuffs. It would also have to possess no properties that would cause problems of over- or underconcentration during food processing (as in the preparation of frozen juice or soup concentrates). I cannot even attempt to put a time estimate on a possible solution to these problems; to me these technical obstacles seem virtually insurmountable.

3. Problems associated with side effects of such an agent—both actual and potential, especially the latter—would be horrendous. No drug is devoid of side effects and, in this instance, the side effects of the sterilant would have to be minimal not only in the sex and age group in which it was supposed to be active but also in all other age groups and in the opposite sex. I will cite just one example illustrating the virtual impossibility of answering all the questions that would be raised: Since humans would be exposed to such an agent within a few months after birth and continuously thereafter, clinical test-

ing would have to involve toxicological studies with infants and would have to continue for at least two decades, through adolescence to adulthood. Who would be willing to carry out such studies? This problem, too, is I believe virtually insurmountable.

4. In contrast to any contraceptive drug now used by humans, which most often is simply a contaminant of an individual's microecology, a contraceptive agent added to a foodstuff or to water would be a general environmental pollutant. It would have to be considered a pesticide, albeit one that is directed primarily at humans. It is exceedingly unlikely that such a compound active in humans would not be effective in at least some other animal species. In fact, since initial biological screening for such an agent would be carried out not in humans but in animals, an agent truly specific for man would completely escape detection!

5. The likelihood of discovering an agent that would reverse the effects of a universally administered sterilant is slight, yet the availability of such a counteragent would of course be an absolute necessity. The only other alternative would be to develop a contraceptive that significantly reduced but did not abolish fertility, the level of escape thus setting the birth rate. Such an alternative might make such an agent acceptable from a demographic standpoint, but hardly from a personal one.

In light of these special problems, which would have to be superimposed on the already formidable difficulties associated with the development of any systemic chemical birth control agent, it is clear that the development of a birth control agent that could be administered to an entire population is, even from a strictly technical standpoint, totally outside the realm of possibility for many decades.

Not everyone agrees with me; as an example I cite these comments from an extraordinarily innovative thinker, John R. Platt, professor of biophysics at the Mental Health Research Institute of the University of Michigan. Upon hearing me deliver a lecture in which I outlined the ideas I have just discussed, he responded:

> I am not interested in imposing a dictatorial method on the world; I am very concerned about side effects and the long-range effects of the large-scale application of compounds to populations. But I am also concerned about our inability to do very much about the population explosion by using our present methods. We have blinded ourselves to the possible degree of public acceptance and to the enormous increase in effectiveness that would result if we could

find oral contraceptives that could be put in salt or other foodstuffs and that could be used voluntarily.

Let me therefore say some favorable things about putting contraceptives in salt. . . . I agree that this method might not work because of lack of effectiveness or uncontrollable side effects, or because the public or their representatives would not accept contraceptives in food—even on a voluntary basis. But since more methods are needed for population control, important additional possibilities should at least be explored in the laboratory.

I agree with Djerassi and others that no contraceptives for large populations should be put into water. It would be both a waste and a danger because water goes to industries and is drunk by animals. The foods that contraceptives could be put into should be so delicious or so expensive that they are not normally thrown out to the chickens or the barnyard animals. They should be factory produced or commercially marketed, even in primitive societies, which limits them to food such as salt, sugar, beer, special breads, polished rice, betel nuts, and perhaps a few others.

Among these, salt is a necessity in every population and, in general, is not manufactured in the home or on the farm but in factories serving large areas. We know how dependent on it populations are—Gandhi's famous march to the sea to break the British salt monopoly and get free of the British factories that were manufacturing it is a good illustration. If there were an effective and safe contraceptive that could be put into salt, it could be put in at a small number of factories, possibly one or two hundred, all over India, for example. It could be monitored by a small number of biochemical technicians, perhaps with master's degrees, just as chlorine and fluoride in our water, Vitamin D in our milk, iodine in our salt, or other "public-health" compounds are monitored in the United States.

This means that such a method would be exceedingly cheap compared with any of our present contraceptive methods, which involve individual application, prescription, or medical examination. If individual examinations or medical applications were needed for birth control in a country the size of India, with over 100 million women of child-bearing age, about 100,000 paramedical personnel would have to be trained and kept in the field. To do that, several hundred training centers would have to be set up, staffed by hundreds or thousands of doctors—who must themselves be trained in advance.

Each step in this process—training the doctors, preparing the centers, training the paramedical personnel, and so on—could take five, seven, or even ten years in order to get the present type of contraceptives out into all the villages. The result is that to the ten or fifteen years needed, as in Djerassi's research and testing program, there must be added twenty or thirty years to organize sufficiently to reach the population, which is increasing all that time. But a method such as an additive to salt, which would require only factory application and about one hundred biochemists, could be a thousand times cheaper and in use ten to twenty years earlier—hundreds of millions of babies earlier.

Platt can afford to make these almost flippant recommendations because he has never had to go through the bracing experience of trying to develop a drug for millions of people and have it pass the scrutiny of regulatory agencies. My response to his extraordinarily optimistic projection is really contained in his own sentence, "*if* [my italics] there were an effective and safe contraceptive that could be put into salt. . . ." It is the little word "if" that pushes any possibility of such an approach well into the twenty-first century.

Alternative Methods of Involuntary Birth Control

In an important article entitled "Beyond Family Planning," Bernard Berelson in 1969 summarized some of the other involuntary fertility control methods that have been proposed seriously from time to time in the scientific literature or in the popular press. Three of these methods merit comment.

One is compulsory sterilization of men with three or more living children. This recommendation is feasible from a hardware standpoint since vasectomies can be performed rapidly on large numbers of men—as has been demonstrated by vasectomy "fairs" in India in which thousands of men were voluntarily sterilized in assembly-line fashion after having been brought together through extensive promotional efforts coupled with modest financial incentives. But as Berelson wisely notes, "In the last analysis, what will be scientifically available, politically acceptable, administratively feasible, economically justifiable, and morally tolerated depends upon people's perception of consequences."

In the mid 1970s the Indian government under Indira Gandhi was about to implement a program of compulsory sterilization that would have involved the loss of seniority or even job jeopardy for civil servants who had more than three children and were unwilling to subject themselves to sterilization. When Mrs. Gandhi was then defeated at the polls by a huge margin, many observers regarded this program to be a contributing factor to her downfall. Here was an instance where a sterilization procedure (vasectomy) was scientifically available, it was almost certainly economically justified, and the Indian government might have made it administratively feasible. It is clear, however, that the majority of citizens considered it neither politically acceptable nor morally tolerable.

A second recommendation, which has been made by Professor William B. Shockley of Stanford, a Nobelist in physics, concerns the possible temporary sterilization, by means of time-capsule contraceptives, of all young women and of any woman after each delivery. Reversibility would be allowed only upon government approval. In addition to the enormous software problems in political, administrative, and moral areas, even the scientific hardware problems of such a method have not been solved. Neither currently available injectable contraceptives nor long-term release capsules under investigation would lend themselves to government-imposed programs, because their side effects—menstrual irregularities—would not be tolerated by many women. Even if a government would consider as draconic a step as compulsory birth control, it is unlikely that it would select a method with unacceptable side effects.

This leaves a third method, which seems more realizable because it bears a close similarity to public health vaccination projects, to which large populations have become accustomed. I am referring to immunological approaches that would make the male or female sterile until the immunization wore off or until a suitable counteragent was administered. Yet it is extremely unlikely that an immunological method could be introduced even under highly restricted and carefully controlled circumstances before the 1990s at the earliest (see Chapter 8), and it would probably require at least another decade of restricted public use before consideration could be given to a massive fertility control program based on immunization.

Of all the potential government-imposed and -implemented approaches to birth control that have been suggested, I believe that for the balance of this century compulsory sterilization is the only method likely o be technically feasible. But even here the larger software questions remain unanswered. Could any massive sterilization program actually be implemented by a government anywhere in the world—and, more important, should it be? Any method of compulsory birth control would encounter enormous moral, social, and political objections, and there would be tremendous public outcries against any such attempts. As Berelson expressed so eloquently in the conclusion of his 1974 evaluation of the effects of worldwide population control programs: "What we seek is human welfare, personal freedom, the quality of life, and demographic trends and changes take on meaning only insofar as they contribute to such ends. Any evaluation should keep that closely in mind—what we are really after. Some costs, in short, are too high, for population control is not the final value."

Operation. Nayarit, classic, *ca.* A.D. 100–400.

Chinesco woman. Nayarit, classic, *ca.* A.D. 100–400.

10

Birth Control in China: The Contraceptive Supermarket

By 1979 SINOPHILIA HAD BECOME a fashionable "disease," at least politically speaking. I myself caught an acute case of it in 1973 while spending a month in eastern China as a guest of the Chinese Academy of Sciences lecturing on future prospects in human fertility control. At that time the People's Republic of China had been opened to Americans for only about a year and a half, and relatively few Americans had received permission to enter the country. During my visit, because of the openness of many Chinese scientists and other professionals with whom I talked and the readiness with which my rather persistent questions were answered and contraceptive samples offered, I was able to learn a great deal about the state of birth control—most of which had been hitherto unknown in the West. Even more important was the fact that my requests to meet certain individuals and to visit given laboratories and pharmaceutical factories were granted without difficulty.

Within a few days after my arrival in China, I became intrigued with putting together the enormous puzzle of the current status of Chinese birth control from little pieces of evidence gathered here and there. It is for this reason that I go into considerable detail in this chapter to give the curious reader a window into how it was possible to gather and assemble evidence upon which I could make some fairly far-reaching conclusions about Chinese birth control practices—including the number of people practicing contraception in the world's most populous country. Regardless of whether or not one has Sinophilia, one cannot help but be impressed by Chinese achievements in fertility control during the past decade— achievements from which the rest of the world is bound to benefit at least indirectly.

In early 1974, Bernard Berelson, then president of the Population Council, wrote in *Studies in Family Planning:*

> How, in theory, can India cut its birth rate in half?—get a major proportion of the labor force into industry and thus sharply raise the standard of living and promote urbanization, give every Indian including the girls at least 6-8 years of schooling, forbid child labor, cut infant mortality to below 25[per 1000], raise the female age at marriage to 25 or so, establish the nuclear family with separate residence, get 35-40 percent of the women of reproductive age into the labor force, set up a functioning system of social security. . . . The point is less that such measures are uncertain of success, than that they cannot be achieved: the policies are reasonably clear, their early implementation is impossible.

Without realizing it, Berelson had described precisely the software components of a remarkable fertility control program instigated in China during the last ten years of Mao Tse-tung's life. In addition to instituting every one of the social changes outlined by Berelson, China also introduced what could be called a "supermarket" approach to contraceptives by making available to the Chinese consumer almost every type of modern contraceptive hardware.

This is all the more remarkable if one considers the absolutely deplorable state of China's health services and the country's enormous health problems just 25 to 30 years ago. At that time some reputable Chinese politicians and newspapers were even willing to recommend seriously the swallowing of live tadpoles as a method of human birth control: "Fresh tadpoles coming out in the spring should be washed clean in cold boiled water, and swallowed whole three or four days after menstruation. If a woman swallows fourteen live tadpoles on the first day and ten more on the following day, she will not conceive for five years. If contraception is still required after that, she can repeat the formula twice, and be forever sterile."

In 1957, 65 women volunteers between the ages of 25 and 40, all of whom were mothers of at least three children, participated in a program organized by the Research Institute in Chekiang to test the effectiveness of this folk remedy. Each woman swallowed 24 and 20 live tadpoles respectively on two successive days after the first day of the menses. Forty-three percent of the women became pregnant within a few months. The following year tadpoles were officially declared to have no contraceptive value. Yet even in 1964, reviewing the progress of steroid oral contraceptives and other modern Western research results of the late 1950s and early 1960s, Cheng Pui-Yuen, a member of the Nanking Pharmaceutical Research Institute, in an otherwise sophisticated article wrote, "Tadpoles have been used clinically. They are also proven to be rather effective. . . . Scientific investigation of their active moiety and purification and characterization of their chemical components may well be fruitful."

Many other indigenous contraceptive folk remedies were circulated during the 1956-57 period. At least one herbal recipe, endorsed by the Hospital of Traditional Chinese Medicine in Peking, is worth notice: "Place 7 [persimmon] stalks on an earth tile. Bake dry on fire, but no metal utensils should be used to touch them. Do not burn stalks. Pulverize. Swallow one whole preparation with yellow wine (millet wine) after the menses. Do not drink yellow wine excessively. (Antidote: persimmons.)" A contraceptive potency of one year was claimed for the persimmon recipe, and it was probably less dangerous to ingest than tadpoles, which might well lead to tapeworm and other parasitic infections.

It is easy to laugh at such recipes, but to dismiss Chinese folk medicine totally would be a mistake. China has combined the use of traditional Chinese and modern Western medicine with results that have paid off in other areas. Dr. E. Grey Dimond of the University of Missouri, the first American physician to enter China in this decade, wrote in the December 1971 issue of the *Journal of the American Medical Association*:

> The entire system of medical care and medical teaching has been changed and no longer can we use our Western terms and concepts to define what is the current, vigorously enforced health program in China. Among these major changes was the requirement that *Western* or modern medicine as we know it must be fully integrated with *traditional* Chinese medicine. Traditional Chinese medicine implies the full range of diagnosis and therapeutics based upon classic teachings of several thousand years including pulse feeling, tongue observation, meticulous interrogation, a vast therapeutic variety of remedies of herb, mineral,

and animal origin, moxa [burning herb on skin], and acupuncture. . . . It is important to understand that this is not simply a polite accommodation but a political requirement, and traditional medicine is now a formal component of the curriculum with faculty and departmental representation.

In light of these considerations it is even more astounding that only 15 years after the public promotion of swallowing live tadpoles for contraception, there were more women taking the Pill in China than in any other country in the world and that all Chinese oral contraceptives were indigenously manufactured rather than imported, a fact that contradicts statements made by those who believe that it is only multinational pharmaceutical companies that are "pushing the Pill."

The introduction and implementation in the People's Republic of China of the social and cultural changes outlined in a hypothetical manner for India by Berelson are now well known. But in the early 1970s, the West knew little about Chinese contraceptive practice, family planning, or population growth. Our lack of knowledge stemmed from two sources. First, after 1966, as a consequence of the Cultural Revolution, Chinese scientists published very little on these or any other technical subjects. Although in the West it is often assumed that not publishing means that no work is being done and furthermore that those who are not publishing are not reading, neither of these assumptions is true in the case of China, at least not in the field of contraceptive technology and medicine.

Second, the Chinese have been remarkably reluctant to publicize their accomplishments in human fertility control, which is less likely attributable to modesty than to a philosophical dilemma. A policy of restricting population growth is not part of Marxist doctrine, and other communist governments are decidedly pronatalist. In fact, the People's Republic of China appears to be the only communist country in the world that preaches the practice of fertility control. The following editorial, from the *Szechuan Daily* (December 22, 1974), was obviously prepared for internal consumption only: "Birth control is a policy decided on by our State. . . . This demands that the growth of the population is compatible with the planned development of the national economy. It will not do for there to be complete anarchy in mankind's reproduction. To advocate late marriage and put into effect birth control are of great significance for socialist revolution and construction, the total emancipation of women, the improvement of the people's living standards, the cultivation and education of the next generation and the improvement of the people's health and the prosperity of the nation."

This is not an isolated statement. As a more recent example, consider the following excerpt from an editorial which appeared on January 27, 1979, in the *People's Daily* of Peking: "The great goals of our country's modernization and economic construction require that the natural population growth rate be controlled at a proper level. It should be lowered to below 1 percent by 1980, and on that basis be further lowered step by step so that our population will grow slowly in a planned manner. This is what we must and can do. By 1978, 11 provinces and municipalities had, ahead of schedule, lowered the natural population growth rate to below 1 percent. This was proof of what could be done."

The Chinese deny that their family planning program is motivated by Malthusian concerns; rather they promote their policy in terms of its benefits to social planning and child welfare, and they emphasize that the ideal family has two children. The adaptation of Marxist doctrine to accommodate Chinese needs for population control is typified by the following remarks, made by a spokesman of the Chinese delegation at an International Conference on Population Planning held in 1973 in Pakistan: "Some Malthusians have prated that China has too many people, the problem of feeding them cannot be solved, that too many people obstruct the progress of society and so on. The revealing facts have thoroughly refuted such nonsense. We hold that, of all things in the world, human beings are the most precious. . . . Our country is a country of socialist system. . . . This requires planned population growth in order to have the population increase well adapted to the planned development of national economy and socialist construction."

The family planning gospel is not only actively preached but also firmly implemented through a variety of incentives that shed light on what Chinese citizens value most: housing, medical care, employment, no family separation. Thus a January 9, 1979, internal broadcast in Kwangtung Province mentions the following features of newly instituted planned parenthood regulations:

> Nursery charges and education fees from primary to senior middle school will be waived for those couples who have produced only one child and who have taken effective steps to insure that they will not have another. In addition, medical treatment for their child will be paid out of public funds up to the age of 18. . . . In assigning urban housing, preference will be given to couples who have produced two

children and to people who marry late. Couples who have only produced one child may be treated as having produced two, for accommodation purposes. In cases of couples who have only produced one child or two daughters, the labor departments should give preference to assigning employment to one of their children so long as they are suitable for labor and employment. . . . Children of urban residents, cadres and workers who have only two need not be sent down to the rural areas. Such children who have already been sent down to the rural areas will be granted preference in being sent back to the towns and reassigned work. . . . The only child of a peasant family should receive an adult's grain ration. . . . The new policy regulations also include measures for sanctions against those who exceed the planned parenthood plans. For instance, they will not be granted subsidies if they are in difficulties.

An English broadcast from Peking on January 21, 1979, included the following statement: "There must be rewards as well as punishments to be determined by the quality of the medical and public health personnel's birth control techniques. Rewards must be given to those who have had no mishap after handling 10,000 cases, while it is necessary to criticize and educate those who are irresponsible. . . . It is essential to do a good job in producing and supplying birth control drugs and devices, strengthen the leadership over scientific research work and actively study how to manufacture highly effective, safe, convenient and economic birth control drugs and devices."

Such broadcasts were essentially unheard of until the early 1970s. Indeed, from the middle 1960s until a few years ago, nearly all Western literature on Chinese contraceptive and family planning practices and estimates of population growth came from professional "China watchers" (almost exclusively social scientists) or from occasional firsthand reports of travelers. With very few exceptions, until that time neither group included experts in contraception and family planning, and hardly anyone seemed to have even inquired about the availability of contraceptive hardware, especially of the sophisticated type such as steroid oral contraceptives. Thus in 1973, I was eager to take advantage of the opportunity to visit China because through the determination of the availability of contraceptive hardware I felt one could gain a real insight into Chinese chemical and clinical competence. Even more importantly, if production figures of such contraceptives could be ascertained, this would be the first hard numerical evidence about the extent of contraceptive practice in the People's Republic.

Availability of Contraceptives and Contraceptive Information

On visiting pharmacies in urban centers such as Canton, Shanghai, Soochow, and Hangchow, I found that condoms, diaphragms, contraceptive foam tablets, and contraceptive suppositories were available at a modest cost (approximately 4¢ for 12 foam tablets and 1¢ for 2 condoms). Oral contraceptives were free (in fact they could not be purchased, presumably because the authorities wished to control their distribution and monitor their use) and were available in every commune, "residential lane," and factory dispensary I visited. A woman using oral contraceptives had her 22-pill supply (usually in paper envelopes or small bottles) replenished on a monthly basis by a "responsible person" or by medical or paramedical personnel (e.g., "a barefoot doctor").

Promotion of family planning was evident everywhere I went. There is extensive—and in the cities apparently successful—encouragement for postponing marriage: it is strongly recommended that the combined ages of bride and groom be at least 50 years. Premarital intercourse is socially unacceptable and hence supposedly very rare. To an American visitor, a society that eschews sex up to the mid twenties—even under conditions of hard work, social pressure, and total political commitment—seems a remarkable phenomenon.

However, in contrast to the pervasive promotion of family planning, dissemination of information on the use of contraceptives is restricted. At every level that I inquired (seminars with physicians and chemists; discussions with interpreters, scientists, students, and professors at Peking University; meetings with a high municipal official in Canton; talks with barefoot doctors) I was given the same reply, namely, that the use of contraceptive methods is not taught in middle schools or universities and that the information is available only for married couples. According to an interpreter in Peking who had recently married, such information is given at the time of marriage at the civil registry and in general is "picked up" from friends and peers. Married couples also attend intensive periodic meetings at various local levels where information concerning contraceptive methods is disseminated. Because of the apparent absence of premarital sex, the present system seems to work.

Condoms, diaphragms, and IUDs (including the delightfully named "Flower of Canton" shown in Fig. 10-1, page 190) are pro-

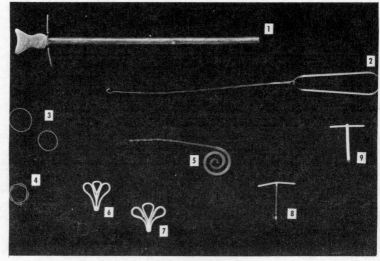

FIGURE 10-1

Intrauterine devices (IUDs) and accessories currently used or under investigation in China. Except for No. 9 (supplied by ALZA Corporation, Palo Alto, California), all are manufactured in China. They are (1) device for inserting IUDs, (2) hook for removing "Flower of Canton" (see No. 7), (3) typical stainless steel coils, (4) typical double stainless steel coil, (5) plastic spiral (Margulies type), (6) "Flower of Canton" IUD (old model), (7) "Flower of Canton" IUD (new model), (8) copper "T" (copper wire wound around plastic T-shaped IUD), (9) ALZA intrauterine progesterone system.

duced in many parts of the world, and their manufacture does not require any special expertise. The complete manufacture of steroid contraceptives, however, requires a totally different level of technical competence, and for this reason later in the chapter I shall describe in some detail the nature and manufacturing practices of oral contraceptives in China.

First, however, I would like to call attention to the meticulous Chinese labeling procedures, which permit even people like myself who do not read Chinese to obtain crucial information. In China all important Western medicines, including steroid contraceptives, carry a Latin name that is usually understandable to the drug expert and Arabic numerals for the quantitative composition of the active ingredients. In addition, labels carry in Chinese the name of the pharmaceutical factory (e.g., Shanghai Pharmaceutical Factory No. 7) and a numerical code that lists the date of manufacture (e.g., 730612 = 12 June 1973). By comparing the location of the factory with the location of pharmacies where I saw such containers I could get a good indication of both the decentralized nature of pharmaceutical manufacture and the range of distribution. The numerical code reveals the rate of use and turnover of a given drug. Thus in a rural commune dispensary I noted containers of male sex hormones such as testosterone propionate with manufacturing dates of the mid 1960s next to an amazing variety of antibiotics all of which were dated after 1970. From this observation one can conclude that in that commune male sex hormone therapy is not practiced very widely in contrast to antibiotic consumption.

Oral Contraceptives

A translation of the Chinese package insert for oral contraceptives follows which describes all three steroid pills used for contraception. It was included with a 1,000-pill bottle and therefore was almost certainly addressed to medical and paramedical personnel since no woman would be given the equivalent of a four-year supply. The Chinese generic name for their most widely used oral contraceptive is *norlutin*. Having participated personally in the chemical discovery of the first oral contraceptive, I was pleasantly amused at this Chinese selection for the generic name, because Norlutin was the trade name first selected by Syntex Corporation in the 1950s for the oral contraceptive norethindrone or norethisterone (see Author's Postscript). The Chinese trade name is of unsurpassed simplicity: Pill No. 1. I leave it up to the individual reader to decide whether the Chinese information is better, worse, or equal in content to what we provide to individual women (pages 101-3) or to medical personnel (page 41).

Instructions for Oral Contraceptive Pills

These tablets have been coated with sugar.

Oral contraceptive pills have been prepared by the working class and scientific technicians under the thought of Chairman Mao. After several years of clinical experiments, they have been proven to be almost 100% effective with no harm to the human body and will not cause damage to future fertility if usage and dosage are followed. The oral contraceptive is so far the best birth control method.

Name:

1. Oral contraceptive pill No. 1 (¼ or ½ dose) (norethindrone).
2. Oral contraceptive pill No. 2 (¼ or ½ dose) (megestrol acetate).
3. Ethynylestradiol pill.

Ingredient:

1. Oral contraceptive pill No. 1 (¼ dose), each pill contains: norethindrone 0.625 mg. and ethynylestradiol 0.035 mg.

Oral contraceptive pill No. 1 (½ dose), each pill contains: norethindrone 1.25 mg. and ethynylestradiol 0.0375 mg.

2. Oral contraceptive pill No. 2 (¼ dose), each pill contains: megestrol acetate 1.0 mg. and ethynylestradiol 0.035 mg.

Oral contraceptive pill No. 2 (½ dose), each pill contains: megestrol acetate 2.0 mg. and ethynylestradiol 0.0375 mg.

3. Ethynylestradiol pill: each pill contains ethynylestradiol 0.005 mg.

Mode of Action: Oral contraceptive pills No. 1 and 2 can suppress periodic flow of eggs and prevent pregnancy (100% effective) if used appropriately. Ovulation resumes and will not cause damage to future fertility when a woman stops using the pill.

Ethynylestradiol pill is a supplementary oral contraceptive drug. It can balance the estrogen of the human body and prevent vaginal bleeding.

Usage and Dosage: Take one pill on the fifth day of menstrual cycle. After taking for 22 consecutive days, wait for the next cycle and start again. Take pills after meal or before bedtime. As long as you take the pill, pregnancy is prevented.

Side Effects: A few women experience some side effects from the pill in the first couple of days. Some of these side effects are similar to symptoms women experience in early pregnancy, such as nausea, dizziness, depression, and vaginal bleeding. Sometimes vomiting, tender breasts, decrease in milk supply, and skin rash may occur. The above side effects occur generally in the first month and may decrease gradually. Some of these side effects may not need treatment and will take care of themselves, otherwise consult your physician.

Important Notes:

1. In order to achieve successful birth control and minimize vaginal bleeding, you should continue taking oral contraceptive pills according to schedule. It is important to form a habit of taking the pill regularly. If you forget to take a pill, you should take it within 24 hours in addition to the regular one.

2. Scanty menstruation or a short period may occur after taking oral contraceptive pills. However, no treatment is necessary.

3. Some women may notice vaginal bleeding because of the imbalance of estrogen in the body. If you have vaginal bleeding, do the following:
    1. Take 1-2 ethynylestradiol pill(s) every day (until the end of the period); minor vaginal bleeding will cease.
    2. In case of minor vaginal bleeding during the last few days of your pill taking, you may not need any ethynylestradiol tablets in addition to the pills, but consider such bleeding as your new period. Take your regular pills on the fifth day of such bleeding.

3. You may stop taking any pills at the end of your period if vaginal bleeding is heavy and consider such bleeding as your period and start taking pills on the fifth day of such bleeding. You may take ethynylestradiol tablets if you notice any vaginal bleeding. In case of frequent vaginal bleeding, you may even start taking ethynylestradiol tablets during your next period.

4. Generally, the menstrual cycle will start in 3-4 days after you stop taking any pills. However, if a new period does not start after 7 days (it is called amenorrhea) you may start taking pills for the next period. If you have amenorrhea for 2-3 months, you should stop taking any pills, wait for a new period, and start again on the fifth day. During the days without pills you should protect yourself from pregnancy by another method of birth control. If you have amenorrhea frequently, you may increase the dose of ethynylestradiol.

5. Patients with acute or chronic hepatitis or nephritis should not use these pills.

6. Patients with uterine tumor and high blood pressure and people having history of liver and kidney diseases may use this pill under the direction of medical authorities.

7. If any effects occur which were not mentioned above, report them to medical authorities so that they can be taken care of.

Storage: Keep closed and keep away from light.

Shanghai Pharmaceutical Factory No. 7

Pills No. 1 and 2

Approximately 70 to 80 percent of all oral contraceptive users in China take the low-dose Pill No. 1, whose label is reproduced in Figure 10-2. A quotation from Chairman Mao, "Bring the emphasis of medicine and hygiene to the countryside," appeared on all bottle labels printed prior to 1972 but is no longer included.

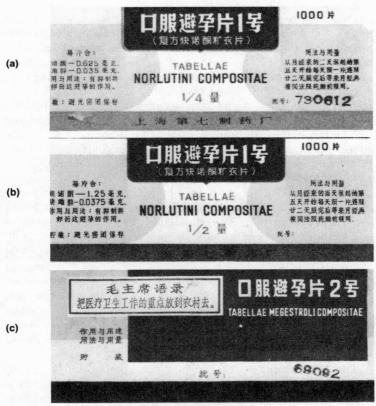

FIGURE 10-2

(a) Bottle label of low-dose Pill No. 1. Translation: "Oral Contraceptive Pill No. 1 (directions for use of sugar-coated norethindrone). Tabellae Norlutini Compositae–1/4 dose. Each tablet contains 0.625 mg. of norethindrone and 0.035 mg. of ethynylestradiol. *Mode of Action:* To suppress periodic flow of eggs and prevent pregnancy. *Usage and Dosage:* Starting on the fifth day of your menstrual cycle take one tablet a day for 22 days. After completing this, wait for the next menstrual cycle and take the medicine in the same way. Take before going to bed. *Storage:* Keep closed and keep away from light. Series Number 730612. Shanghai Pharmaceutical Factory No. 7. (b) Bottle label of high-dose Pill No. 1. Text identical to (a) except for dosage. (c) Bottle label of Pill No. 2. Text identical to (a) except for date and content description: "1 mg. of megestrol and 0.035 mg. of ethynylestradiol." The material in the left square is absent in labels printed after 1971, such as (a) and (b), and reads as follows: "*Chairman Mao's Quotation:* 'Bring the emphasis of medicine and hygiene to the countryside.'"

The woman Pill user is generally first given the low-dose Pill No. 1.

If bleeding irregularities are noted, she is shifted to the high-dose Pill No. 1, and if this is not satisfactory, then to the low-dose Pill No. 2 containing megestrol and ethynylestradiol. (Megestrol was the active ingredient of some oral contraceptives marketed in Europe and to a minor extent in the U.S., but it was withdrawn from the market in the mid 1970s because of increased incidence of mammary tumors in beagles.)

Of interest to Western readers (and probably totally unknown to most Chinese patients and even physicians) is the meaning of the puzzling notation in the package insert (also see labels in Fig. 10-2) referring to ¼ and ½ dose. As I will explain, this notation tells us something about the speed with which China, compared to the U.S., is prepared to act on dosage modifications. The original Chinese clinical work on oral contraceptives began in 1963 or 1964 with a variant of Pill No. 1 consisting of 2.5 mg. of norethindrone and 0.5-0.6 mg. of ethynylestradiol. Although it is conceivable that the steroid active ingredient was imported into the People's Republic for the original clinical work, I suspect that it was manufactured indigenously since in 1963-64 nowhere else in the world was norethindrone combined with the estrogen ethynylestradiol (but rather with its methyl ether, mestranol). This 2.5 mg. version of Pill No. 1 (similar in strength to pills used in the early 1960s in North America and Europe) was tested for efficacy in Shanghai on nearly 30,000 women over a two- to three-year period. In 1965, clinical work in Shanghai was started with Pill No. 1 containing 1.25 mg. of norethindrone and 0.035 mg. of ethynylestradiol (hence the notation "½ dose" in the translation of the general package insert for oral contraceptives), and in 1967, during the Cultural Revolution when supposedly the birth control program was ignored but not abandoned, the ¼ dose corresponding to the present low-dose version of Pill No. 1 was introduced into clinical work.

The development of the low-dose Pill is important on several grounds. First, the rapid and early introduction into wide clinical use of the low-dose Pill demonstrates that less stringent safety regulations in China allowed the introduction of a new drug earlier than is possible under a stricter regulatory climate. The Chinese were the first in the world to have used a low-dose combination of norethindrone and an estrogen (ethynylestradiol). Not until the mid 1970s did the FDA approve comparable low-dose contraceptive pills in the U.S. (see Chapter 4). In other words, American women got the "Chinese" dosage of the "American" Pill five to six years later!

Second, thromboembolism, a major side effect of the relatively high-dose Western contraceptive pills, is supposedly insignificant in China, where 70 to 80 percent of all contraceptive users are on the low-dose Pill. In addition to the remarkably reduced dosage (¼ the American dose at that time), other possible explanations for the observed lack of thromboembolism include genetic factors, nutritional factors, differences in the amount of physical exercise, inadequate statistical studies on the occurrence of thromboembolism in China, and use of ethynylestradiol as the estrogen component of the Chinese Pill (rather than the more common mestranol used in American oral contraceptives prior to 1973).

During the 1960s in Taiwan, where oral contraceptives were imported from the West, a higher incidence of side effects was observed than in China. Since genetic and nutritional factors cannot possibly be responsible for this apparent difference, it seems likely that this greater incidence of side effects in Taiwanese women was attributable to the higher-dose Western oral contraceptives. (As Chinese women are generally of smaller size and weight than the average European or American woman, the low-dose regimen makes sense even on a mg./kg. body-weight basis.) The contrast in the Taiwanese and P.R.C. experiences with oral contraceptives over roughly the same period of time also provides an instructive example of the potential advantages of indigenous family planning efforts as opposed to reliance on foreign imports.

Further reduction of the low-dose Pill No. 1 was attempted in Shanghai (probably prior to 1970) but the ⅛ dose (0.312 mg. norethindrone with 0.035 mg. ethynylestradiol) apparently caused too many difficulties, notably with respect to irregular bleeding. Inspection of Chinese package inserts and numerous discussions with Chinese gynecologists and other physicians indicate that menstrual irregularities are the side effect of greatest concern to Chinese women. The other side effects listed (such as nausea) are the same as noted in the West, but it is likely that they are of much less concern to Chinese women for two reasons. First, all literature and promotional material emphasize that the Pill should be taken at bedtime, when side effects such as nausea are least likely to be noted; ingestion in the morning is more frequent in Europe and America. Second, Chinese women on the average probably work harder than their American and European counterparts, and because of this they may simply not focus on, or complain about, some of the so-called minor side effects.

The rapid reduction in dosage of Pill No. 1 in China was not necessarily motivated by a desire to find the lowest effective therapeutic dose. A second and perhaps even more important factor was undoubtedly the need to disseminate the available steroid raw material to as many people as possible. By using only 25 percent of the then-accepted North American steroid dose, the Chinese were able to provide contraceptive protection to four times as many women.

Injectable Steroid Contraceptives

The Chinese have become quite interested in injectable steroid preparations because they eliminate daily Pill taking and can be administered particularly efficiently in such a well-organized and highly supervised living and working environment. The original Chinese clinical work on injectable contraceptives again started in Shanghai around 1964 or 1965 and was clearly patterned on European and American research, although the currently recommended Chinese dosage is exactly half that of the original American regimen. Larger-scale distribution of injectable steroids in China occurred in 1969 but these injections were primarily used for treatment of menstrual disorders rather than for fertility control.

Since 1970 the long-acting progestational agent 17-hydroxy-progesterone caproate has been used in these injectable contraceptives but has found only limited acceptance, presumably because of bleeding irregularities. In fact, the clinical results in the United States and Germany in the early 1960s with this particular agent (using twice the P.R.C. dose) were sufficiently discouraging for its production to be discontinued completely by the Western manufacturer. A translation of the package insert accompanying an injectable Chinese steroid contraceptive preparation follows because it represents an instructive example of the ingenious use by the Chinese of contraceptive hardware and software components.

Instruction for Birth Control Injection No. 1 (17-hydroxyprogesterone caproate formulation)

"Bring the emphasis of medicine and hygiene to the countryside."—Chairman Mao.

Birth Control Injection has been invented by the working class and revolutionary technicians, under the thought of Chairman Mao, based on the success of the birth control pill and with the cooperation of workers, peasants, soldiers, and revolutionary technicians. After more than five thousand clinical experiments, it has been proven to be 98.59% effective with no side effects and will not cause damage to future fertility. After approval by the authority concerned, this injection has been considered as a more convenient and simpler method. It has been well accepted by the public, hence can be widely used under the direction of medical technicians.

Name: Birth Control Injection No. 1 (17-hydroxyprogesterone caproate formulation)

Ingredient: 17-hydroxyprogesterone caproate and estradiol valerate (250 mg. 5 mg./ampule)

Mode of Action: By suppressing the

periodic flow of eggs, this medicine prevents pregnancy.

Usage and Dosage: Injections are only effective on a monthly basis. The directions are as follows: Initially on the fifth day of menstrual cycle, take two injections (or take one injection on the fifth and fifteenth days). For the subsequent months, the injection (only one) should be made on the 10th-12th day of your menstrual cycle. (For people with short menstrual cycle, the injection should be taken on the 10th day.) These injections should be continued on a monthly basis for protection.

Adverse Reactions: The major side effects are those associated with menstruation, such as lengthening of cycle, shortening of period, irregular menstrual flow. After six months, the magnitude of these effects should decrease. Some people may feel sick, nauseated, dizzy, weak, have swelling in the breast, rash, etc. Do not worry about these minor side effects; they will disappear by themselves. Take medical advice if necessary.

Precautions:

1. In order to optimize the effect of the injection and minimize side effects, injections should be carried out regularly and thoroughly.

2. If variation in menstruation occurs:
   a. If the period is lengthened, take birth control Pill No. 1 or 2, one or two tablets per day for four days; this should stop the flow. Or take the pill a week before the menstrual cycle for four days. This will prevent bleeding. If bleeding reoccurs, repeat the same procedure.
   b. If bleeding occurs after the period, take ethynylestradiol 0.0125-0.025 mg. till the next injection time arrives. If the bleeding occurs

very close to injection time, do not worry about it.
   c. If the menstrual cycle is shortened, start taking the birth control pill ten days after the injection, one to two tablets per day for four to six days.
   d. If after injections continuous bleeding occurs, take the birth control Pill No. 1 or 2 for four days. When bleeding stops, take one injection of birth control injection No. 1; eleven days later take the pill, one to two tablets per day for four days, to prevent further bleeding.

3. For those people whose period has been lengthened to more than ten days, the injection should be made seven days after the flow has stopped.

4. Each injection is good for 14 days. If you miss your period after an injection, wait for 28 days before you take your next injection. If two consecutive periods are missed, no further injections should be made. Another method of contraception should be employed until your period reoccurs. Then start injection sequence over from beginning.

5. People with acute or chronic hepatitis or nephritis or lumps in the breast should not use this injection. (If during this process lumps in the breast develop, stop usage immediately.)

6. If any effects occur which were not described above, report them to medical authorities so that they can be taken care of.

7. If solidification of the medicine occurs in the bottle, melt in hot water, shake well, and use.

Packaging: Each box contains ten ampules of one ml. each. Keep away from light.

Shanghai Pharmaceutical Factory No. 9.

The first portion of the package insert appears almost ludicrous when read superficially by the average Western reader. Many American women nowadays are even suspicious of the technical contributions of male scientists and physicians; it is unlikely that they could conceive of anyone feeling more reassured to learn that soldiers and peasants have also contributed to the development of an injection that they were about to get. Similarly a statement that any drug is "98.59 percent effective" is meaningless, and the phrase "with no side effects" is preposterous. Yet on further reflection one realizes that these statements are the essential political software component of the contraceptive hardware, there to assure the recipient that this contraceptive, like all others, reflects the State's interest in family planning and the total commitment of all citizens (workers, peasants, soldiers, and revolutionary technicians) to the limitation of population growth. The highly quantified index of efficacy (98.59 percent, as if any biological effectiveness could be expressed to the second decimal point) and the claim of total absence of side effects are there to reassure the woman.

However, a few paragraphs later the woman is also told the truth—in a detailed but simple description of adverse reactions and an even more complicated detailed description of precautions. This package insert offers good support for China specialist Leo Orleans's conclusion in his 1974 report to Congress: "Reinforced by Party philosophy and propaganda which took the mystery out of medicine, the people assume responsibility both for themselves and for those around them. . . . Health in China is everybody's business."

New Chinese Contraceptive Developments

Thus far, the entire discussion of contraceptive hardware has focused on methods that originated in the West and were introduced with relatively minor modifications into China. It is worthwhile to consider two others that, although not chemically new, are innovative in that they seem to be responsive to problems of the local society, as well as a third method that is not only novel but could also have a major impact abroad.

The Chinese Paper Pill

By far the most interesting contraceptive formulation that I encountered, and one that had never been mentioned in the Western literature or newspapers prior to my China trip in 1973, is a paper formulation referred to as "Sheet Type Oral Birth Control Pills" (see Fig. 10-3) developed at Shanghai Pharmaceutical Factory No. 7, supposedly by one of the local technicians. A roll of paper, approximately 50 cm. wide and consisting of water-soluble carboxymethylcellulose, is passed mechanically through a dryer, then through a pan

(a)

(b)

(c)

FIGURE 10-3

Sheet Type Oral Contraceptive Pill No. 2 showing both sides of insert, (a) and (b), and one month's actual supply consisting of 22 squares of paper (c). Translation: (a) "Sheet Type Oral Birth Control Pill No. 2 Series Number 73047–Shanghai Pharmaceutical Factory No. 7; (b) "The color of this oral birth control sheet No. 2 (megestrol) is yellow. Each square contains 1 mg. of megestrol and 0.035 mg. of ethynylestradiol. *Mode of Action:* Oral birth control sheets No. 1 and 2 can suppress periodic flow of eggs and prevent pregnancy. *Side effects and points for attention:* See the instructions on the original sugar-coated contraceptive pills. The same. *Usage and Dosage:* Take one square on the fifth day of your menstrual cycle. After taking 22 squares, wait for the next cycle and start again. Take one small square every day before bedtime, chew slightly and swallow with water."

containing an edible dye, again through a dryer, and finally through a pan containing an alcoholic solution of the active ingredients of the standard steroid oral contraceptive. After drying, the colored roll of paper impregnated with the drug is placed in a machine that cuts it into strips and then perforates it like stamps into "daily squares." The monthly sheet containing 22 squares, together with the package insert (the same color as the medicated paper), is then packaged mechanically in a cellophane envelope.

The entire process described above is handled by one operator; his homemade "Rube Goldberg" machine is shown below. This operator, who seemed to have been involved in the original development of the paper pill, listed four advantages of this novel formulation: 1. The manufacturing process affords greater protection for the workers, who are much less exposed to large quantities of the active ingredients than in tablet manufacture. In view of the minimal Chinese safety precautions, this is indeed an important advantage. 2. The formulation is much lighter and smaller and thus easier to ship and store. 3. The product is supposedly more uniform. 4. Money is saved on raw material (no tablets, bottles, etc.), and the technology is much simpler, requiring fewer people and much less equipment and space, which considering the number of Chinese oral contraceptive consumers is a significant saving of both time and money.

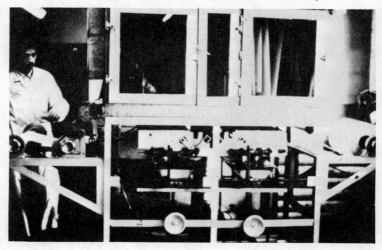

Given the apparent advantages of this ingenious paper formulation—especially the fact that it would permit decentralization of contraceptive manufacture by having such simple homemade machines set up in many different locations and simply shipping the alcoholic solutions of active ingredients to them—one would have expected the Chinese to publicize and distribute these paper pills widely. Yet according to Leo Orleans this does not seem to be the case; they are now rarely mentioned in Chinese publications. Perhaps some unexpected stability or acceptability problems were encountered. It is pertinent to note that a clinical trial comparing the standard oral contraceptive tablet and a paper pill manufactured for the WHO in Germany is currently being conducted under WHO auspices in nine different centers (Alexandria, Chandigarh, Ibadan, Karachi, Manila, New Delhi, Santiago, Seoul, and Stockholm) involving over 1,000 women. Particular emphasis is being placed on acceptability since efficacy is likely to be very similar to that of standard oral contraceptives. This study is supposed to be completed by late 1979, and it would be ironic if this Chinese development should in the end be acceptable in other countries, but not in the People's Republic of China.

The Chinese Vacation Pill

Most of the information on the Chinese vacation pill, a synthetic steroid with the formidable name $2\alpha,17\alpha$-diethynyl-A-norandrostane-$2\beta,17\beta$-diol dipropionate, also called Anordrin, comes from the 1977 report of the National Academy of Sciences' steroid chemistry and biochemistry delegation to the People's Republic of China. This is basically a postcoital pill that was developed specifically for married couples who live apart for extensive periods (mostly because of work assignments in different locations) and who meet only once or twice a year for vacations, generally for periods of four weeks. According to the instructions, the vacation pill should first be taken immediately after coitus and then again the following morning; it is recommended primarily for couples who have "frequent" (?) intercourse ("six to eight times per month") because the pill appears less effective if used only sporadically. Since each tablet contains 7.5 mg. of the active steroid ingredient, the cumulative dose within one menstrual cycle could approach or exceed 200 mg. per month depending on the frequency of sexual intercourse, one of the reasons why this type of postcoital pill is unlikely to be acceptable for general use in countries such as the United States.

The active steroid on which the Anordrin preparation is based was synthesized in France by Jean Jacques of the College de France in the 1950s and was tested biologically in the U.S. Its presumed estrogenicity was considered an undesirable feature which led to discontinuation of these studies for contraceptive purposes. The precise mechanism of action of Anordrin is not well understood, and although it may inhibit ovulation (as do the usual steroid oral contraceptives), its principal mode of action seems to be to block production of the natural female hormone progesterone, thereby preventing the implantation of the fertilized egg in the uterus.

The chemical work on Anordrin was initiated in the late 1960s at the Institute of Organic Chemistry of the Chinese Academy of Sciences in Shanghai. Whereas acute and short-term toxicity studies were carried out in both dogs and rhesus monkeys, chronic toxicology was performed only in rats for about a year and a half after which, in 1971, clinical work began. Two years later, in June 1973, the clinical data were reviewed at a symposium, which recommended the drug for general use. These recommendations were approved in January 1974 by the Office of Planned Births of the State Council. Compared to the time-consuming development process that exists in Japan, Western Europe, and the U.S. in particular, where such a development would have taken well over a decade, the speed of the Chinese approval process leaves one almost breathless.

The Chinese Male Pill

On January 5, 1979, the *New York Times* and many other U.S. newspapers ran the headline "Visitors Say Chinese Report They Have a Safe and Effective Birth Control Pill for Men." The accompanying article began: "Chinese scientists say that they have developed the first safe and effective birth control pill for men, it was reported here today. The contraceptive is 99.8 percent effective, does not interfere with sexual activity and has no serious side effects, the Chinese told a group of visiting family planning experts from the United States." The background to this story is worth telling, for this new advance is of interest in several respects.

First and foremost is the intrinsic importance of the development itself—a new, nonsteroidal oral contraceptive for males—and the fact that it is totally original Chinese work, rather than a Chinese adaptation of a Western discovery. Second, here we again see how rapidly clinical work is able to be instigated in a country that lacks a strict regulatory apparatus such as the FDA. This raises the question whether we are paying too high a price for caution or whether the Chinese are risking too much by rushing into clinical trial too early. Third, this work sheds interesting light on current Chinese publication practices.

This new Chinese male pill was discussed in detail in an article entitled "Gossypol—A New Antifertility Agent for Males" (*Chinese Medical Journal,* November 1978), which was mailed to me in January 1979 by a former Chinese associate in Peking who responded to my inquiry about technical details of this work. I was able to obtain additional information from colleagues who visited China early in 1979. Briefly, the story is the following.

In 1969 a Chinese Academy of Sciences expedition to Hopei Province examined the outbreak among peasants (male as well as female) of a disease characterized by fever, general malaise, and burning sensations. It was eventually traced to the cottonseed oil that formed part of their daily diet; long-term consumption affected both cardiac muscles and genital organs, resulting in infertility. Apparently peasants traditionally boiled the cottonseed before pressing it, whereas under the more modern commune system the production was centralized and the cottonseed was pressed cold. Evidently, the original boiling step inactivated the cottonseed oil constituent that was responsible for the disease studied by the Academy expedition.

In 1971 the Chinese researchers conducted experiments with rats that demonstrated that gossypol (a constituent of cottonseed first isolated in 1899 in Germany and whose chemical structure was established by Roger Adams at the University of Illinois in 1938) was the active material responsible for the antifertility effect. Though gossypol can be synthesized in the laboratory, it is much easier to isolate it from cottonseed, which contains from 0.4 to 1.7 percent of this substance. Potentially, there is an almost unlimited amount of gossypol available. The current world production of cottonseed amounts to approximately 25 million tons per annum, which corresponds to at least 100,000 tons of gossypol! If the future of the world's population problem depended on the availability of gossypol as a male contraceptive, we would have no supply shortage to worry about.

The chemical constituents of cottonseed have been the subject of chemical, physiological, metabolic, and toxicological studies in the West for the past 50 years. Because cottonseed could be used as an important protein supplement in developing countries, the dietary role of cottonseed meal and its principal constituents has received particular attention. A great deal of biological and toxicological work with gossypol has been carried out on ruminant livestock (for which cottonseed meal is used as a protein supplement) as well as on poultry, swine, fish, dogs, rats, and even humans, and a wide variety of toxic effects in experimental animals has been reported. The predominant ones are loss of appetite, reduction in growth rate, diarrhea, vomiting, anemia, and, when high doses are given, cardiac irregularity, which can cause death.

However, in moderate doses, gossypol has not produced noticeable toxic effects in humans, especially if given in the presence of certain minerals such as iron salts, which bind gossypol and make it biologically inactive. Cooking or moist-heat treatment during the processing of cottonseed renders gossypol nontoxic and this chemical alteration of gossypol may explain why the Chinese noted lowered fertility rates only in those areas of the country where *unrefined* cottonseed was consumed. (Because high doses of gossypol produce appetite loss in experimental animals, during the 1940s U.S. scientists pursued this lead to determine whether gossypol could act as an appetite depressant in humans, but this did not prove to be the case.)

The Chinese rat studies, which were very detailed and fairly sophisticated, included nine-month toxicological studies as well as studies following three generations of rats born to females that had been mated with gossypol-treated male rats. This experimental work demonstrated that nontoxic doses of gossypol caused infertility within a period of two to four weeks and that fertility gradually was restored after stopping the treatment. Although the mechanism of action is not completely clear, gossypol seems to interfere with sperm production in the seminiferous tubules and results in nonviable sperm.

What is extraordinary is that in 1972, within a year after the initial animal toxicology began, the first clinical experiments with gossypol were under way. By 1979, over 4,000 healthy men had been on gossypol for more than six months, over 2,000 of them already for two years, and some for as long as four years. The initial human dosage was 20 mg. per day, given orally in tablet form, and judging from semen analysis, infertility was achieved within two months, whereupon the maintenance dose could be reduced to one fourth of the starting dose. After discontinuation of gossypol treatment, sperm production gradually resumed and within three months both morphology and number of sperm appeared to be normal. According to my Chinese correspondent, this conclusion is not based only on semen examination but also on subsequent successful pregnancies and normal offspring: "Many children were born and they are normal in every respect."

Just as in the case of the Chinese vacation pill, the speed with which the Chinese progressed from initial animal toxicology to human experiments is truly remarkable. The results published to date about this development are clearly of such interest that the work will undoubtedly be repeated in the United States and elsewhere, but I suspect that in the U.S. it will take several years before initial clinical experiments will be permitted. The final proof of the pudding, of course, is what the long-term consequences of gossypol ingestion by humans are, how reversible the procedure is in terms of the normalcy of offspring produced after men have been on this pill for years, and, most importantly, whether many men are prepared to take it. According to the *New York Times,* one Chinese doctor told his American visitors, "The men are not very enthusiastic yet."

Regardless of the eventual practical outcome of this Chinese development, the preliminary results are clearly exciting. Gossypol is an important new lead in male contraception, and its chemical structure, a polyhydroxylated binaphthalene derivative, is totally different from that of other substances hitherto studied that interfere with spermatogenesis. If gossypol should ultimately prove unsatisfactory, there is little doubt that chemical modifications of this substance will be examined, which may lead to better alternatives.

Chinese Publication Practices

Why is it that such an exciting scientific development, which has been under way for several years, was kept under wraps until late 1978? The Western publish-or-perish syndrome and the need for rapid preliminary announcements of promising new developments as well as the desire for immediate peer recognition have probably not been eliminated completely in China, but they have certainly been repressed. The internal communication network in China is based not so much on scientific publication as on personal communication between the relatively few research institutes active in a given field such as human fertility control. Even more striking than the delay in announcing gossypol's fertility control use is the fact that the original article in the *Chinese Medical Journal* names no individual author or authors, but rather carries the byline "National Coordinating Group on Male Antifertility Agents." This display of deliberate anonymity—virtually unheard of in Western scientific circles—has become a common, but probably temporary, practice in recent Chinese scientific publications.

Chinese scientific publication practices have come a long way since the 1960s when every article (usually bearing actual authors' names rather than the names of groups) paid long and effusive homage to Chairman Mao. This practice continued into the early 1970s when journal publication was resumed after the hiatus of the Cultural Revolution. Thus, the distinguished Chinese research journal *Scientia Sinica,* in one of its first post-Cultural Revolution issues (February 1973), included in its contents an article entitled "Using Chairman Mao's Philosophical Thinking to Guide Scientific Experiment in Peanut Cultivation." The article began with the startlingly short and disarming statement "I am a peasant." I doubt whether *any* scientific journal anywhere in the world in recent years has used these words, and one wonders whether Chinese journals in the post-Mao period will again contain them.

The current tendency in China is to publish factual scientific content without political messages, but the appearance of articles authored primarily by anonymous groups of scientific workers is almost certainly on the decline. Since 1978 there have been several authoritative articles denouncing the practice of forcing scientists to present their findings as collective units or to share credit with people who did not contribute to the results. The majority of scientific articles now list authors by name and this is described as a way to acknowledge contributions of individuals to the development of the country. In short, authorship and publication are now viewed as a means of rewarding and providing incentive to researchers, which is not very different from current practice in the West.

Current Usage of Contraceptives

I was convinced when I returned from China in 1973, as I am today after studying the relevant literature published in the intervening years, that it is impossible to write a definitive treatise on contraceptive practice in the People's Republic. The country is too large, national statistics are totally unavailable, many areas are not yet open to foreigners, and the extent of contraceptive usage— qualitatively and quantitatively—is still uneven.

Given the paucity of hard facts, current contraceptive usage in China is clearly the most difficult topic to cover even semiquantitatively. All one can do today is obtain as many anecdotal reports from as many different locations as possible and try to determine whether any trends are discernible. Virtually all travelers to China are currently restricted to the eastern and primarily urban centers of the country; those rural communes that have been visited are generally not too distant from the major cities (Canton, Shanghai, Peking) and thus may not be very representative. Attempting to make precise extrapolations to the entire country would therefore be preposterous.

In the urban centers (e.g., in residential units, factories, etc.) remarkably detailed figures are now available about the use of contraceptives because individual file cards are kept for each married woman of reproductive age (generally considered in China to be up to 45 years). In my experience, in the rural communes replies about contraceptive practices were usually worded in much more general terms and depended on the hierarchical position of the respondent.

Table 10-1 (pages 208-9) summarizes the results of my 1973 trip interviews and those of three other groups that visited China in 1972 and 1973. In spite of the limitations of the data, some trends in 1973 can be discerned that are rather different from the situation existing prior to 1969 (as gleaned from the literature of the mid 1960s). Abortions, for which only the woman's consent is required, are carried out by vacuum aspiration (a technique invented in the Soviet Union, but first used widely in China before becoming the method of choice for early abortion in the rest of the world). Judging from Table 10-1, the incidence of abortion appears to be relatively low in the better-organized urban residential sections; however, I state that conclusion with great reservation since most respondents provided only qualitative answers ("very few," "some"), which may have been colored by the official party line favoring preventive medicine (i.e., contraception or sterilization) rather than abortion.

Sterilization, primarily in females, is remarkably high in urban centers (which is qualitatively similar to the situation in the U.S.) and reflects the government's policy encouraging such a drastic step among parents of two or more children. The apparent receptivity of Chinese parents, notably working mothers, to sterilization may in part be attributable to the much greater stability of Chinese marriages compared to American or European marriages (nearly 50 percent of U.S. marriages terminate in divorce)—hence the lesser concern that one of the partners may wish to have children again in another marriage. The trend in urban centers away from IUDs and toward oral contraceptives is unmistakable. It is substantiated quite clearly by oral contraceptive production figures cited below. The Chinese urban population is estimated at approximately 125 million, which should yield approximately 15 million married women of reproductive age. (Even if one assumes overoptimistically that as many as 50 percent are using oral contraceptives, the 1972 production of Shanghai's Pharmaceutical Factory No. 7 alone could comfortably take care of the total urban oral contraceptive requirements.)

As far as rural areas are concerned, except for the qualitative statement that at this time IUD usage still predominates over oral contraceptive consumption, comments must be made with great reservations because of the extremely limited data base. This is an area where future visitors can make particularly useful contributions, even if they provide only anecdotal reports from geographi-

TABLE 10-1

Extent of Sterilization, Contraception, and Abortion in Selected Communities

Community	Population	Households	Married Women under 45 yrs.	Sterilized	Contraceptive method % Oral Contracep.	IUD	Condom or Diaphragm	Injectable	Abortions per yr.
A	11,717	3,291	1,229	31	19	4	20	2	Very few
B	8,700	1,718	1,080	44	23	3	18	2	Very few
C	68,000	15,000	NA		Most	Some	Some		?
D	8,000	NA			Most	Some	Some	Some	Very few
E	17,000	3,700	2,200	55*	22	6	9		
F	20,500	4,600	3,220	ca. 20	>60	<10	<5		40-50
G	22,631	5,400		62*	16	9	15	1	
H	68,000	NA	8,978	43	14	4		1	
I	6,400		3,920	10	Most			1	80
J	3,710		427	6	30	12	1		10-20
K	30,000				Most				
L	3,916	NA	3,320	17	45	7	25		
M	13,000	3,600	1,300	36	32	13	11		?
N	1,700	NA	<850	20	10	20	<50		Very few
O	28,000	7,400	2,920	20	25	5	19	<1	186

			>50	<40	<40	1-2
P	3,014		Low		Very few	Very few
Q	705	378	30	>50	Very few	Very few
R	63,000	15,900	>10	<10	Most	
S	21,000		Some	Some	Most	
T			Low	Some	Most	20
U	65,000	NA	Most	Some	Some	Some

* Includes males

A. Lane of Chang-chia-ch'ai Street Revolutionary Committee, Shanghai.
B. Street Committee of Fan Kwa Lüng Workers New Housing, Shanghai.
C. Tsao Yang Workers Village, Shanghai.
D. Shanghai Diesel Engine Works.
E. Pon Pu New Village (factory workers' residence), Shanghai.
F. Hsü Hang People's (Rural) Commune 40 km. northwest of Shanghai.
G. Tongwan People's (Rural) Commune 40 km. south of Shanghai.
H. Shanghai Street and Lane Health Station No. 2.
I. Peking Textile Factory No. 3.
J. "Model Commune" of Peking Capital Hospital.
K. Peking Municipal Children's Hospital Health District.

L. Peking factory served by Peking Obstetric and Gynecological Hospital.
M. Street Committee in Nanking.
N. Silk Brocade Mill, Hangchow.
O. Shao Yun Shang urban residential section, Hangchow.
P. Estimate by group of family planning physicians for urban area of Canton.
Q. Estimate by group of family planning physicians for rural area near Canton.
R. Sha Ch'i brigade of Da Shi People's (Rural) Commune (40 km. from Canton), Kwangtung Province.
S. Ta Li People's (Rural) Commune, Kwangtung Province.
T. Ma Chi Za People's (Rural) Commune, Shensi Province.
U. Wuhan Iron and Steel Works, Hupei Province.

SOURCE: C. Djerassi. "Some Observations on Current Fertility Control in China." The China Quarterly, no. 57, January/March 1974, pp. 40-62.

cally different rural areas. However, it is safe to assume that although many highly organized urban areas may approach 90 percent contraceptive coverage in the relevant age group, the 20 percent figure provided for the Da Shi People's Commune in Kwangtung Province is probably a more realistic one for the Chinese rural population. The latter amounts to over 700 million people of which about 85 million may be assumed to be the female target population. If 20 percent of the women in that group practice contraception, we would be talking about 17 million women. If half of these women used oral contraceptives—which is almost surely much too high a figure—that would yield about 8.5 million women Pill users in the rural population. This figure, combined with the 7.5 million estimated urban Pill users (probably a maximum figure), would lead to a conceivable total of 16 million oral contraceptive consumers in 1972, a figure very close to my independently calculated estimate for the 1972 Chinese production of oral contraceptives. To my knowledge this is still the only quantitative figure for Chinese oral contraceptive use that has been put forward in conjunction with supporting evidence. In terms of hard data, I consider these projections to be the most significant outcome of my China trip, since they provide insight into Chinese technical competence at a very high level of chemical sophistication and at the same time afford a minimum numerical value for current oral contraceptive use in the People's Republic. This, combined with the data summarized in Table 10-1, allows us to obtain at the least a semiquantitative picture of contraceptive consumption in the urban areas of China.

The large-scale production of steroid oral contraceptives is among the most difficult technical operations in the chemical industry, in part because of the large number of separate chemical steps involved. That the People's Republic is completely self-sufficient in this respect is remarkable—both from a qualitative and quantitative viewpoint. The production of all pharmaceuticals, including steroids, in China is decentralized and occurs in various sections of the country, although Shanghai has a heavy concentration of pharmaceutical companies (at least 12). To my knowledge, based largely on inspection of bottle labels, at least three of these Shanghai factories are involved in various stages of contraceptive manufacture; the account that follows is based on a discussion with technicians from Factory No. 9 and a visit to Factory No. 7.

Factory No. 9 is concerned with the difficult stage of production of the chemical ingredients of Pill No. 1, whereas Factory No. 7 is one of several factories that deal exclusively with formulations (production of ampules, tablets, etc.) and final packaging of six major groups of drugs, one of which is oral contraceptives (Pills No. 1 and 2).

The finishing process I observed in Factory No. 7 was carried out in one room containing eight rotary pans, each with a capacity of one million tablets. Two batches per pan are completed in one working day, thus giving this factory a daily production capacity of 16 million pills. Since the factory operates for 300 days per year, the *potential* annual capacity of Shanghai Factory No. 7 can be calculated (one million pills can provide contraceptive coverage to about 4,000 women for a year) to satisfy the annual oral contraceptive needs of over 19 million women. When I presented the vice-chairman of the Revolutionary Committee of the factory with this calculation, he remarked that the oral contraceptive department within the factory did not work all year but operated only until the requisite annual quota of tablets was satisfied. The quota is established by the "authorities" who also supply the active ingredient, which is manufactured by other factories (such as No. 9). When I asked directly about the actual 1972 production quota rather than potential production capacity, I was told that it amounted to 200 million tablets per month, which corresponds to 2.4 billion tablets per year. This amount is sufficient to supply approximately 9.6 million women, which thus should be considered a firm minimal annual production figure for the P.R.C. at that time (1972). Although I do not know how many other factories manufacture Pills No. 1 and 2, at least one (Shanghai Factory No. 11) and probably several others also did so in 1973. If their cumulative production equaled that of Factory No. 7, then the production of oral contraceptives in China in 1972 was theoretically sufficient to supply 20 million women. Since one can assume that at least 25 percent of any annual production is in the pipeline at any given time, unless an unusually high number of pills is stored or remains unused, one can arrive at a *consumption rate* of at least 15 million women.

Using these ballpark figures, which can be refined rather easily during future visits to additional pharmaceutical factories (the National Academy of Science's steroid chemistry delegation in 1976 was unable to secure production figures, hence my 1973 figures are still the most recent) and more extensive discussions with family planning and health ministry personnel, one can tentatively project that up to one third of the Chinese population of active reproductive age is now practicing birth control in one way or another. How do I arrive at this conclusion? Assuming that out of the total Chinese population approximately 100 million women are married and of reproductive age and that 15 to 16 million are on oral contraceptives with an equal number using other birth control methods, then approximately 30 million women would have been covered in 1973 and probably a much higher number in 1979.

Using 1963 as a reference point, the Chinese accomplishments during the past decade and a half have been unsurpassed in terms of magnitude, intensity, and total self-sufficiency. These remarkable achievements in the most highly populated country in the world augur well for further progress in the next decade. China apparently has achieved, or will soon achieve, the production capacity to fulfill all its contraceptive hardware needs. The chief remaining problem for that country is to ensure greater penetration of the family planning gospel to the rural areas.

From an analytical standpoint the ultimate proof of the efficacy of family planning efforts lies in population statistics. Much has been written about the uncertain state of current knowledge of China's population, birth rate, death rate, age distribution, etc., but in the absence of national statistics, anecdotal reports, which represent the grist for the mills of professional China watchers, must suffice. In some of the highly organized rural communes, such as Tongwan People's Commune near Shanghai, detailed population and birth figures (including a comparison of yearly "planned" births vs. actual births) are recorded on public posters (see entry G in Table 10-1; note the extraordinarily high incidence of sterilization). These figures, if correct, are impressive. Particularly interesting is Table 10-2, which lists the birth rate of that commune for a period of ten years and shows a dramatic decrease from 45 per 1,000 in 1963 to 10.4 per 1,000 in 1972, coupled with an interesting fluctuation during the period 1966-70. This fluctuation is almost certainly a consequence of the Cultural Revolution and can be interpreted either as an abnormal drop in the birth rate in 1967, attributable to family disruptions at the start of the Cultural Revolution, or else as a temporary rise in 1968-69, associated with reduced attention to birth control programs.

Quite recently, the Chinese authorities have publicized their family planning successes on a much broader scale with the outside world in mind. Thus in an English language broadcast on January 21, 1979, Radio Peking reported: "The population growth rate was under 1 percent in Peking, Shanghai, Tientsin, Szechuan, Hopei, Kiangsu, Shantung, Chekiang, Hupeh, Shansi, and Shensi. It was 0.8 percent for Szechuan, China's most populous province. The 11 provinces and municipalities have reached their 1980 target in birth

TABLE 10-2
Birth Rate (1963-72) of Tongwan People's Commune
(40 km. south of Shanghai)

Year	Birth Rate (per thousand)	Year	Birth Rate (per thousand)
1963	45	1968	21
1964	35	1969	20
1965	23	1970	15
1966	20	1971	13
1967	17	1972	10.4

control. . . . The conference [on family planning held from January 4 to 18, 1979, in Peking] discussed measures for bringing down the *national population growth rate* [my italics] to below 1 percent by 1980."

I have gone into such great detail about contraceptive practices in a single country, the People's Republic of China, because what happens in China has a bigger impact on the world than what happens in any other country since one fourth of the world's population lives there. The obvious question remains: is the Chinese experience in any way transferable to other developing countries, notably the world's second most populous state, India? Personally I doubt it. The peculiarities of the Chinese social and political setting place China in a unique position, at least on its grand scale. We must turn to ministates such as Singapore to find such impressive success stories, and it is perhaps no surprise that the cultural setting is similar. As stated so succinctly by Leo Orleans, "It is the Chinese society itself that gives public health most of its structure and order. The Chinese are a disciplined people living in a disciplined society." Still, I consider China the example par excellence on a grand scale of the pragmatic combination of relevant contraceptive hardware and software to accomplish a national goal.

Pensive man. Nayarit, classic, *ca.* A.D. 100–400.

11

Strategies for the Future

REP. McCLOSKEY: What should be the priorities of the Congress [with respect to supporting birth control research]?

DR. DJERASSI: You must answer a question for us, first. What are the objectives of Congress? What is it you want to accomplish?

If you want to get a new practical contraceptive— practical from the standpoint of being used—during the next five years or so, that's one thing; if you want it in the next ten years, that's another thing; if you talk about the year 2000, that's a third thing. You have to tell us what your objective is.

If your objective is to do something during the next five years or so, then you can forget about basic research. That will have no impact whatsoever. In fact, you're not going to get any new method.

REP. McCLOSKEY: Well, let me ask you that. I don't think there is anyone in the Congress, let alone on this committee, who has yet made the choice: Do we want to develop better and safer contraceptives in five years, or do we want to develop a wholly safe, effective, and acceptable contraceptive in 15 years?

DR. DJERASSI: There is no such thing as a wholly safe contraceptive.

Testimony from hearings of the House Select Committee on Population, 95th Congress, March 8, 1978

THE AMERICAN PUBLIC, NOT JUST CONGRESS, must make up its mind about its objectives and priorities in the area of birth control. If there has ever been a double-barreled question to which all the inhabitants of the earth should wish a satisfactory answer it is this: How many men and women can live on this planet? What will be the quality of all of their lives? This is not an area where we can shrug our shoulders and say, "Let someone else worry," because we would do so at the peril of our children and grandchildren.

Clearly the course of human fertility control for the balance of this century has virtually been determined. Because of the exceptionally long lead times involved in developing new contraceptive measures, what we do now will just barely affect the future contraceptive practices of children born today. Given present public attitudes and the current regulatory climate, with the overriding emphasis on safety, we can expect that taxpayers will spend more and more on government-sponsored contraceptive research and have less and less to show for it. Such increased government expenditures are appropriate, but because we are still talking about piddling sums here, they will be inadequate to do the job. I maintain that we can—and *must*—do better than this.

I cannot conceive of a single *new* nonsurgical contraceptive procedure—chemical or nonchemical—that could be brought to the public without the participation of the pharmaceutical industry. This is true in socialist countries as well as in capitalist ones. Those people who harangue against private industry, in this instance the pharmaceutical industry, should realize this. I am not implying that all new practical work in the field of contraception must be done by the existing mechanism of the private pharmaceutical industry, although I believe that it is far more efficient and cost effective than other alternatives. My point here is not to sing the praises of the free enterprise drug industry or to protect its profits, but rather to try to ensure that it continues to be possible to develop drugs that are needed for human well-being. To accomplish this we must devise strategies that will help create an effective partnership between government and industry, on the model of other major technological efforts such as the space program, or undertake the difficult and even more costly steps that would be involved in the socialization of the drug industry in areas where drug development is especially lengthy. Personally, I consider this latter alternative counterproductive.

What I do feel strongly about is that we must get on with the job. Just spending more and more of the taxpayers' money is not an answer unless these expenditures are made within the proper institutional and operational framework. The present framework is clearly not a desirable one. The pharmaceutical industry in general, and not just in the U.S., is simply no longer putting the effort behind fertility control research that it once did and that it continues to do in other health areas. Yet we have not yet set up an alternative institutional mechanism in this country to fill this void in contraceptive research and development. The Center for Population Research of the National Institute of Child Health and Human Development is now over a decade old, and it does represent a positive step in providing outside funds in the field of birth control. However, in contrast to many other biomedical efforts of the National Institutes of Health (e.g., National Cancer Institute), where outside funding is complemented by significant high-caliber in-house research, such intramural operational efforts in birth control are minimal. Under existing governmental constraints, about all the Center for Population Research has been able to do in the birth control area is to let cumbersome contracts for fairly specific jobs.

The Consumer Advocate

Before discussing specific strategies for establishing a viable cooperative relationship between government and industry, let us first look at some of the factors that have helped create our current problems. The chief reasons for the pharmaceutical industry's lack of interest in contraceptive research and development are the absence of financial incentives and, even more important, the antagonistic climate toward risk taking in this country, which—at least in the biomedical area—is also spreading rapidly to other technologically advanced nations (e.g., Japan and West Germany). One significant factor contributing to this risk-averse climate has been the arrival on the scene of the *virulent* consumer advocate. I emphasize the adjective because the advent of the *constructively critical* consumer advocate was one of the more refreshing and societally significant developments of the 1960s. Now, however, consumer advocacy has become a business with its own momentum, bureaucracy, and vested interests. Unfortunately, among its members are persons who have sufficient formal technical training to ask all the questions but not the foggiest idea of or interest in how to answer them. They have become experts at asking what one of the wise men of American science, Alvin Weinberg, has called "trans-scientific" questions. According to Weinberg's definition, trans-scientific questions are epistemologically matters of fact, yet they are beyond the competence of science. In 1977 he pointed out in *Interdisciplinary Science Reviews* that unanswerable trans-scientific questions are usually asked of science by policymakers because

> public policy generally demands from science prediction rather than observation. And since science is generally less proficient in predicting than it is in observing, public policy often asks science more than science can give. This is not to say that the predictions of science are always so fragile as to be useless in formulating public policy . . . but increasingly, as public policy concerns itself with the deleterious side effects of technology, it asks science to make predictions about the rare events. . . . We ask for the effects of small insults, or the probabilities of rare events, or social consequences in inherently complex, intransitive systems; or we ask about events on a global scale where direct experimentation is too risky. These generally are trans-scientific, not scientific matters.

Weinberg then proceeds to the subject of the trans-scientific debate, an activity engaged in with increasing frequency by some scientifically trained members of various consumer and environmental movements. Again, Weinberg is right on the mark as he explains: "When a scientist speaks in a scientific forum he is judged by his peers who demand proof; when he speaks in a public forum he can hardly be kept honest by his scientific peers. Thus the trans-scientific debate, conducted in public nonscientific forums, invites irresponsibility."

I am critical of such trans-scientific debates because I feel that those who ask questions that either border on or already fall into the realm of trans-science should have the obligation at the same time to indicate what *they* think can be done to obtain the answers to the questions they ask. They should go through the intellectual rigor and discipline of constructing, for the information they desire, the equivalent of critical path maps of the type outlined in Chapter 5. Only then can they determine—or can society determine—whether a desired additional increment of information is worth the price. Let me cite a recent relevant example in the field of birth control.

At the instigation of many developing countries, the WHO has sponsored extensive trials with the injectable steroid contraceptive Depo-Provera, developed by the Upjohn Company. Even though the drug is used in nearly 60 countries, it has not been approved for contraceptive indications in the U.S., despite the fact that Upjohn has attempted to obtain FDA approval for ten years after having conducted phase III clinical trials under FDA-approved protocols. Yet two members of the Public Citizen Health Research Group in Washington, Sidney M. Wolfe, M.D., and Anita Johnson, Esq., wrote on December 16, 1976, to the Assistant Secretary for Health of HEW that "at least 10,000 women were given this drug for contraceptive purposes last year, and FDA has taken no steps to curtail exposure." Furthermore, they demanded "thorough medical follow-up for at least *40 years* [my italics] of the thousands of women who have already gotten Depo-Provera" and stated that "this follow-up should be financed by Upjohn, but should be controlled by independent scientists, so that Upjohn's financial interest in the drug does not bias the results of the study." The demand that the developer of the drug should pay for 40 years of follow-up on thousands of women in the absence of any evidence that such women have been harmed is a simplistic and populist argument, but is it a reasonable one? The Upjohn Company carried out the requisite clinical work in an approved manner. Following thousands of people for 40 years would be incredibly expensive, and what would it prove? If it is cancer that one is concerned about, then clearly 40 years of follow-up research on thousands of people is a requirement that one could make of any drug that is given to healthy people for long periods of time. If this demand of Wolfe and Johnson is the price that any developer (industry or government or nonprofit research institute) must pay for clinical research, would any institution be prepared to carry out such work? Who benefits by such irrational shooting from the hip?

That a certain backlash to some of the stands taken by consumer advocates and environmentalists may actually be in the offing is suggested by a recent news item from *Science* describing defections from certain environmental groups: "In popular lore, the environmentalist has the soul of St. Francis and the nerve of a lion tamer. He is not driven by a lust for wealth or glory, but by a vision of a world in which men live in harmony with nature. Given that the environmentalists share something with the saints, it is surprising to learn that many scientists who once counted themselves friends now consider themselves adversaries of groups such as the Natural Resources Defense Council, the Environmental Defense Fund, and Friends of the Earth. The new adversaries are not industrialists, but pure research scientists, primarily academics."

The Pharmaceutical Industry

Having presented some aspects of the adversary climate in which industry in general and the pharmaceutical industry in particular currently function, I realize that what I am about to propose—a more effective collaboration between government (i.e., the taxpayers) and the pharmaceutical industry in certain areas which are of major societal benefit—will be neither popular nor even palatable to many people. Nonetheless, it is critical that we devise ways to enlist more intimate involvement of the pharmaceutical industry in practical research on new contraceptive approaches.

The costs of developing a new contraceptive agent have risen so dramatically over the past two decades that they are beginning to outstrip the financial capabilities of an individual company and to reduce greatly the company's chance of recovering such costs after the drug has been approved by the government for marketing to the public. For instance, if 10 to 15 years of research by one company, costing up to $50 million, results in the development of a "once-a-month" pill, is it likely that the public, the press, or possibly even the legislature will tolerate a price of several dollars for a single pill when the final manufacturing cost of a chemical ingredient may be only 2 to 5 percent of that amount? Yet unless such a price were charged, the prospects of a firm's recovering the research expenditure, let alone making a profit on the investment, would be negligible.

The reason for the tremendous costs and for the long experimental periods associated with the development of a new contraceptive agent is that such a drug, which is administered to a large population of healthy people, must present minimal risks. The chances of developing such drugs are correspondingly smaller than those of developing other drugs, and in my opinion it is only reasonable that the public (that is, the taxpayer, by way of the government) should bear part of this development cost. The special features responsible for the extraoradinary costs of birth control drugs are the very long trials required to determine toxicity (unlike those for other drugs) and the very large and long phase III trials in humans, accompanied by an ever-increasing number of follow-up clinical laboratory examinations ranging from important observations (effects on endocrine organs, liver, kidneys, serum lipids, coagulation and clotting factors, blood pressure, and the eye) to the trivial (including the effect on wax in one's ear). It is a portion of these aspects of phase III clinical research, rather than the chemical, biological, short-term toxicological, or even phase II clinical studies, that I believe should be funded by the public. One indirect means of partially funding such research would be to alter the current drug approval procedures to allow conditional marketing approval by the FDA.

The consumer suffers from the delusion that drug safety and drug efficacy are all-or-nothing propositions. That people experience side effects from "safe" drugs should be no more surprising than the fact that occasionally some people die when "safe" airplanes crash. This evaluation leads to the following recommendation for a change in procedure that could facilitate and stimulate research not only on contraceptive drugs but also on other drugs in preventive medicine involving long-term administration to normal populations (note that all members of a normal population are not necessarily healthy in all respects). For such drugs, the conventional FDA approval process as it applies to ordinary medicines designed for sick people is totally inadequate in that it is not responsive to the real problems of drugs given to "healthy" people for long periods of time and to the legitimate concerns about the occurrence of rare but serious side effects. In my opinion the existing phase III clinical program for such agents should be reduced to meticulously planned, moderate-sized clinical studies of limited length (two years would be adequate in most instances) which would disclose whether a new agent had any conspicuous toxicity. Efficacy could clearly be established under such conditions. But the question of whether the drug had any low-incidence toxicity would remain. Work with oral contraceptives has taught the medical profession the important fact (well known to statisticians) that large samples are needed to demonstrate small effects reliably and that it is extremely difficult and costly to accumulate such samples in a premarketing phase.

It is at this stage that the FDA could introduce the concept of *conditional approval* of a drug, somewhat analogous to the FAA's Certificate of Provisional Airworthiness. During such use testing, the agent could be marketed, but some of the profits from sales would be used for structured follow-up studies of sizable populations consisting of the subjects put on medication. The FDA could assign a permanent monitor to coadminister such programs; this would be far superior to the present monitoring through the collection of anecdotal reports of side effects which may or may not be drug related. Under the proposed scheme—which the FDA has tried in a few other fields (e.g., Parkinson's disease) since I first proposed it in 1970, but never in contraception—one avoids the need to collect, during the phase III clinical trials, tremendous quantities of information on people who are well and reacting favorably to the drug.

Instead, attention is focused during the "provisional-approval-for-marketing" phase on the few individuals who do poorly, and it is possible to determine more quickly whether their reactions are drug related. Basically, I am saying that obvious side effects—especially if they occur in a significant number of people—can be detected quickly in relatively small numbers of people who are studied very carefully. *Rare* side effects—even though serious—are unlikely to be noted until the drug has been administered to large numbers of people, numbers that usually can be reached only after a drug is on the market. Merely delaying the time of such introduction tells us very little. I suspect that in areas such as developing fundamentally new approaches to fertility control, the slightly increased risk of such a procedure is well worth the price in terms of years saved and of unwanted births prevented.

If the drug survived a well-designed follow-up study, then it could be given full approval by the FDA, and continuing large studies financed by the sponsor would not be required. Implementation of such a recommendation could markedly speed up the time required to develop a practical contraceptive agent from my current estimate of 12-20 years to possibly half that time.

Another possibility is that a pharmaceutical company could be given the option of applying to a government agency for full financial support of the long-term toxicity studies (which could actually be performed elsewhere under contract) and of all phase II and phase III clinical work. If the research should lead to development of a commercial product, then the company would be obligated to repay the government agency on an annual royalty basis. If all of the money was repaid and the drug was still being sold commercially, it might be reasonable to expect a continued royalty payment on a reduced basis for the life of the commercial product. In other words, during the first years of such a system, funds would only be outflowing from the government agency, but after a certain period an equilibrium would be reached, and under extremely favorable circumstances the flow might even turn in favor of the government agency. Such a proposal may appear unprecedented in the drug field, but it has a striking precedent in the U.S. government's interaction with the aerospace and defense industries.

As an additional and fairly simple incentive to industry I would like to suggest a modification in the patent law that would alter the patent lifetime of drugs in the area of birth control and in other fields where very long-term premarketing investigation is required. At present the life span of a U.S. patent is 17 years. Clearly, if a pharmaceutical firm invests millions of dollars in research over a period that consumes most of the lifetime of the patent (a circumstance that may easily occur when a 10- to 15-year period of premarketing research and development is required), then a crucial incentive is removed. One possibility is to offer use-patent protection for such products for, say, 10 years, starting with the date of the *approved* NDA (New Drug Application). Such an alteration would work to everyone's benefit—it would give industry an assured period of proprietary position and yet reduce the overall lifetime of a patent, thereby reducing the length of this legal monopoly.

Encouraging participation by the pharmaceutical industry in birth control research is of direct significance only in the highly developed countries, notably the U.S., whereas the effect on lesser-developed countries is more indirect. However, there is another recommendation which, although addressed to U.S. policymakers, would make itself felt very quickly in the rest of the world. I am referring to our minimal involvement with the World Health Organization in the area of human fertility control and to means of altering this state of affairs.

The World Health Organization

Because birth control is a global problem, not a national one, I put contraceptive agents in a completely different category from any other drug. The results of effectively controlling fertility in one country but not in others eventually will be felt everywhere (for instance, does anyone really believe that the projected growth of Mexico's population from 67 million today to somewhere between 300 and 600 million in 70 years will not have an enormous impact in the U.S.?), whereas this is usually not the case with diseases controlled in one country but not in another. Therefore I would like to suggest that a completely different regulatory approval mechanism be developed for contraceptives—one that is internationally rather than nationally based. The WHO is the obvious body to perform this regulatory function because it has representatives from virtually all countries and currently sponsors a large number of clinical trials in the field of contraception in many parts of the world. (A modest precedent exists in the Codex Alimentarius, which establishes and enforces international standards on food and is operated jointly by the WHO and the United Nations Food and Agricultural Organization.) A birth control agent tested under WHO auspices would not suffer from the stigma of being developed in an affluent country (i.e., the U.S.) and then being tested and used abroad when it has not even been approved for use in the country of its origin because it is presumably too risky. I doubt whether the WHO would have much lower safety standards than those in the U.S., but it might well act faster than does the FDA. In any event, the WHO's standards would apply to all inhabitants of the globe and not just to those of one country. (Because people make individual choices about birth control, the more birth control methods we have available, the more choices are available to the person desiring contraception. A method or procedure—even though approved—if perceived to be risky in a given country or by a certain population group is unlikely to be used widely by them. Yet that is no reason to ban such an agent if it fulfills specified safety standards established by an international organization.)

Given the crucial importance of development time in the context of contraceptive research, relegating approval of new contraceptives on a worldwide scale to the WHO would be a constructive step. This recommendation is based in part on the considerable success of the ever-increasing cooperative clinical testing program under way in dozens of locations throughout the world under WHO auspices (see Table 8-1). Simultaneous international testing of a new contraceptive approach is desirable not only on ethical and moral grounds but also on scientific ones, because at an early stage in the epidemiological studies one can incorporate geographical, racial, nutritional, and other health parameters that would be very difficult to study otherwise or that would prolong the studies. Considering how much money our government is spending annually in the birth control field (see Table 5-4), one would think that the U.S. would be a major contributor to the WHO program in this field. Nothing could be further from the truth. Until 1978 we not only had not contributed any funds, but scientists in the U.S. had received more money for research in the birth control field *from* the WHO than had scientists in any other country in the world. The total budget of the WHO for birth control research in 1978 was on the order of $16 million. In 1977 and 1978 the United States was indirectly the largest recipient (10-12 percent) of that money, yet the United States was the only major Western country that had not participated in this program financially.

In late 1978 the U.S. considered for the first time contributing funds to the WHO birth control program, but as of mid 1979 nothing had progressed beyond the talking stage. I find this situation shocking because the program is designed to develop *new* contraceptive agents, particularly for the Third World, and is funded largely by Western European countries. Congress should do something about this—at the very least appropriate a sum of money back to the WHO that is directly or indirectly spent by that organization in the U.S. We should support this WHO program annually on a generous scale, not by withholding funds from other U.S.-sponsored efforts, such as those of the Agency for International Development (AID) or the National Institutes of Health, but by incrementally increasing our contributions to WHO (e.g., on the order of the annual equivalent of one fourth of the cost of a single sophisticated fighter plane).

Prognosis for the Future

What is the likelihood of some or all of these recommendations being implemented? I suspect that it is minimal. The American consumer today is unlikely to approve of the most expeditious ways to encourage new research in practical birth control: taking more risks in clinical research, giving up some national regulatory function to an international body, offering incentives to the pharmaceutical industry to encourage it to become more actively involved in fertility control development. Barbara Seaman's comment at the March 9, 1978, hearings of the House Select Committee on Population, though somewhat strong, is probably not atypical: "If you are considering giving any more tax rebates or any extra tax help to the drug companies, I'm going to stop paying my taxes, that's what I mean. To me it's as bad as funding the Viet Nam War." To me the entire scenario seems déjà vu. I made many of these suggestions in 1970, together with a rather dismal prognosis for the development of new contraceptive agents during the coming 15 years if none of the steps were implemented. Have Americans become more globally oriented in the intervening years? I have no reason to believe so. Our myopia is not confined to the birth control field; we approach energy problems with the same ostrich-like stance.

Wallace Stevens, the great American poet and incidentally an employee and later vice-president of the Hartford Accident and Indemnity Company for nearly 40 years, wrote in "The Pure Good of Theory":

> It is time that beats in the breast and it is time
> That batters against the mind, silent and proud,
> The mind that knows it is destroyed by time.

In birth control, time is *the* most expensive commodity. Every day 350,000 babies are born in this world but only 200,000 persons die. Yet we act as if we had an unlimited amount of time. We do not, which is why I have written this book.

Incense burner. Mayan, classic, *ca.* A.D. 700–900.

The Chemical History of the Pill

> *Most of us choose birth control—and immediately find our-*
> *selves confronted by a problem that is simultaneously a puzzle*
> *in physiology, pharmacology, sociology, psychology and even*
> *theology. "The Pill" has not yet been invented.*
>   Aldous Huxley, *Brave New World Revisited*, 1958

WITHIN TWO YEARS OF THE TIME that Aldous Huxley hypothesized about a pill to be used in birth control, "the Pill" was introduced into medicine. Just as relatively few persons know the origin of the coinage of the term *the Pill*, few laymen know the history of the active ingredient that made Huxley's Pill a reality.

Actually there is no such thing as *a* history of *the* Pill. First, there were two Pills and second, pieces of the history are missing as not all of the participants in this scientific development have told their story. Many of the journalistic accounts have been unmitigated hack jobs—with Paul Vaughn's *The Pill on Trial* (1970) being a notable exception. What follows is my attempt to tell one part of the story of the very beginning of the Pill—its chemical development—the part with which I was associated personally.

The biological and clinical work leading to the development of steroid oral contraceptives has been ably summarized by one of the key actors in the oral contraceptive drama, the late Gregory Pincus, formerly scientific director of the Worcester Foundation for Experimental Biology and a long-time scientific consultant to G.D. Searle & Company, the Chicago-based pharmaceutical firm that first marketed an oral contraceptive. However, in Pincus's magnum opus, *The Control of Fertility,* written in 1965, there cannot be found a single reference to any chemist or to how the steroid chemical contained in the Pill actually arrived in his laboratory—to me, a psychologically intriguing omission. The active chemical ingredient of the Pill did not occur in nature, nor was it bought in a drugstore. How did Pincus get it?

By definition, every synthetic drug must originate in a chemist's laboratory. However, what happens to this chemical entity after it has been synthesized—how it ultimately becomes a drug that reaches the consumer—depends very much on circumstances. For instance, frequently a substance is synthesized in connection with some specific chemical problem and as an afterthought, sometimes even years later, is then submitted for wide pharmacological screening in the hope that some biological activity will be noted as an extra bonus. (For example, the insecticidal activity of DDT was discovered through such biological screening decades after the substance was first synthesized in a German university laboratory for a totally different purpose.) Alternatively, a given substance may be synthesized for a specific biological purpose, found to be inactive in that regard, and then exposed to wider, random pharmacological scrutiny in the hope that something useful might be salvaged from an apparently unsuccessful piece of research. The literature of medicinal chemistry is replete with accounts of instances where such accidental screening uncovered unexpected biological activity that provided the necessary impetus for further chemical, pharmacological, and clinical work.

It is hardly surprising that the modern medicinal chemist is unhappy with this state of affairs, as predictability rather than serendipity is the leitmotif of science in general, and of chemistry in particular. Since the early part of this century, beginning with Paul Ehrlich, the founder of modern chemotherapy, the chemist has attempted to establish relationships between chemical structure and biological activity that would lead to the *a priori* prediction of a potentially useful drug. The development of steroid oral contraceptives represents a telling example of this approach; it was one of the few instances in medicinal chemistry where chemists deliberately set out to synthesize a substance with a given biological endpoint—in this instance, to mimic the biological action of the female sex hormone progesterone when administered orally (progesterone itself is essentially inactive by this route unless given in huge doses)—and succeeded. Thus, a complete history of the Pill must start with its chemical history—the portion skipped so completely and surprisingly in Pincus's *The Control of Fertility*—and to do this one needs to talk steroid chemistry.

Steroid Chemistry: A Primer for the Nonchemist

The term *steroid* is derived from the Greek, meaning "like a sterol." Sterols, in turn, are certain solid alcohols that occur widely in plants and animals—the best known being cholesterol, which is the most abundant sterol in man and other vertebrates. The term steroid has no biological implication; it is based on a purely chemical definition. All steroids (and all sterols) are substances based on the chemical skeleton pictured in Fig. 1, which has the formidable generic name perhydrocyclopentanophenanthrene.

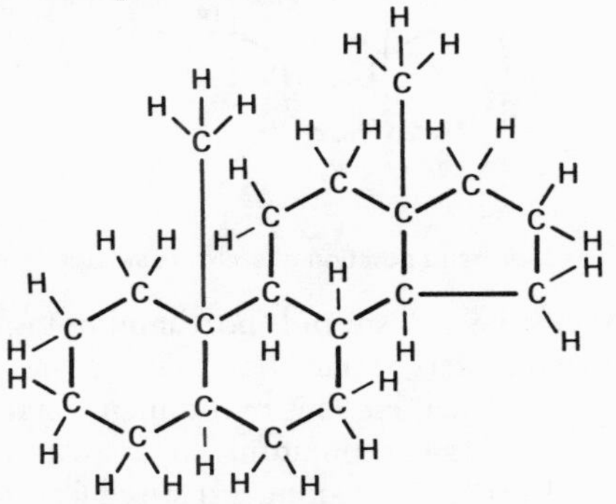

FIG. 1
Steroid skeleton

Steroid chemistry is very complicated for chemists because of its extraordinary subtlety—there are thousands upon thousands of synthetic and hundreds of natural compounds based on that simple steroid skeleton that differ only by some very minor variations in their chemical structure. However, such variation not only alters the chemical properties of the molecule, but, as will be shown below, also can produce dramatically different biological results. To oversimplify, it is like having to write the entire Bible with a very limited alphabet, which complicates life for the writer and biblical scholar but not for the general reader.

The steroid skeleton as drawn in Fig. 1 consists solely of carbon and hydrogen atoms. Such a picture is extraordinarily cumbersome, so steroid chemists use a chemical shorthand in which the symbols for carbon (C) and hydrogen (H) are dropped, and the fact that carbon is tetravalent (i.e., four bonds are connected to each carbon) is taken for granted.

This shorthand representation is shown in Fig. 2. All that the nonchemist need remember is that *by definition* all steroids must possess this skeleton, which consists of three six-membered rings and one five-membered ring. In this shorthand notation each corner of the rings is assumed to be a carbon atom and the valence of each carbon is assumed to be satisfied by hydrogen atoms, which are not written. The carbon atoms are numbered from 1 to 19, with atoms 18 and 19 being not part of a ring but rather attached as methyl groups (CH_3 in Fig. 1); the rings are identified by the letters A, B, C, and D.

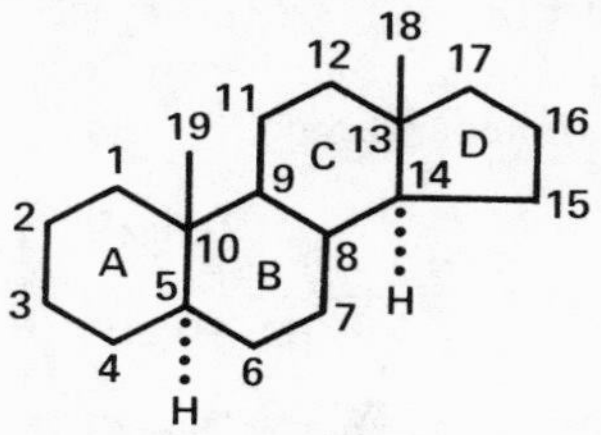

FIG. 2
Shorthand notation of steroid skeleton

The only other aspect of steroid shorthand notation that need be mentioned concerns stereochemistry, that is, the position of the atoms in space. As drawn, Fig. 2 is two-dimensional, but in fact one should visualize the ring carbon atoms to be located in the plane of the paper and all other connecting substituents (for instance, the hydrogen atoms) projecting either above or below the plane of the paper. Usually this planar location is indicated only for those atoms to which one wants to call attention: the conventional shorthand notation employs a solid line (also called β) for bonds above the plane (e.g., carbon atoms 18 and 19 in Fig. 2) and a dotted line (also called α) for substituents below the plane of the paper (e.g., hydrogen atoms attached to positions 5 and 14 in Fig. 2).

Many of the most important biologically active molecules in nature are based on this steroid skeleton. Examples are the male and female sex hormones, bile acids, vitamin D, the cardiac-active constituents of digitalis, and the adrenal cortical hormones (related to cortisone and usually referred to generically as corticosteroids). The wide variations in the biological activity of steroids (e.g., why one steroid is responsible for male secondary sexual characteristics and another for female secondary sexual characteristics) are associated with the introduction of a third atom, oxygen (O), located in special positions of the steroid skeleton. To return to the Bible analogy, nature has written the entire steroid bible with only a three-letter alphabet (C, H, and O), the location of O being used predominantly to express the type of biological activity. Examples of such variations in oxygen-containing steroids follow and, to make reading easier, those portions of the structural formulae to which I wish to call attention are printed in bold.

For instance, the only chemical difference between testosterone (Fig. 3), the male sex hormone, and progesterone (Fig. 4), one of the two female sex hormones, is the nature of the oxygen-containing substituent at position 17. On the other hand, the second female sex hormone, estradiol (Fig. 5), and the other steroid estrogens are unique among steroids in that their ring A is a *benzene* ring, otherwise known as an aromatic ring, which consists of three alternating double bonds contained in a six-membered ring. In order to incorporate such a benzene (aromatic) ring into ring A of the steroid skeleton (Fig. 1) and still retain the tetravalent character of carbon, no additional substituent can be attached to position 10. Therefore the estrogens (Fig. 5) lack carbon atom 19, attached to position 10 of testosterone (Fig. 3) or of progesterone (Fig. 4), because these two steroids have a "nonaromatic" ring A.

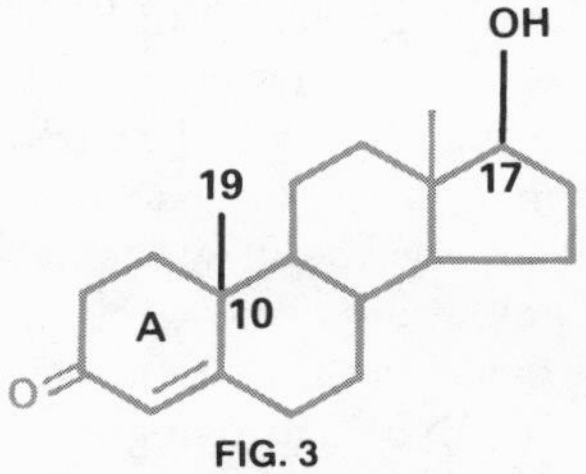

FIG. 3
Testosterone
(male sex hormone)

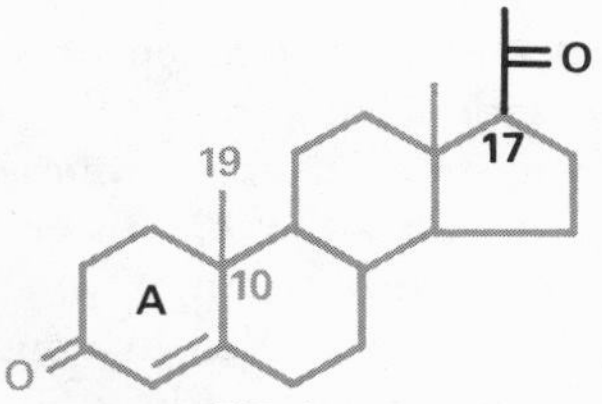

FIG. 4
Progesterone
(female progestational hormone)

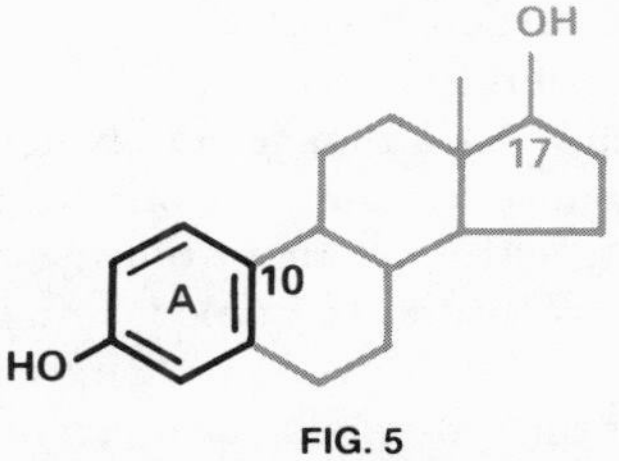

FIG. 5
Estradiol (female estrogenic hormone)

As the reader will see, these chemical symbols are by no means as formidable as they may look at first glance. Though the rest of the story can be read without paying attention to these figures, in doing so the important nuances of the chemical history of the Pill and of other steroids would be missed. It would be like reading a book on art history without looking at a single illustration! Thus, having ended my primer for the chemical virgin, I will proceed with my story.

Mexico: A Steroid Chemist's Paradise

In the spring of 1949 I was a 25-year-old chemist, four years out of graduate school, who had been working as a research chemist in New Jersey at the American branch of the Swiss pharmaceutical company Ciba. I was getting impatient with the comfortable industrial setting and was anxious for an academic job. I had no luck. In fact, I still remember the rather brusque way in which I was turned down by Iowa State College when I applied for a faculty opening. I thought I was rather good. I had finished my Ph.D. at the University of Wisconsin shortly before my twenty-second birthday with a thesis on a very difficult problem in the steroid field—namely, the chemical conversion of the male sex hormone testosterone (Fig. 3) into the estrogenic hormone estradiol (Fig. 5). At Ciba I had worked on various aspects of medicinal chemistry, was a codiscoverer of one of the first antihistamine drugs (Pyribenzamine), and had also published a number of papers on steroid chemistry.

Sensational news about the beneficial effects of the adrenal steroid cortisone in the treatment of rheumatoid arthritis had appeared only a few months earlier. Cortisone was hailed as an apparent "cure" for one of the most common of crippling diseases and as a discovery that, to many, rivaled in importance the successful treatment of infectious diseases with antibiotics. Not surprisingly, I was very anxious to try my luck in that area of steroid chemistry. Unfortunately, the powers that be at Ciba did not agree, because all work dealing with adrenal corticosteroids was carried out at that time at Ciba's Swiss headquarters in Basel.

In short, I was ready for a change, and when the telephone rang that spring and a chemist acquaintance of mine asked me whether I would consider an attractive job offer from a company called Syntex in Mexico City, I did not hang up immediately.

Under ordinary circumstances doing chemistry in Mexico seemed preposterous at that time; "serious" chemistry supposedly stopped north of the Rio Grande. This assumption was based not just on

Yankee arrogance but also on the fact that practically no significant chemical publications emanated from Latin American laboratories. However, the invitation was very open and tempting: "Just come to Mexico City to visit us with all expenses paid." Since I had never been to Mexico nor ever heard of Syntex, I was curious. I went, but to be honest, I did so primarily with a tourist's motives and did not really expect to find acceptable working conditions. A couple of days in beautiful Mexico City (at that time smog-free and relatively un-crowded) and especially my conversation with Dr. George Rosen-kranz, the 32-year-old vice-president and technical director of Syn-tex, were persuasive.

Rosenkranz, a first-class steroid chemist of Hungarian descent, basically made me an offer that I could not refuse. Specifically, he asked me—who had always worked alone or with one or two technicians in the laboratory—to head a research group that would attempt a practical synthesis of cortisone as well as work on other aspects of steroid chemistry that interested me—and to do this in surprisingly well-equipped laboratories. These research opportuni-ties and the likelihood that I would learn another language appealed to me. Nevertheless, when I returned to the United States and told my friends at the University of Wisconsin and Harvard of the reasons for my decision, they thought that I could not possibly be serious.

I must now turn to major chemical breakthroughs in steroid chemistry in the 1930s and 1940s in order to explain why this company, Syntex, had been established in Mexico to do steroid chemistry and was now about to embark on a project that, according to *Fortune* magazine in 1951, created "the biggest technological boom ever heard south of the border."

In the context of steroid chemistry, the 1930s could be called the decade of the sex hormones. The structure of the steroid skeleton was not elucidated until 1932, when the German chemist Heinrich Wieland demonstrated that the most common sterol in the animal kingdom, cholesterol, possessed the structure shown in Fig. 6. Within a few years, chemists in Germany (Karl Slotta and Adolf Butenandt), Switzerland (Leopold Ruzicka and Tadeus Reichstein), and the United States (Edward Doisy, Edward Kendall, and Oskar Wintersteiner) demonstrated that the sex hormones testosterone (Fig. 3), progesterone (Fig. 4), and estradiol (Fig. 5), and the adrenal hormone cortisone (Fig. 7) all were based on the steroid nucleus (Fig. 1). Although the work in the United States was carried out exclu-sively in academic environments, the European studies involved an intimate collaboration between industry and universities. And it was the European pharmaceutical companies—notably Ciba in Switzerland, Schering in Germany, and Organon in Holland—that introduced the sex hormones into medical practice in the late 1930s, primarily for replacement therapy in patients suffering from some type of hormone deficiency.

Chemists at these companies were able to synthesize testosterone (Fig. 3) and progesterone (Fig. 4) by laborious processes from cholesterol (Fig. 6)—the main difficulty being the transformation of the 8-carbon side chain of cholesterol attached at position 17 into the oxygen-containing side chains of testosterone and progesterone. Estradiol, the third hormone that had been introduced into medicine by that time, was not synthesized from cholesterol but rather was isolated from the urine of pregnant mares; at that time it was not known how to generate chemically the aromatic ring A of estradiol (Fig. 5) from the nonaromatic ring A of the standard steroids such as cholesterol (Fig. 6). The meager yields from the laborious chemical conversion of cholesterol to the sex hormones testosterone and progesterone and the cumbersome nature of the isolation of minute amounts of the estrogen estradiol from thousands of gallons of pregnant mares' urine explain why these hormones, though used in medicine, were very expensive to produce.

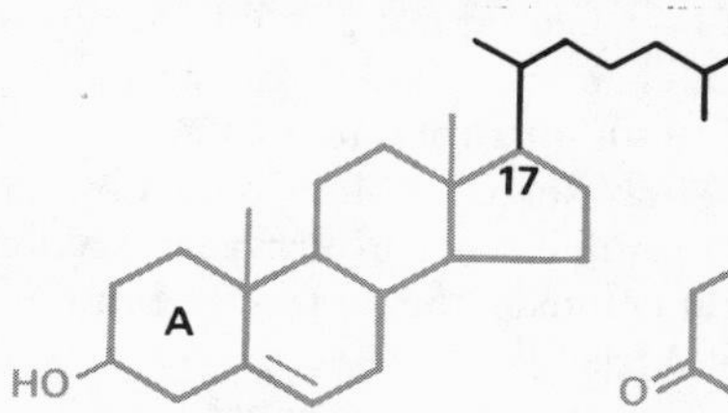

FIG. 6
Cholesterol

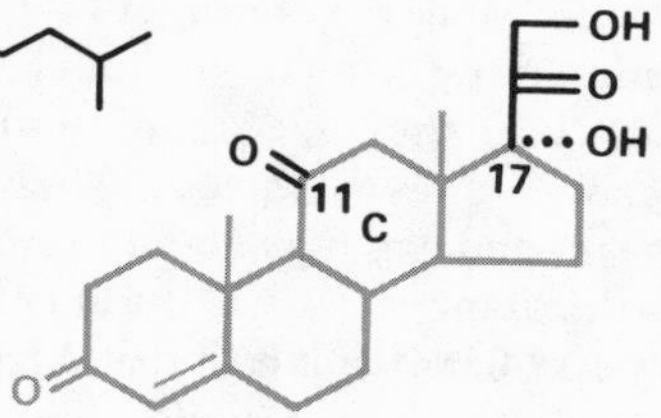

FIG. 7
Cortisone

All these limitations in steroid production changed during the 1940s, which could be called the decade of the cortical hormones or, even more appropriately, the decade of Mexican jungle chemistry. In the late 1930s and very early 1940s Russell E. Marker, a brilliant but unorthodox professor of chemistry at Pennsylvania State University, conducted research on a group of steroids called *sapogenins,* compounds of plant origin that bear their name because of the soaplike quality of their aqueous suspensions. In fact, natives of Mexico and Central America, where sapogenin-containing plants occur wildly and in abundance, had used substances derived from these plants as soap substitutes for doing laundry and to kill fish (the water-soluble forms of sapogenins, called saponins, are toxic). Chemically, the unusual feature of the sapogenins is the additional two rings (marked E and F in Fig. 8) attached to positions 16 and 17 of the standard steroid ring skeleton.

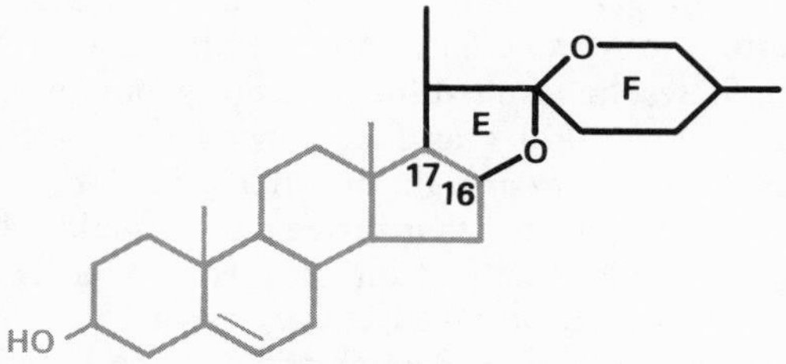

FIG. 8
Diosgenin (from Mexican yams)

Marker concentrated particularly on the chemistry of a sapogenin called *diosgenin* (Fig. 8), which has exactly the same steroid nucleus as cholesterol (Fig. 6) but a different side chain. Through a brilliant series of investigations, Marker discovered an exceedingly simple process whereby the two complex E and F rings (from our standpoint, molecular garbage) could be degraded very simply to a substance that was then easily transformed chemically into the sex hormone progesterone (Fig. 4).

More stories—many of them apocryphal ones—have been told about Marker's life during the 1930s and 1940s than about almost any other chemist. I met with Marker in October 1979 and among the true stories, he said, is that he never received his Ph.D. degree from the University of Maryland, in spite of an excellent doctoral thesis, because he was unwilling to take a required course in physical chemistry, which bored him. He ignored his professor's warning that without a doctoral degree he "would end up as a urine analyst" and in 1935, after a short stint in industry and six years at the Rockefeller Institute, he accepted an $1,800 research fellowship at Pennsylvania State University because it permitted him to carry out independent research in the newly blossoming field of steroid chemistry.

Marker was not only a maverick, he was also an entrepreneur. He discovered that diosgenin was particularly abundant in certain types of yams that grow wildly in Mexico, and he urged the American pharmaceutical company Parke-Davis, which had supported his research at Pennsylvania State University, to capitalize upon his discovery through the industrial manufacture of progesterone from diosgenin. Parke-Davis was interested neither in Marker's proposal nor even in bothering to take out patents in Mexico to protect his discoveries. Not one to be thwarted by industrial shortsightedness, Marker went to Mexico on his own to collect 10 tons of plant material, which he then extracted in a rented laboratory in Mexico City. After returning with the syrupy extract to the States, he isolated the pure diosgenin and eventually transformed it into 3,000 grams of progesterone—at that time worth nearly $80 per gram—in the industrial laboratory of a friend. Having demonstrated that progesterone could be prepared easily on a relatively large scale from diosgenin, Marker sought to establish a production facility in Mexico, closer to the site of the plant raw material. Looking through the Mexico City telephone directory under the heading "Laboratorios," he noticed the name "Laboratorios Hormona." Drs. Emeric Somlo and Federico Lehmann, the two owners of Hormona, hardly believed Marker's claim to have synthesized so much of the precious hormone from yam-derived diosgenin in so short a period, but after his delivery of 2 kg. of progesterone to Hormona's office in New York City, Syntex (from *Syn*thesis and *Mex*ico) was formed as a production company on January 21, 1944, on the premises of Laboratorios Hormona, with Marker retaining a 40 percent ownership of the new company.

Within a year, the partners had a major disagreement and Marker left the company, taking his know-how with him. However, early in his academic career, he had published a scientific description of his chemical processes in the *Journal of the American Chemical Society,* and since no one had taken out patents in Mexico for his discoveries, the commercial production of progesterone from diosgenin in that country was up for grabs. (Four years later Marker quit chemistry abruptly and totally, dedicating himself for the next 30 years to commissioning Mexican-made replicas of antique European silver works. His last scientific publication, in 1949, in the *Journal of the American Chemical Society,* had the unique distinction of not listing a laboratory address but simply the notation "Hotel Geneve, Mexico City." Marker is now 79. No public recognition was given to this remarkable chemist until 1969 when the Mexican Chemical Society presented him with a special award [in the form of a silver tray] at an international steroid symposium in Mexico City. His discovery of steroid sapogenins as a starting material for hormone synthesis should have resulted in a flood of honors such as election to academies, honorary degrees, and awards. I have the feeling, somehow, that Marker is less bothered by this than I am.)

The pharmaceutical giants apparently did not recognize the importance of Marker's work. Parke-Davis had already missed the boat, and the European hormone cartel consisting of Ciba, Organon, and Schering apparently had not paid any attention to Marker's discoveries—perhaps owing to the disruption of the war.

In any event, Somlo and Lehmann, looking for another chemist who could reestablish the manufacture of progesterone from diosgenin at Syntex, met Dr. George Rosenkranz in Havana and recruited him to the firm. Rosenkranz had immigrated to Cuba a few years earlier from Switzerland, where he had received his Ph.D. degree under Leopold Ruzicka, one of the giants of early steroid chemistry. Rosenkranz's thesis had dealt with another group of sapogenins, not related to the steroids, but he was well acquainted with Marker's work. Within two years Rosenkranz had not only reinstituted the large-scale manufacture of progesterone from diosgenin but, even more importantly, also achieved the commercial synthesis of the male sex hormone testosterone from these same Mexican yams. Both syntheses were so much simpler than the traditional methods involving cholesterol—used by the European pharmaceutical companies —that in a short while tiny Syntex broke the international hormone cartel. This resulted in both considerable lowering of prices and greatly increased availability of these hormones.

At that time Syntex served only as a supplier to other pharmaceutical companies throughout the world, which purchased the steroid hormones from Syntex and then packaged them in their own formulations under their own labels—exactly the opposite of the usual process in which a pharmaceutical firm in a lesser-developed country imports the active ingredients for its medicinal products from the U.S. or Europe and simply reformulates them. Consequently, few people outside the pharmaceutical industry even knew of the existence of this small chemical manufacturing operation in Mexico City, which soon was to revolutionize steroid chemistry and the steroid industry all over the world. Needless to say, in the late 1940s little love was lost between the major international pharmaceutical giants and the small Mexican upstart, Syntex.

Cortisone in Mexico

Independently of these steroid developments in Mexico, whose worldwide impact was not felt until the 1950s (when over 50 percent of the world's supply of steroids was produced in Mexico from the yam-derived diosgenin starting material), a second event occurred in the 1940s which changed the entire historical course of steroid chemistry and medicine.

Although the structure of the adrenal hormone cortisone had been elucidated in the late 1930s by the Swiss chemist Tadeus Reichstein, cortisone had not been used in medicine—in part because of the extraordinary difficulty in synthesizing this hormone, which differs from all of the other steroids discussed so far in that it has an oxygen atom in ring C at position 11 in addition to a rather complicated oxygenated side chain at position 17 (Fig. 7). During World War II rumors had spread that German aviators were given cortisone for increased resistance to stress which supposedly enabled them to fly at altitudes above 40,000 feet. Though this rumor subsequently proved to be false, it was responsible for a substantial effort in the United States to achieve a chemical synthesis of this rare adrenal hormone, and it eventually stimulated major American pharmaceutical companies—Merck, Upjohn, Lederle, and Squibb—to enter the steroid field.

Through an amazing tour de force, Lewis H. Sarett, a young American chemist working for Merck, in 1944 accomplished the first synthesis of cortisone from deoxycholic acid, which was derived from cattle bile purchased from slaughterhouses. Sarett chose a bile acid as the starting material because it is one of the few naturally occurring steroids that bears an oxygen atom in ring C (Fig. 9). Although its oxygen atom is not at position 11, where it is required for cortisone (Fig. 7), Sarett worked out a procedure for moving the oxygen atom from position 12 in the bile acid to position 11. He was able to introduce the other structural features of cortisone, notably the highly oxygenated side chain at position 17, by procedures that had been developed earlier in other laboratories.

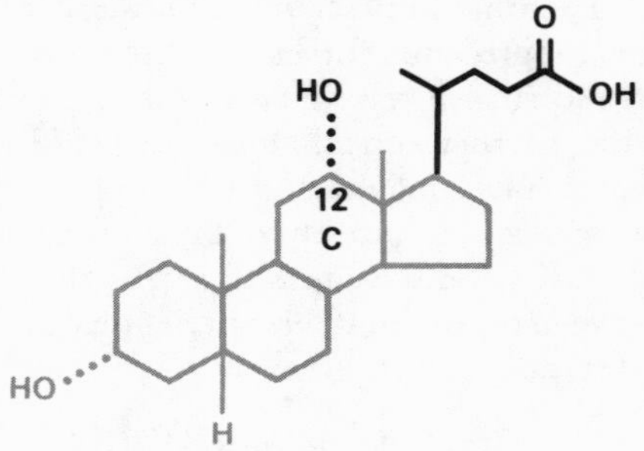

FIG. 9
Deoxycholic acid (from cattle bile)

Cortisone synthesized by Sarett at Merck was first used at the Mayo Clinic by Drs. Philip S. Hench and Edward C. Kendall, who announced in early 1949 that cortisone had apparently miraculous effects in the treatment of rheumatoid arthritis. This discovery won

Hench, Kendall, and Reichstein (who had established the structure of cortisone in the late 1930s) a Nobel Prize. The therapeutic effectiveness of cortisone in rheumatoid arthritis hit the pharmaceutical industry and indeed the whole lay public like a bombshell. Newspaper articles featured crippled arthritics who were able to dance within a few days or weeks after cortisone therapy. Cortisone was hailed as a new miracle drug, which the pharmaceutical companies saw as a potential bonanza (to be used by millions of patients) and the public saw as a reaffirmation of its faith in the magic of modern medicine (as usual, the serious side effects of this potent drug became apparent only after several years of extensive use). The race was on to develop a better and cheaper method of synthesizing cortisone than the extraordinarily laborious 36-step sequence originally worked out by Sarett from bile acids.

This was the state of the art when I received the offer from Syntex in the spring of 1949 to launch a chemical research program to develop a synthesis of cortisone from the abundant yam-derived plant steroid diosgenin (Fig. 8), which was already the starting material for all progesterone and testosterone manufactured by Syntex. It was through the initial sales of these hormones (probably on the order of $3 to $5 million per year) that the owners of Syntex felt they could afford a research effort in the cortisone field. I was convinced that the best route to an academic job, which until then had eluded me, was to establish a scientific reputation in the literature, and even though my friends thought me mad for trying to do this in Mexico, I felt intuitively that this was the right place. After all, the goal—a new and more productive synthesis of cortisone from a plant raw material—was one of the hottest scientific topics in organic chemistry at that time.

Both Syntex and I had a common objective: to establish a scientific reputation. I was young and willing to gamble on a few years in Mexico—partly because living in another country appealed to me and also because I felt that any scientific achievement from a laboratory in Mexico was likely, upon publication, to make a much bigger impression on academia than one coming from the usual laboratories in North America or Europe.

Consequently, I really had only one requirement before I accepted the Syntex job offer and that was the opportunity to publish any scientific discoveries promptly in the chemical journals. Syntex agreed to this and stuck to its bargain, and I certainly had my own personal incentive to make good on it. From my previous industrial experience I fully understood that discoveries had to be patented by the firm in whose laboratory the work was performed before they were written up for publication. However, instead of having patent attorneys run the show in terms of deciding if and when to publish, we operated in the reverse manner at Syntex. Here the chemists told the patent attorneys, only half jokingly, "You better patent quickly or we'll publish anyway."

This was extraordinarily unusual for a pharmaceutical company. As a result of this policy, during my first two years at Syntex we published more rapidly in the chemical literature than did any other pharmaceutical company, or possibly even many university laboratories. Thus, long before Syntex sold any drugs under its own name in the open market in order to become known to the medical profession, its international scientific reputation in chemistry was well established. (Syntex's extraordinarily liberal publication policy had an important effect upon its much larger competitors, such as Upjohn, Merck, and Pfizer in the U.S., and their European counterparts. Since other steroid chemists did not want to be scooped, they were equally interested in publishing quickly, which they did.) In 1959, Professor Louis F. Fieser of Harvard University, the author of the most famous book in the steroid field, reported at an international steroid conference about his analysis of the origin of the references in the latest (1959) edition of his book *Steroids*. He had broken down the several thousand references by origin into those from academia and those from industry and then had analyzed them even further by institutional origin. Even though the survey was made only about nine years after the founding of Syntex's research department, he pointed out that no other laboratory in the world—academic or industrial—had published as much in the steroid field during that period as had Syntex. Chemistry south of the Rio Grande had finally made the grade in the international arena.

To return to cortisone and late 1949, the race to synthesize this rare hormone from a source more readily available than bile acids was international: it included two teams from Harvard, one from Oxford, one from the Federal Institute of Technology in Zurich, and groups from various pharmaceutical companies (Merck being one of the key ones). The race was won by our group at Syntex—won in the sense of first publication in the *Journal of the American Chemical Society* in 1951 announcing that we had succeeded in completing the laboratory synthesis of cortisone from yam-derived diosgenin. A few months later, we reported a second synthesis of cortisone, this time starting with another steroid sapogenin, hecogenin, which was available from the waste products of Mexican sisal production (in the late 1950s the British firm Glaxo used this process under license from Syntex for the industrial synthesis of cortisone from East African sisal).

Our synthesis of cortisone from a plant raw material, rather than from animal-derived bile, not only made scientific headlines but even resulted in articles in *Fortune* and *Life;* the latter showed us in a silly picture posed around a bare conference table supporting a huge Mexican yam from which we supposedly made cortisone. George Rosenkranz, the only person in that group over the age of 28, is holding a test tube of cortisone (my vague recollection is that the tube was filled with salt since we had only made a minute quantity of cortisone at that time), and we seem to be mesmerized by this huge and somewhat ominous-looking yam.

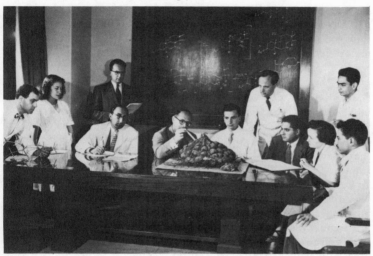

In the end, although this was one of the key events that put Syntex on the international steroid map, our achievement proved to be purely a scientific one. It had no direct commercial consequence because within months of our chemical discovery, a group at the Upjohn Company reported an extraordinarily innovative way of solving the most difficult aspect of the synthesis of cortisone, namely, the introduction of the oxygen atom into position 11 (Fig. 7). They accomplished this difficult feat by introducing microbiological fermentation technology into the steroid field—the first time this had been done industrially—through exposure of the female sex hormone progesterone (Fig. 4) to certain microorganisms, which specifically introduced an oxygen atom into position 11 in high yield in one single operation. (A key factor in this work was the use of a very sensitive method, called paper chromatography, for the separation and detection of trace quantities of steroids. The application of this technique in the steroid field was pioneered by Dr. Alejandro Zaffaroni, an Uruguayan biochemist from the University of Rochester, who was later to play an important role in the commercialization of Syntex's oral contraceptive.)

Ironically, the Upjohn discovery of a simplified means of cortisone synthesis had an enormous commercial impact on Syntex because in order to exploit its fermentation procedure industrially, Upjohn suddenly needed tonnage quantities of progesterone—amounts that were totally unheard of prior to that time. In 1951, Syntex was the only company in the world that had the technology to synthesize progesterone on that scale from yam-derived diosgenin, and Syntex thus suddenly found itself to be the key supplier of the new raw material for cortisone synthesis.

The Chemical Origin of the Pill

In addition to providing a challenging chemical problem, my move to Mexico City had another attractive component. For the first time in my career I had ample laboratory manpower at my disposal, even though most of it consisted of locally trained technicians rather than professionals. This enabled me, together with George Rosenkranz, to institute other projects in the steroid field in addition to concentrating on a new means of cortisone synthesis. For instance, I was able to pursue my first love in the steroid field, namely, the possible chemical production of the estrogenic hormones from the much more readily available male sex hormone testosterone (which had been the chief topic of my Ph.D. dissertation). As I mentioned earlier, in contrast to the sex hormones testosterone and progesterone, which were synthesized in the 1930s from cholesterol, the third sex hormone used in medicine, estradiol, was derived from pregnant mares' urine because of the great difficulty in synthesizing it chemically from a more readily available steroid.

At the start of World War II, a group at Schering in Germany had discovered a chemical method to accomplish this goal, and Syntex was clearly interested in having an alternative procedure at its disposal. One of our first publications in 1950, in fact, dealt with an innovative solution to the problem of the chemical synthesis of the estrogenic hormones from the more readily available testosterone. In the technical jargon, what we had accomplished was the *aromatization* of ring A of testosterone (Fig. 3) into the *aromatic* benzene ring A of estradiol (Fig. 5)—that is, we discovered a way of selectively expelling the methyl group (carbon number 19) attached at position 10 of testosterone, which was nature's barrier to the simple transformation of its ring A into a benzene ring. As will become apparent shortly, this discovery led chemically almost directly to the Pill.

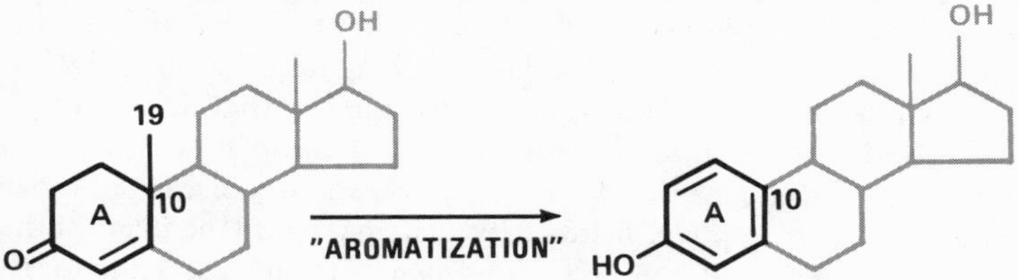

FIG. 3
Testosterone
(male sex hormone)

FIG. 5
Estradiol
(female estrogenic hormone)

At the beginning of this chapter I indicated that when a chemist attempts to synthesize a biologically active compound, he often tries to predict what its biological modes of action might be; at times these predictions are correct and at others they are not. I now provide an example of the latter. We decided to apply our recently discovered aromatization procedure by removing the carbon number 19 substituent attached to position 10 of progesterone (Fig. 4), thus synthesizing a hybrid molecule (Fig. 10) that possessed the aromatic ring A characteristic of estradiol (Fig. 5) as well as a side chain at position 17 typical of progesterone.

Our naive hope was that this chemical Siamese twin (Fig. 10) might exhibit biological properties of both progesterone and estradiol; as it turned out, this synthetic hybrid was devoid of any interesting biological activity whatsoever. Nevertheless, this investigation, which appeared to be a dead end, proved to be the key to all subsequent chemical work leading to the development of an orally active ovulation inhibitor.

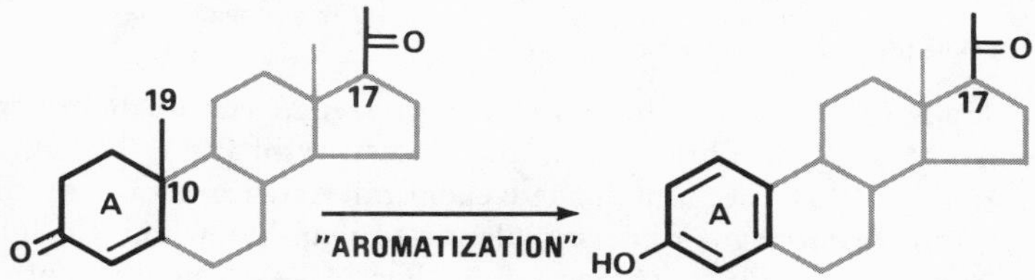

FIG. 4
Progesterone
(female progestational hormone)

FIG. 10
Synthetic hybrid of
progesterone and estradiol

By 1950, the multiple biological functions of the female sex hormone progesterone were well known; among them, maintenance during pregnancy of the proper uterine environment for the development of the fetus and inhibition of further ovulation during pregnancy. Accordingly, progesterone was sometimes referred to as "nature's contraceptive," and some suggestions had appeared in the literature in the preceding two decades—notably by the Austrian endocrinologist Ludwig Haberlandt—that progesterone might be useful in fertility control. Were it not for the fact that, in order to be orally active, progesterone needs to be given in enormous quantities, it is quite conceivable that it might have found practical application as an oral contraceptive. Instead, its principal use in medicine at that time was for the treatment of various menstrual disorders and for the prevention of certain types of miscarriage.

Until the middle 1940s it had been assumed that progesterone's biological activity was extremely specific and was limited to progesterone itself (now rewritten as Fig. 11 in order to emphasize that the hydrogen attached to position 14 is behind the plane of the paper) and some analogs that had an additional carbon-carbon bond between the 6-7 or 11-12 positions. The belief in this extreme structure specificity of progesterone was supported by the observation by a Swiss group that even so close a relative as 17-isoprogesterone (Fig. 12), which differs from the parent hormone progesterone (Fig. 11) in stereochemical detail at only one center (position 17), exhibits no noticeable progestational activity.

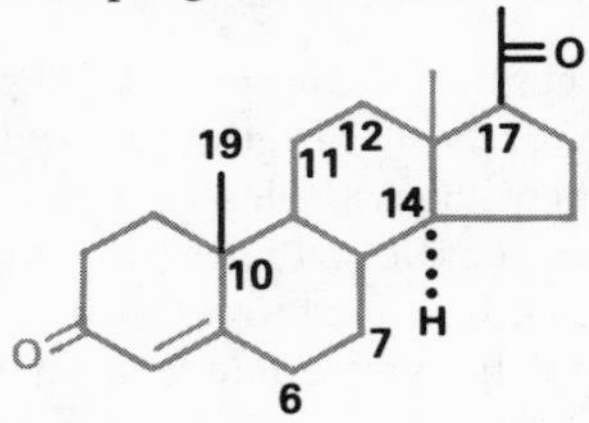

FIG. 11
Progesterone
(female progestational hormone)

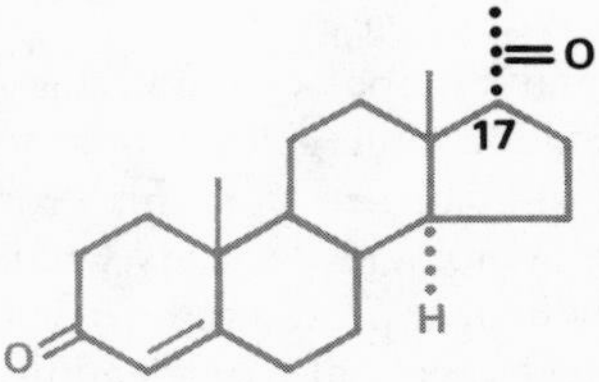

FIG. 12
17-Isoprogesterone

It was for this reason that I was so impressed as a graduate student when Maximilian Ehrenstein at the University of Pennsylvania reported in 1944 the complicated chemical transformation of the naturally occurring cardiac stimulant strophanthidin (Fig. 13) into an oily mixture of 19-norprogesterone (Fig. 14)—so called because it lacked the methyl carbon atom number 19 ("nor" meaning "less"). Ehrenstein's substance differed from the natural hormone progesterone (Fig. 11) in three important respects:

1. The synthetic steroid (Fig. 14) had the *wrong* orientation at

position 17. In other words, the substituent at that position was behind the plane of the paper (dotted line or "α") rather than above it (solid line or "β") as in progesterone (Fig. 11).

2. It had the *wrong* orientation at position 14: the hydrogen atom in Ehrenstein's substance is above the plane of the paper (solid line) whereas in the natural hormone progesterone the hydrogen atom is below the plane (dotted line).

3. Most importantly, there was a *structural* difference in that the carbon atom number 19 attached to position 10 in the natural hormone progesterone was now replaced by a hydrogen atom (see position 10 in Fig. 14).

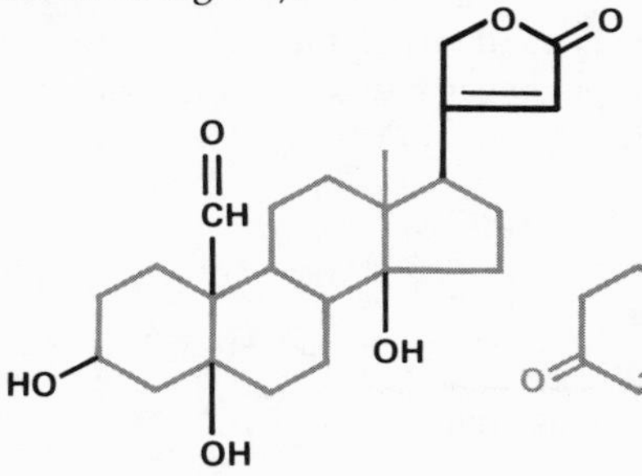

FIG. 13
Strophanthidin

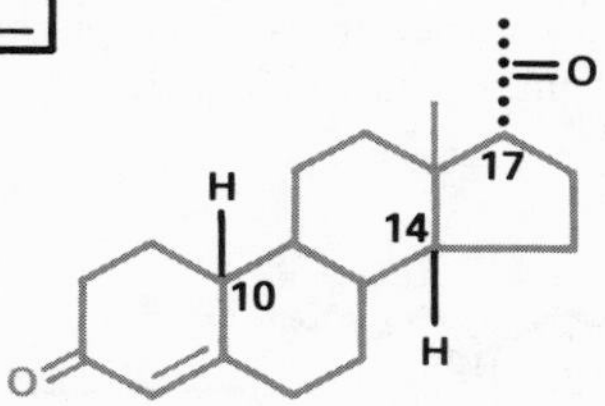

FIG. 14
Ehrenstein's 19-norprogesterone
(14-iso-17-iso-19-norprogesterone)

Ehrenstein's minute amount of oily product, more precisely called 14-iso-17-iso-19-norprogesterone, was only sufficient to be tested for biological activity in two rabbits, and it exhibited a high progestational effect in one of them. Under ordinary circumstances, doing such an experiment with only two rabbits would be totally unacceptable, but that is all the material that was available. Strophanthidin proved to be hopeless as a starting material because its chemical structure is so different from that of progesterone or even 19-norprogesterone that it took Ehrenstein a full ten years of work to repeat even the synthesis he had achieved in 1944. Thus in 1951 the question remained: was the high progestational activity that had been observed in one rabbit in 1944 a fluke, or was it real? If real, retention of biological activity in spite of extensive structural changes clearly upset the then-prevailing assumption that any chemical alteration in the structure of progesterone would automatically lower or abolish its biological activity. It was this apparent contradiction of a generally held dogma that had intrigued me as a graduate student.

What in retrospect appears to me to have been a very naive attempt to make a hybrid molecule containing the structural features of both female sex hormones (progesterone and estradiol) had led to our synthesis at Syntex of substantial quantities of the aromatic analog of progesterone (Fig. 10). A year earlier, the Australian chemist Arthur J. Birch had developed a chemical procedure, using metals (such as sodium) and liquid ammonia, to *dearomatize* molecules such as estradiol—that is, to construct the *nonaromatic* ring A of testosterone (Fig. 3) from the benzene ring A of estradiol (Fig. 5).

We immediately applied this chemical procedure to our synthetic hybrid (Fig. 10), and the result was crystalline, pure 19-norprogesterone (Fig. 15), which was in all respects identical to the natural hormone progesterone except that it had a hydrogen atom rather than a methyl group attached to position 10.

FIG. 10	FIG. 15
"Aromatic" progesterone	Authentic 19-norprogesterone

In 1951 we had no facilities at Syntex in Mexico City to test for biological activity of this substance, and therefore we sent it immediately to a commercial laboratory in Madison, Wisconsin, with the request that it be tested for progestational activity. The compound proved to be highly active, thus confirming the important observation of Ehrenstein seven years earlier that the removal of carbon atom 19 from progesterone not only did not diminish biological activity, as might have been expected from prior work, *but in fact augmented it.*

We also sent some of our synthetic crystalline 19-norprogesterone to Dr. Roy Hertz of the National Cancer Institute in Bethesda, Maryland, because interest had been expressed at that time in the treatment of cervical cancer through local injections of high doses of progesterone. This was a painful procedure, and it was clearly desirable to consider a more potent progestational compound that might be useful in such treatment. Hertz confirmed the progestational activity of our substance—in fact, he showed that when given by injection it was four to eight times as active as the natural hormone, thus making it the most powerful progestational agent known at that time. We submitted our work for publication to the *Journal of the American Chemical Society* on May 21, 1951, and immediately set out to develop an approach to synthesize an orally effective progestational analog.

Here again there was a lead from the scientific literature that expedited our work greatly, thus illustrating how in science one invariably builds on the work of predecessors. Over a dozen years earlier, just before the outbreak of World War II, Hans H. Inhoffen and his colleagues in the research laboratories of Schering had introduced acetylene (written as HC≡CH, in other words, two carbon atoms connected by a triple bond) into position 17 of the estrogenic hormone estradiol and the male sex hormone testosterone. The resulting product in the estrogenic series, called 17α-ethynylestradiol (Fig. 16), surprisingly showed increased oral estrogenic activity. (Twenty-five years later this was to become one of the estrogenic components of the combination oral contraceptive pill.) The product resulting from the addition of acetylene into position 17 of the male sex hormone testosterone, 17α-ethynyltestosterone (Fig. 17), displayed totally unanticipated properties—serendipity at its best.

Not only was this synthetic steroid orally active but it also exhibited perceptible *progestational* (female sex hormone) activity rather than the expected androgenic (male sex hormone) activity. This was the first observation that an orally effective progestational compound could be synthesized, and though this synthetic steroid (Fig. 17), also known generically as *ethisterone*, never found great utility in medicine, it was precisely the hint that we needed in the summer of 1951.

Having found that the removal of the 19-methyl group of progesterone (Fig. 11), leading to 19-norprogesterone (Fig. 15), greatly increased progestational activity by the injectable route, it did not take us long to predict that removal of the 19-methyl group of orally active ethisterone would increase its progestational activity while, we hoped, retaining its oral efficacy. Using the chemical methodology developed in synthesizing 19-norprogesterone (Fig. 15), Luis Miramontes, a young Mexican chemistry student carrying out his bachelor thesis in the Syntex laboratories under the direction of George Rosenkranz and myself, succeeded on October 15, 1951, in synthesizing 19-nor-17α-ethynyltestosterone (Fig. 18), generically known as *norethisterone* or *norethindrone*. Not in our wildest dreams did we imagine that eventually this substance would become the active progestational ingredient of over 50 percent of currently used oral contraceptives.

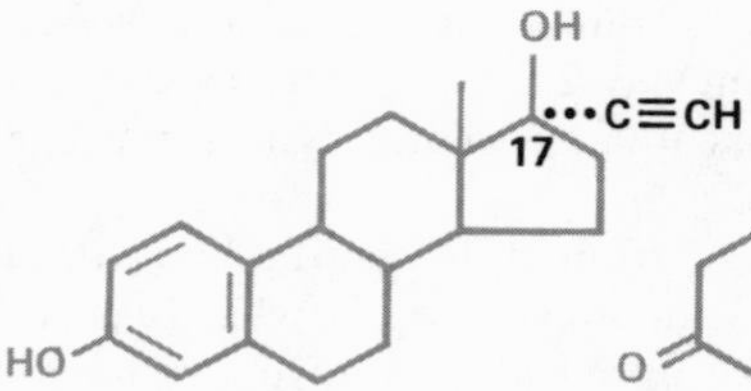

FIG. 16
17α-Ethynylestradiol

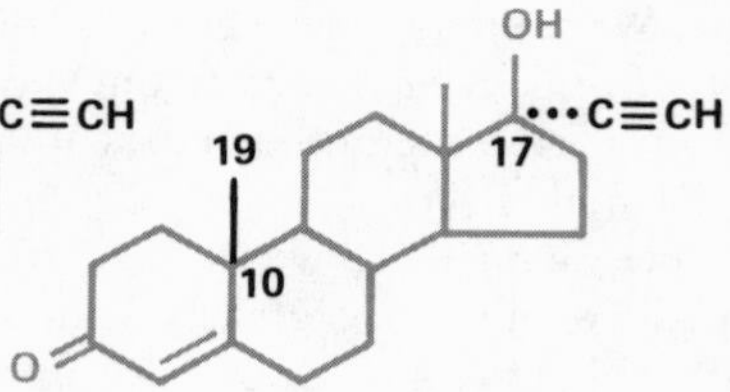

FIG. 17
17α-Ethynyltestosterone;
ethisterone

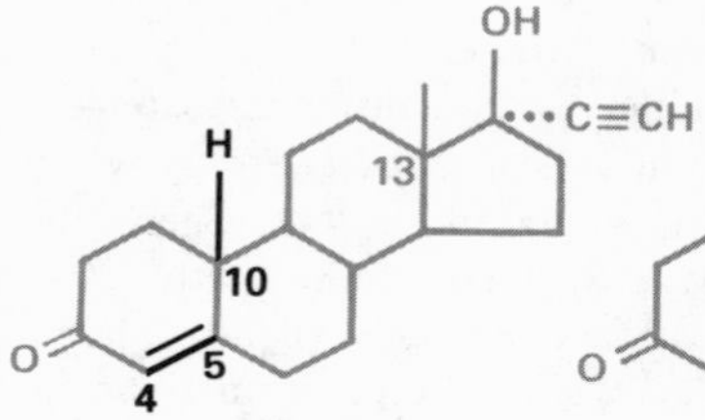

FIG. 18
Norethisterone or norethindrone
(19-nor-17α-ethynyltestosterone)

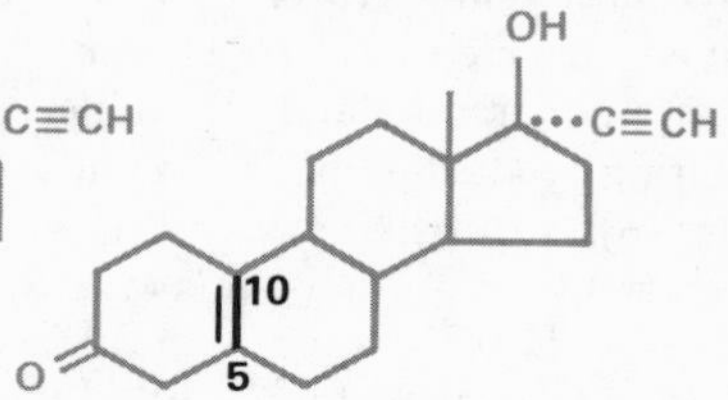

FIG. 19
Norethynodrel

We immediately submitted the compound to a commercial testing laboratory for biological evaluation and gloated happily when the report came back that it was more active as a progestational hormone by the oral route than any other steroid known at that time. In less than six months, we had accomplished our predicted goal of synthesizing a superpotent orally active progestational agent.

We filed our patent application for norethindrone on November 22, 1951 (it is the only patent for a drug listed in the National Inventors Hall of Fame in Washington), and I reported the details of our chemical synthesis together with the substance's biological activity at the April 1952 meeting of the American Chemical Society's Division of Medicinal Chemistry in Milwaukee, Wisconsin. The abstract of this report was published in March of 1952, and the full article with complete experimental details appeared in 1954 in the *Journal of the American Chemical Society.*

A few weeks after having synthesized the substance, we sent it to various endocrinologists and clinicians—first to Roy Hertz at the National Cancer Institute and Alexander Lipschutz in Chile, later to Gregory Pincus at the Worcester Foundation in Shrewsbury, Massachusetts, Robert Greenblatt in Georgia, and Edward Tyler in Los Angeles. In fact, it was Dr. Tyler of the Los Angeles Planned Parenthood Center who in November 1954 presented the first clinical results with norethindrone for the treatment of various menstrual disorders and fertility problems.

On August 31, 1953, well over a year after my first public report on norethindrone, Frank D. Colton of Searle filed a patent for the synthesis of a very closely related compound (Fig. 19), generically known as *norethynodrel,* which differed from norethindrone (Fig. 18) only by the location of the double bond between positions 5 and 10 rather than positions 4 and 5. Mild treatment of Colton's norethynodrel with hydrochloric acid or, in fact, even as weak an acid as human gastric juice, converts it to a large extent into norethindrone.

Both the Syntex and Searle compounds, together with many other steroids, were tested for ovulation inhibition during 1953-54 by Gregory Pincus and his collaborators at the Worcester Foundation. Pincus and Dr. John Rock, a clinician at Harvard, were interested in ovulation inhibitors as possible agents for contraception (eventually turning into a reality Haberlandt's prediction, made 20 years earlier, that a substance with the biological properties of progesterone might be a useful contraceptive) and found that Syntex's norethindrone and Searle's norethynodrel were the two most active steroids in that respect.

Pincus, a consultant for Searle, understandably picked the Searle compound for use in his further biological and clinical studies. In the meanwhile Syntex—a minute company compared to other pharmaceutical enterprises, with no biological laboratories and no marketing sales force—went its own way in trying to convert this laboratory discovery into its first proprietary commercial product. As indicated earlier, we were able to handle the absence of biological laboratories efficiently and without difficulty by sending the synthetic steroids we developed to various outside investigators who then carried out the biological and clinical studies. However, our lack of a marketing organization required that we collaborate with another pharmaceutical company. For an interesting historical reason, Syntex chose Parke-Davis for this collaboration.

No great affection existed between the two companies during the late 1940s through the mid 1950s primarily because Parke-Davis, one of the most conservative of all pharmaceutical companies in the United States, had totally missed out in the steroid field, as mentioned earlier, by not backing Marker's intitial steroid work in Mexico. We felt that one way of making up for this loss and the resulting resentment of Syntex was to offer an exclusive license to Parke-Davis to market norethindrone. After some rather intense negotiations, an agreement was reached in 1956. Parke-Davis received an exclusive license to market norethindrone in return for purchasing it from Syntex at a price that bore a fixed relationship to Parke-Davis's final sales price. In other words, Syntex had a major financial stake in Parke-Davis's commercial success.

I participated in these negotiations because although I had left Syntex in 1952 to teach at Wayne State University in Detroit (next door to Parke-Davis), I had retained a close relationship as a consultant to the Mexican company. (I returned to Syntex in 1957, where I stayed for another three years, after which I accepted an offer of a chemistry professorship from Stanford University. What neither Stanford nor I anticipated was that my move to California would lead Syntex itself to transfer most of its facilities and personnel to the Stanford Industrial Park three years later. By 1979, Palo Alto, California, had become the de facto world headquarters of this multinational pharmaceutical corporation with worldwide sales approaching the half-billion-dollar mark.)

We provided Parke-Davis with all the laboratory and preliminary clinical data that we had accumulated through our outside investigators, and after doing some additional required toxicology and monkey experiments, Parke-Davis received FDA approval for norethindrone in 1957—at the same time as did Searle for their compound—for the treatment of menstrual disorders and for certain conditions of infertility. Thus, both norethindrone and norethynodrel went on the market independently in the same year.

An interesting side excursion into the occasionally murky waters of industrial patents is warranted at this point. As I explained earlier, we at Syntex had filed a patent application on norethindrone in November 1951 and published the results the following year, whereas Searle did not submit its patent application on norethynodrel until August 1953. To what extent their work was prompted simply by a wish to circumvent our patent priority will probably never be known, because Searle never chose to publish any of Colton's chemical research in the scientific literature, although Searle scientists were otherwise well known for publishing their results widely. Suffice it to say that since their norethynodrel (Fig. 19), which was not covered by Syntex's patent, is transformed into our patented norethindrone (Fig. 18) by gastric acid after ingestion, one could raise an interesting legal question. Is synthesis of a patented compound in the stomach an infringement of an issued patent? I urged that we push this issue to a legal resolution, but Parke-Davis did not concur. Searle was selling a very important anti-motion-sickness drug, Dramamine, which contained Parke-Davis's antihistamine Benadryl, and our norethindrone in 1957 seemed small potatoes over which it was not worth fighting with a valued customer.

We can now return to the clinical studies that eventually led to FDA approval of norethynodrel and norethindrone for another and much more important clinical indication—birth control. (In certain countries, such as Spain or Italy, where contraceptive use of these steroids was not approved for many years because of religious opposition, the euphemism "menstrual regulation"—for which these compounds had been approved in the U.S. already in 1957—served to hide their much wider contraceptive usage.)

Preliminary clinical experiments by Pincus, Rock, and their associates in Puerto Rico had demonstrated that the ovulation inhibition properties of these substances could be employed for contraceptive purposes as well as for menstrual regulation. Pincus, who was a remarkable entrepreneur, convinced Searle that the commercial potential of an oral contraceptive warranted some risk taking. He deserves a great deal of credit for persuading that firm to proceed, ignoring fears of potential consumer backlash to other Searle drugs that might result from the Catholic Church's opposition to birth control. Syntex, of course, had no such problem since it had no other drugs on the market that could be the object of any real or imagined boycott. We had a much bigger problem—no marketing organization—but we did not lack entrepreneurs.

The entrepreneurial counterpart to Pincus at Syntex was Dr. Alejandro Zaffaroni, who had joined Syntex in 1951 to head a newly formed biochemical department. Though he was not involved with the original scientific work on oral progestational steroids, Zaffaroni was the driving force behind parallel clinical experiments conducted on behalf of Syntex by clinicians in Mexico City, San Antonio, and Los Angeles in order to accumulate the necessary human data for FDA approval of norethindrone as a contraceptive agent. At this stage, in the late 1950s, just as it became obvious that oral contraception was about to become a practical reality, Parke-Davis got cold feet and refused to even *consider* marketing norethindrone as an oral contraceptive. Thus, while Searle was proceeding full steam ahead toward FDA approval, Syntex suddenly had to find an alternative marketing outlet or be excluded from deriving any financial benefit from a field in which, relatively speaking, it had committed a larger proportion of its resources than had anybody else.

Parke-Davis's apprehension about a possible boycott of some of its other products as a result of a potential Catholic backlash was perhaps not unreasonable, but such a consumer backlash never developed. Actually, three years earlier, Charles Pfizer & Company had an option from Syntex to market norethindrone, but Pfizer had not exercised it because its president, who was a very active Roman Catholic lay person, felt that Pfizer should not touch any agent even potentially related to birth control.

Thus, it was up to Zaffaroni to start almost from scratch to find another marketing candidate. He made a brilliant choice by negotiating a very favorable contract with the Ortho Division of Johnson & Johnson, probably the most effective and important marketer of contraceptive hardware devices at that time. But a monumental snag was about to occur. Parke-Davis refused to release to Ortho the monkey studies that it had completed on norethindrone. I can only speculate on the reason for this refusal: "If I dare not eat this tempting cake, why should I help someone else buy it? What's more, though the cook offered it to me first, I still don't like him."

As a result, Ortho had to repeat a number of studies that had already been carried out. This backtracking prevented Ortho from receiving FDA approval to market Syntex's norethindrone for contraceptive use until 1962 (under the trade name Ortho Novum), two years after Searle first hit the market with their oral contraceptive norethynodrel (under the trade name Enovid). In 1964, Parke-Davis finally woke up to the facts of life and decided to enter the contraceptive market after all. After obtaining a license from Syntex for a derivative of norethindrone—norethindrone acetate—they received FDA approval to market the compound as an oral contraceptive. Thus, though initially Searle had the oral contraceptive market to itself, by the mid 1960s Syntex—through its two licensees, Ortho and Parke-Davis, as well as through its own sales force established in 1964 through the initiative and under direct supervision of Dr. Zaffaroni—had gained the major share of the U.S. oral contraceptive market.

In short, the first oral contraceptive chemical, norethindrone, was synthesized at Syntex in Mexico City in 1951. Searle's steroid, norethynodrel, was synthesized at least a year and a half later but there is no question that Searle deserves full credit for marketing the first oral contraceptive in 1960. I am firmly convinced, though admittedly biased, that even if no contraceptive work had ever been done at Searle, the marketing of the Pill would have been delayed by only a couple of years, at the most.

Other Steroid Oral Contraceptives

Although this ends the story of the origin of the Pill, readers may well wonder what has happened subsequently with regard to the development of other steroid oral contraceptives. In the late 1950s and early 1960s, four additional 19-norsteroids were synthesized by different groups and eventually were introduced into medical practice. The first of these was norethindrone acetate (Fig. 20), which was synthesized in the Schering laboratories in Germany and which was known to biodegrade in the body to norethindrone (Fig. 18). Schering marketed this compound worldwide under license from Syntex (this was the substance that Parke-Davis used when they finally entered the oral contraceptive market in the U.S.).

A more interesting variant of the norethindrone molecule is lynestrenol (Fig. 21), which was synthesized in the Organon laboratories in Holland and which differs from norethindrone in that an oxygen atom has been removed from position 3. This substance has never been introduced into contraceptive practice in the U.S., but it is marketed elsewhere. What is interesting about lynestrenol is that the body itself can reintroduce the oxygen atom at position 3—which the Dutch chemists had removed so laboriously to circumvent Syntex's norethindrone patent—so that biologically much of lynestrenol is transformed into norethindrone once it is ingested.

The third steroid is ethynodiol diacetate (synthesized in the late 1950s at Searle to replace norethynodrel) which differs from norethindrone acetate (Fig. 20) only in a minor way by the nature of the substituent at position 3 (Fig. 22). Here again the body largely metabolizes ethynodiol diacetate back into norethindrone. Roughly speaking, therefore, we can say that the Pill—at least much of what floats around in a woman's body—is norethindrone and that at least metabolically speaking, the body's chemists (i.e., the enzymes that are responsible for these metabolic changes) pay little attention to patents.

One last substance merits mention, namely, norgestrel (Fig. 23), synthesized in the early 1960s by the British chemist Hershel Smith and first introduced in the United States commercially by Wyeth Laboratories in 1968. In contrast to the other 19-norsteroids, norgestrel is not transformed in the body into norethindrone. Norgestrel differs from the latter by having a two-carbon chain attached at position 13. The body has no biochemical mechanism to convert this two-carbon chain into the one-carbon unit present in the other oral contraceptives, and it is this molecular difference that apparently is

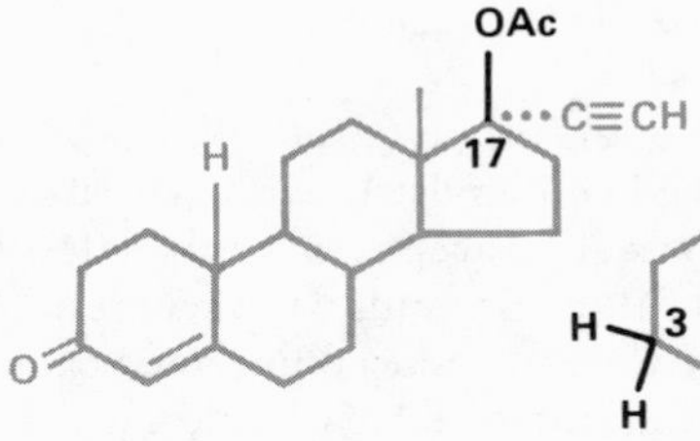

FIG. 20
Norethindrone acetate

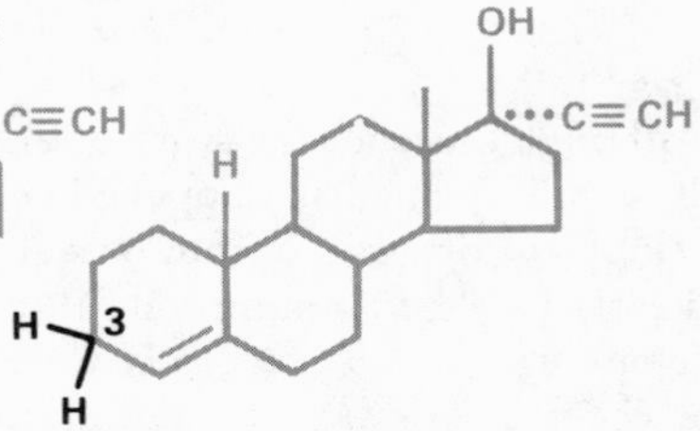

FIG. 21
Lynestrenol

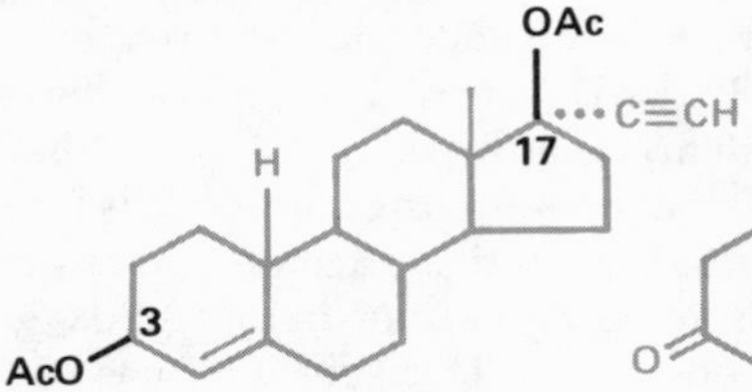

FIG. 22
Ethynodiol diacetate

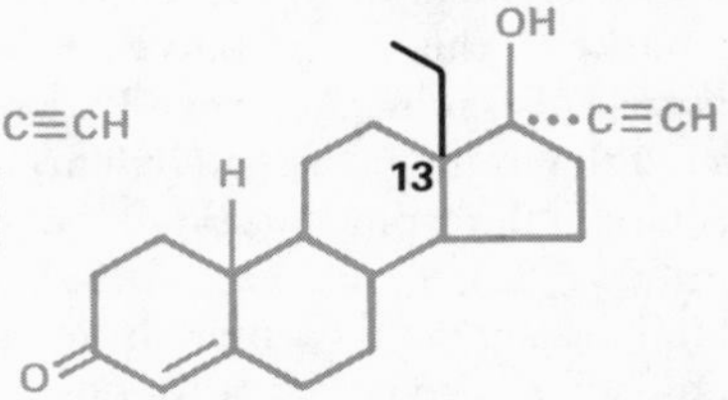

FIG. 23
Norgestrel

responsible for the fact that norgestrel is active at a somewhat lower dose than are the other 19-norsteroid oral contraceptives.

In terms of active ingredients, norethindrone is still the leading compound used in oral contraceptives. Ortho and Syntex together account for approximately 40 percent of the U.S. oral contraceptive market, with Parke-Davis (marketing norethindrone acetate), Lederle, and Mead-Johnson accounting for another 11 percent. The remaining 49 percent of the U.S. market is divided between Wyeth's norgestrel (28 percent) and Searle's ethynodiol diacetate (21 percent). The original norethynodrel developed by Pincus and his collaborators is hardly used anymore.

In addition to this private oral contraceptive market, there is a substantial international public sector market in the U.S. because, since 1972, the Agency for International Development has been purchasing large amounts of oral contraceptives. (For the last three years, Syntex has won all of the government contracts, amounting on an average to 100 million cycles per year, which corresponds to about eight million women being protected annually in a contraceptive sense by norethindrone.) Norethindrone's patent coverage, of course, has long since expired—one of the reasons why it has found such favor among public agencies. However, a more important reason for its popularity, which accounts not only for the paucity of active ingredients in the various existing oral contraceptives but also for the fact that no drug company has a new oral contraceptive of the progestational type under development, is the following.

By now it will have become obvious to every reader that questions about actual and potential side effects of the Pill—foremost of which are concerns about possible carcinogenicity—cannot be answered until a very large population group has been on a given agent for years. It is likely that a larger body of such epidemiological evidence is being accumulated about norethindrone than about any other steroid agent because not only is it the active ingredient in over 50 percent of the world's oral contraceptives but, even more importantly, it has been used longer than any other agent that is still being sold. Given a few more years, definitive evidence concerning norethindrone will be available. If it is demonstrated that there is little or no association between this agent and cancer, then—given norethindrone's generic availability (i.e., the absence of patent protection)—it is probable that norethindrone will become the agent of choice for public sector work in most parts of the world. To displace it by a new product, not yet on the market, that works by a similar biological mechanism would then become so prohibitively expensive as to be totally unjustified.

Of the money now being spent on new contraceptive development, essentially none is being allocated to developing new chemical entities suitable for ovulation inhibition by the progestational hormone mechanism. Therefore, the next hormonal Pill for women—if there is going to be a next—is unlikely to be a steroid.

Reader's Guide

SINCE MOST OF THE CHAPTERS in this book can be read independently, I am listing—in the order in which they appear in the text—leading references to support most factual statements and/or specific quotations.

Chapter One

C. Djerassi. "Birth Control After 1984." *Science,* vol. 169, 1970, pp. 941–51.

U.S., Congress, House, Select Committee on Population, *Hearings on Fertility and Contraception in America,* 95th Cong., 1978, vol. III, p. 150.

M. Potts. "Against Nature" (10th Darwin Lecture in Human Biology). *Biologist,* vol. 17, 1970, pp. 143–51.

F. Miller and R. Sartorius. "Population Policy and Public Goods." *Philosophy and Public Affairs,* vol. 8, no. 2. Princeton: Princeton University Press, 1979.

Chapter Two

World Health Organization. *Special Programme of Research, Development and Research Training in Human Reproduction,* 7th Annual Report, Geneva, November 1978.

M. Potts (International Fertility Research Program, Research Triangle, N.C.), private communication, February 12, 1979.

M.C. Stopes. *Contraception—Its Theory, History and Practice.* London: Bale and Danielsson, 1923.

R.V. Short. "The Evolution of Human Reproduction." *Proceedings of the Royal Society of London,* vol. B. 195, 1976, pp. 3–24.

N.B. Loudon, M. Foxwell, D.M. Potts, A.L. Guild, and R.V. Short. "Acceptability of an Oral Contraceptive That Reduces the Frequency of Menstruation." *British Medical Journal,* vol. 2, 1977, pp. 487–90.

S. Nilsson and K.G. Nygren. "Transfer of Contraceptive Steroids to Human Milk." *Research in Reproduction,* vol. 11, no. 1, 1979, pp. 1–2.

N.E. Himes. *Medical History of Contraception.* New York: Schocken Books, 1970.

P.D. Harvey. "Condoms—A New Look." *Family Planning Perspectives,* vol. 4, no. 4, 1972, pp. 27–30.

A.D. Sollins and R.L. Belsky. "Commercial Production and Distribution of Contraceptives." *Reports on Population/Family Planning,* no. 4, 1970, pp. 1–23.

R.T. Ravenholt (Office of Population, Agency for International Development, Washington, D.C.), private communication, February 2, 1979.

V. Jorgensen. "Adolescent Contraception." In *Hormonal Contraceptives, Estrogens and Human Welfare,* M.C. Diamond and C.C. Korenbrot, eds., p. 111. New York: Academic Press, 1978.

U.S., Congress, House, Select Committee on Population, *Hearings on Fertility and Contraception in America,* 95th Cong., 1978, vol. III, p. 131.

M. Elstein and R.A. Sparks. *Intrauterine Contraception.* Montreal: Eden Press, 1977.

M.J.K. Harper. "Contraception—Retrospect and Prospect." *Progress in Drug Research,* vol. 21, pp. 293–407. Basel: Birkhäuser, 1977.

M. Requena. "Chilean Program of Abortion Control and Fertility Planning: Present Situation and Forecast for the Next Decade." In *Fertility and Family Planning,* S.J. Behrman, Leslie Corsa Jr., and Ronald Freedman, eds., p. 485. Ann Arbor: The University of Michigan Press, 1969.

"Induced Abortion." *World Health Organization Technical Report Series,* no. 623, 1978.

C. Tietze. "Induced Abortion: 1977 Supplement." *Reports on Population/Family Planning,* no. 14, 1977.

T.M. King. "Abortion and Abortifacients." *Improving Contraceptive Technology,* Draper Fund Report, no. 6, Washington, D.C., 1978, p.28.

C. Djerassi. "Fertility Control Through Abortion—An Assessment of the Period 1950–1980." *Bulletin of the Atomic Scientists,* vol. 28, no. 1, 1972, pp. 9–14, 41–45.

"Menstrual Regulation: The Method and the Issues." *Studies in Family Planning,* vol. 8, no. 10, 1977.

Chapter Three

World Health Organization. *Special Programme of Research, Development and Research Training in Human Reproduction,* 7th Annual Report, Geneva, November 1978.

K. Ford. "Contraceptive Use in the United States 1973–1976." *Family Planning Perspectives,* vol. 10, no. 5, 1978, p. 264.

S.M. Keeny, ed. "East Asia Review." *Studies in Family Planning,* vol. 9, no. 9, 1978, p. 235 (Indonesia), p. 246 (Singapore).

G.B. Baldwin. "The McCormick Family Planning Program in Chiang Mai, Thailand." *Studies in Family Planning,* vol. 9, no. 12, 1978, pp. 300–313.

A. Gallegos, J.G. Pena, J.A. Solis, and A. Keller. "Recent Trends in Contraceptive Use in Mexico." *Studies in Family Planning,* vol. 8, no. 8, 1977, p. 197.

A. Bamisaiye, C. de Sweemer, and O. Ransome-Kuti. "Developing a Clinic Strategy Appropriate to Community Family Planning Needs and Practices: An Experience in Lagos, Nigeria." *Studies in Family Planning,* vol. 9, nos. 2–3, 1978, pp. 44–48.

B. Berelson, ed. *Population Policy in Developed Countries.* New York: McGraw-Hill, 1974.

U.S., Congress, Senate, Subcommittee on Monopoly of the Select Committee on Small Business, *Hearings on Competitive Problems in the Drug Industry,* 91st Cong., 1970, vol. 2, pp. 6755, 6780–81.

R. Richter et al. "Report from Five Swiss Centres on Two Comparative Trials with Oral Contraceptives." In *Modern Techniques of Controlling Human Reproduction,* pp. 121–26. Hertford, U.K.: Stephen Austin & Sons, Ltd., 1966.

The Royal College of General Practitioners. *Oral Contraceptives and Health.* London: Pitman Medical, 1974.

C. Tietze. "The Pill and Mortality from Cardiovascular Disease: Another Look." *Family Planning Perspectives,* vol. 11, no. 2, 1979, pp. 80–84.

M.A. Belsey, Y. Russell, and K. Kinnear. "Cardiovascular Disease and Oral Contraceptives: A Reappraisal of Vital Statistics Data." *Family Planning Perspectives,* vol. 11, no. 2, 1979, pp. 84–89.

M.P. Vessey and R. Doll. "Is the Pill Safe Enough to Continue Using?" *Proceedings of the Royal Society of London,* vol. B. 195, 1976, pp. 69–80.

E.B. Connell. "The Pill: Risks and Benefits." In *Hormonal Contraceptives, Estrogens and Human Welfare,* M.C. Diamond and C.C. Korenbrot, eds., pp. 1–6. New York: Academic Press, 1978.

G. af Geijerstam. "Fertility Control by Induced Abortion." In *Nobel Symposium 15: Control of Human Fertility,* E. Diczfalusy and U. Borell, eds., p. 224 (estimated number of illegal abortions in 1967). New York: Wiley Interscience, 1971.

C.F. Westoff and E.F. Jones. "The Secularization of U.S. Catholic Birth Control Practices." *Family Planning Perspectives,* vol. 9, 1977, pp. 203–7.

"Birth Control in Amerika." *Science for the People,* vol. II, no. 4, 1970, pp. 28–31.

U.S., Congress, House, Select Committee on Population, *Hearings on Fertility and Contraception in America,* 95th Cong., 1978, vol. III, p. 130.

F.S. Jaffe. "Hormonal Contraceptives in Fertility Control Programs." In *Hormonal Contraceptives, Estrogens and Human Welfare,* M.C. Diamond and C.C. Korenbrot, eds., pp. 113–21. New York: Academic Press, 1978.

Chapter Four

P.B. Hutt. "Unresolved Issues in the Conflict Between Individual Freedom and Government Control of Food Safety." *The Food Drug Cosmetic Law Journal,* vol. 33, 1978, pp. 560–62 (list of common carcinogenic food components), p. 568 (annual cancer risks associated with various human activities and exposures).

M. Mintz. *St. Louis Globe-Democrat,* November 5, 1969, p. 5.

"Hormonal Steroids in Contraception." *World Health Organization Technical Report Series,* no. 386, 1968, p. 23.

B.N. Ames. "Identifying Environmental Chemicals Causing Mutations and Cancer." *Science,* vol. 204, 1979, pp. 587–93.

M.H. Briggs and E. Diczfalusy, eds. *Pharmacological Models in Contraceptive Development—Animal Toxicity and Side-Effects in Man.* WHO Research and Training Center of Human Reproduction, Karolinska Institutet, Stockholm, 1974, pp. 251, 262, 264.

U.S., Congress, House, Select Committee on Population, *Hearings on Fertility and Contraception in America,* 95th Cong., 1978, vol. III, pp. 150–51.

World Health Organization. *Special Programme of Research, Development and Research Training in Human Reproduction,* 7th Annual Report, Geneva, November 1978, p. 34.

E. Diczfalusy. "Second Gregory Pincus Memorial Lecture." 5th International Congress on Hormonal Steroids, New Delhi, October 30, 1978.

"Steroid Contraception and the Risk of Neoplasia." *World Health Organization Technical Report Series,* no. 619, 1978.

D. Seigel and P. Corfman. "Epidemiological Problems Associated with Studies of the Safety of Oral Contraceptives." *Journal of the American Medical Association,* vol. 203, 1968, pp. 950–54.

J.L. Marx. "Estrogens: Hormones Link to Cancer Disputed." *Science,* vol. 202, 1978, pp. 1270–71; see, however, *Science,* vol. 203, 1979, p. 348.

U.S., Congress, Subcommittee of the Committee on Appropriations, *Hearings on 1975 Appropriations,* 93rd Cong., 1974, pp. 131–32.

Chapter Five

U.S., Congress, House, Select Committee on Population, *Hearings on Fertility and Contraception in America,* 95th Cong., 1978, vol. III, pp. 2, 173, 183, 578.

O. Harkavy, F.S. Jaffe, M.A. Koblinsky, and S. Segal. "Funding of Contraceptive Research." *Proceedings of the Royal Society of London,* vol. B. 195, 1976, pp. 37–55.

C. Djerassi. "Prognosis for the Development of New Chemical Birth-Control Agents." *Science,* vol. 166, 1969, pp. 468–73.

C. Djerassi. "Mao Tse-tung says 'Mankind ought to exercise self-control.' Freeman Dyson asks 'What are the hidden costs of saying no?'" *Chemistry and Industry,* London, 1975, pp. 593–95.

C. Djerassi. "Birth Control After 1984." *Science,* vol. 169, 1970, pp. 941–51.

J.H. Abeles. "New Drugs: Prospects and Perspectives." Text of speech delivered at Financial Analysts Federation Health Care Seminar, November 14, 1978, and distributed as a research report by Kidder, Peabody & Co., New York, November 28, 1978.

R.O. Greep, M.A. Koblinsky, and F.S. Jaffe. *Reproduction and Human Welfare: A Challenge to Research.* Cambridge: MIT Press, 1976.

Chapter Six

U.S., Congress, Senate, Subcommittee on Monopoly of the Select

Committee on Small Business, *Hearings on Competitive Problems in the Drug Industry,* 91st Cong., 1970, vols. 1, 2, 3 (Oral Contraceptives).

"Wave of Alarm Over the Pill." *San Francisco Sunday Examiner & Chronicle,* January 18, 1970, p. 2.

"The Pill—A New Poison Hazard." *Modern Medicine,* May 9, 1966, p. 28.

H.L. Verhulst and J.J. Crotty. "Survey of Products Most Frequently Named in Ingestion Accidents in 1965." *Journal of Clinical Pharmacology,* vol. 7, 1967, pp. 9–16.

Jack Anderson. "Merry-Go-Round: New Frightening Dangers of 'the Pill.'" *San Francisco Chronicle,* April 29, 1970, p. 41.

J.J. Bonica and G.D. Allen. "Drugs for the Relief of Pain." In *Drugs of Choice, 1966–1967,* W. Modell, ed., p. 205. St. Louis: C.V. Mosby, 1966.

"New Method of Birth Control." *San Francisco Chronicle,* December 2, 1978, pp. 1, 3.

"Consumer Group Says Caffeine Poses Peril to Pregnant Women." *New York Times,* February 4, 1976, p. 35.

J.S. Greenstein. "Studies on a New, Peerless Contraceptive Agent." *Canadian Medical Association Journal,* vol. 93, 1965, pp. 1351–55.

E.T. Tyler. "Antifertility Agents." *Annual Review of Pharmacology,* vol. 7, 1967, pp. 395–96.

"Humouring the Physician." *Canadian Medical Association Journal,* vol. 93, 1965, p. 1370.

Chapter Seven

Chemical and Engineering News, October 25, 1971, p. 25.

"Endocrine Approaches to Male Contraception." *International Journal of Andrology,* supplement 2, 1978. Proceedings of 5th Annual Workshop on the Testis, Geilo, Norway, 1978.

U.S., Congress, House, Select Committee on Population, *Hearings on Fertility and Contraception in America,* 95th Cong., 1978, vol. III, pp. 87, 463.

A. Banks. "The Pill for Men?" *Boston Magazine,* February 1977.

S.J. Segal. "The Physiology of Human Reproduction." *Scientific American,* September 1974, pp. 53–62.

R. Guillemin and A.V. Schally. Nobel Prize addresses on hypothalamic hormones in *Les Prix Nobel 1977,* pp. 160–93, 201–34. Stockholm: Almquist and Wiksell, 1978.

D.W. Fawcett. "Prospects for Fertility Control in the Male." In *Hormonal Contraceptives, Estrogens and Human Welfare,* M.C. Diamond and C.C. Korenbrot, eds., pp. 57–74. New York: Academic Press, 1978.

I. Lubell and R. Frischer. "The Current Status of Male and Female Sterilization Procedures." *Proceedings of the Royal Society of London,* vol. B. 195, 1976, pp. 93–114.

J.F. Hulka and J.E. Davis. "Sterilization of Men." In *Human Reproduction,* E.S.E. Hafez and T.N. Evans, eds. New York: Harper and Row, 1973.

D.M. de Kretser. "The Regulation of Male Fertility. The State of the Art and Future Possibilities." *Contraception,* vol. 9, 1974, pp. 561–600.

K.S.K. Tung. "Human Sperm Antigens and Antisperm Antibodies. Studies in Vasectomy Patients." *Clinical and Experimental Immunology,* vol. 20, 1975, pp. 93–104.

J.M. Loe. U.S. Patent No. 3,731,670 (May 8, 1973).

T.S. Lardner. "Bioengineering Aspects of Reproduction and Contraceptive Development." In *Frontiers in Reproduction and Fertility Control,* R.O. Greep and M.S. Koblinsky, eds. Cambridge: MIT Press, 1977.

"Schering Workshop on Contraception: The Masculine Gender." *Advances in the Biosciences,* G. Raspé and S. Bernhard, eds., vol. 10. Oxford: Pergamon Press, 1974.

C. Holden. "Sperm Banks Multiply as Vasectomies Gain Popularity." *Science,* vol. 176, 1972, p. 32.

R. Ansbacher. "Artificial Insemination with Frozen Spermatozoa." *Fertility and Sterility,* vol. 29, 1978, pp. 375–79.

R. Witherington, J.B. Black, and A.M. Karow. "Semen Cryopreservation: An Update." *Journal of Urology,* vol. 118, 1977, pp. 510–12.

"Sperm Banks Win New Acceptance." *New York Times,* January 14, 1979, p. 22E.

World Health Organization. *Special Programme of Research, Development and Research Training in Human Reproduction,* 7th Annual Report, Geneva, November 1978, pp. 91–98.

R.V. Short. "Healthy Infertility." *Upsala Journal of Medical Sciences,* supplement 22, 1978, pp. 23–26.

M.C. Diamond and C.C. Korenbrot, eds. *Hormonal Contraceptives, Estrogens and Human Welfare*, p. xii. New York: Academic Press, 1978.

J.M. Davidson. "Gonadal Hormones and Human Behavior." In *Hormonal Contraceptives, Estrogens and Human Welfare*, M.C. Diamond and C.C. Korenbrot, eds., pp. 123–26. New York: Academic Press, 1978.

S.B. Schearer. "Current Efforts to Develop Male Hormonal Contraceptives." *Studies in Family Planning*, vol. 9, no. 8, 1978, pp. 229–31.

Chapter Eight

A. Lein. *The Cycling Female—Her Menstrual Rhythm*. San Francisco: W.H. Freeman, 1979.

R.B. Greenblatt, R.H. Asch, V.B. Mahesh, and J.B. Bryner. "Implantation of Pure, Crystalline Pellets of Estradiol for Conception Control." *American Journal of Obstetrics and Gynecology*, vol. 127, 1977, pp. 520–24.

World Health Organization. *Special Programme of Research, Development and Research Training in Human Reproduction*, 7th Annual Report, Geneva, November 1978, pp. 19–117.

R.O. Greep and M.A. Koblinsky, eds. *Frontiers in Reproduction and Fertility Control*. Cambridge: MIT Press, 1977.

C. Grobstein. "External Human Fertilization." *Scientific American*, vol. 240, no. 6, 1979, pp. 57–67.

E. Diczfalusy. "Improved Long-Acting Fertility Regulating Agents. What Are the Problems?" *Journal of Steroid Biochemistry*, 1979, in press.

G.W. Duncan et al., eds. *Fertility Control Methods—Strategies for Introduction*, p. 130 (J.F. Marshall). New York: Academic Press, 1973.

"Biology of Fertility Control by Periodic Abstinence." *World Health Organization Technical Report Series*, no. 360, 1967.

S. Nilsson and K.G. Nygren. "Transfer of Contraceptive Steroids to Human Milk." *Research in Reproduction*, vol. 11, no. 1, January 1979, pp. 1–2.

E. Diczfalusy, ed. *Immunological Approaches to Fertility Control*. Karolinska Institutet, Stockholm, 1974.

WHO Task Force on Immunological Methods for Fertility Regulation. "Evaluating the Safety and Efficacy of Placental Antigen

Vaccines for Fertility Regulation." *Clinical and Experimental Immunology,* vol. 33, 1978, pp. 360–75.

U.S., Congress, Senate, Subcommittee on Monopoly of the Select Committee on Small Business, *Hearings on Competitive Problems in the Drug Industry,* 91st Cong., 1970, vol. 2, p. 6616.

S.J. Segal. "New Approaches to Contraception." *Clinical Obstetrics and Gynecology,* vol. 17, no. 1, 1974, pp. 157–66.

Chapter Nine

B. Berelson. "An Evaluation of the Effects of Population Control Programs." *Studies in Family Planning,* vol. 5, no. 1, 1974, pp. 2–12.

M.M. Ketchel. "Should Birth Control Be Mandatory?" *Medical World News,* October 18, 1968, pp. 66–71.

C. Djerassi. "Birth Control After 1984." *Science,* vol. 169, 1970, pp. 941–51.

G. Orwell. *1984.* New York: Harcourt, Brace and Co., 1949.

A. Huxley. *Brave New World.* New York: Harper and Row, 1932.

A. Huxley. *Brave New World Revisited.* New York: Harper and Row, 1958, pp. 10–11, 138–39.

B.T. Feld and G.W. Szilard, eds. *The Collected Works of Leo Szilard: Scientific Papers,* pp. 506, 508, 514. Cambridge: MIT Press, 1972.

L. Szilard. *The Voice of the Dolphins and Other Stories.* New York: Simon and Schuster, 1961, pp. 23–24.

H. Brown and E. Hutchings, eds. *Are Our Descendents Doomed?,* pp. 164–73 (J.R. Platt). New York: Viking Press, 1972.

B. Berelson. "Beyond Family Planning." *Science,* vol. 163, 1969, pp. 533–43.

Chapter Ten

B. Berelson. "An Evaluation of the Effects of Population Control Programs." *Studies in Family Planning,* vol. 5, no. 1, 1974, pp. 2–12.

H.Y. Tien. "Sterilization, Oral Contraception and Population Control in China." *Population Studies,* vol. 28, no. 3, 1965, pp. 215–35.

Cheng Pui-Yuen. "Advances in the Research of Oral Contraceptives." *Acta Pharmaceutica Sinica,* vol. XI, no. 12, 1964, pp. 842–58.

E.G. Dimond. "Medical Education and Care in the People's Republic of China." *Journal of the American Medical Association,* vol. 218, 1971, pp. 1552–63.

"Strengthen Leadership and Do a Good Job of Birth Control Work." Editorial, *Szechuan Daily,* December 22, 1974, as broadcast by Szechuan Provincial Radio and translated in Foreign Broadcast Information Service's *Daily Report: People's Republic of China,* December 24, 1974, pp. J2–J3. Springfield, Va.: National Technical Information Service, U.S. Department of Commerce.

Speech of the Chinese Delegation. International Conference on Population Planning for National Welfare and Development, Lahore, Pakistan, September 25, 1973.

"Kwangtung Issues New Planned Parenthood Regulations." January 6, 1979, as broadcast by Kwangchow Radio and translated in Foreign Broadcast Information Service's *Daily Report: People's Republic of China,* January 9, 1979, p. H3. Springfield, Va.: National Technical Information Service, U.S. Department of Commerce.

"National Planned Parenthood Conference Held in Peking." January 26, 1979, as broadcast by New China News Agency and translated in Foreign Broadcast Information Service's *Daily Report: People's Republic of China,* January 31, 1979, pp. E10–E15. Springfield, Va.: National Technical Information Service, U.S. Department of Commerce.

C. Djerassi. "Fertility Limitation through Contraceptive Steroids in the People's Republic of China." *Studies in Family Planning,* vol. 5, no. 1, 1974, pp. 13–30.

C. Djerassi. "Some Observations on Current Fertility Control in China." *The China Quarterly,* no. 57, January/March 1974, pp. 40–62.

Pi-Chao Chen. "China's Birth Control Action Programme, 1956–1964." *Population Studies,* vol. 24, no. 2, 1970, pp. 141–50.

L.A. Orleans. *The Role of Science and Technology in China's Population/Food Balance.* Prepared for Subcommittee on Domestic and International Scientific Planning, Analysis and Cooperation, House Committee on Science and Technology. Washington, D.C.: U.S. Government Printing Office, September 1977.

Oral Contraceptives and Steroid Chemistry in the People's Republic of China. Committee on Scholarly Communications with the PRC, Report No. 5. Washington, D.C.: National Academy of Sciences, 1977.

P. Crabbé, H. Fillion, Y. Letourneaux, E. Diczfalusy, A.R. Aedo, J.W. Goldzieher, A.A. Shaikh, and V.D. Castracane. "Chemical Synthesis and Bioassay of Anordrin." *Steroids,* vol. 33, 1979, pp. 85–96.

World Health Organization. *Special Programme of Research, Development and Research Training in Human Reproduction,* 7th Annual Report, Geneva, November 1978, pp. 22–23, 114–15.

"Visitors Say Chinese Report They Have a Safe and Effective Birth Control Pill for Men." *New York Times,* January 6, 1979, p. 20.

National Coordinating Group on Male Antifertility Agents. "Gossypol—A New Antifertility Agent for Males." *Chinese Medical Journal,* New Series, vol. 4, no. 6, 1978, pp. 417–28.

M.B. Abou-Donai. "Physiological Effects and Metabolism of Gossypol." *Residue Reviews,* vol. 61, pp. 125–60. New York: Springer Verlag, 1976.

L.C. Berardi and L.A. Goldblatt. "Gossypol." In *Toxic Constituents of Plant Foodstuffs,* I.E. Liener, ed., pp. 211–66. New York: Academic Press, 1969.

L.A. Orleans. *Health Policies and Services in China, 1974.* Prepared for Subcommittee on Health, Senate Committee on Labor and Public Welfare, p. 40. Washington, D.C.: U.S. Government Printing Office, 1974.

Chapter Eleven

U.S., Congress, House, Select Committee on Population, *Hearings on Fertility and Contraception in America,* 95th Cong., 1978, vol. III, pp. 388–89.

A.M. Weinberg. "The Limits of Science and Trans-Science." *Interdisciplinary Science Reviews,* vol. 2, no. 4, 1977, pp. 337–42.

D. Maine. "Depo: The Debate Continues." *Family Planning Perspectives,* vol. 10, no. 6, 1978, pp. 342–45.

E. Marshall. "Environmental Groups Lose Friends in Effort to Control DNA Research." *Science,* vol. 202, 1978, p. 1265.

C. Djerassi. "Birth Control After 1984." *Science,* vol. 169, 1970, pp. 941–51.

World Health Organization. *Special Programme of Research, Development and Research Training in Human Reproduction,* 7th Annual Report, Geneva, November 1978.

W. Stevens. *The Palm at the End of the Mind.* New York: Alfred A. Knopf, Inc., 1971, p. 265.

World Population 1977. U.S. Department of Commerce, Bureau of the Census, Washington, D.C., 1978.

Author's Postscript

A. Huxley. *Brave New World Revisited*, p. 138. New York: Harper and Row, 1958.

P. Vaughn. *The Pill on Trial*. New York: Tower Publications, 1970.

G. Pincus. *The Control of Fertility*. New York: Academic Press, 1965.

C. Djerassi. "Steroid Oral Contraceptives." *Science*, vol. 151, 1966, pp. 1055–61.

"Mexican Hormones." *Fortune*, May 1951, pp. 86–90, 161–68.

R.E. Marker. "Steroidal Sapogenins, Part 173." *Journal of the American Chemical Society*, vol. 71, 1949, p. 3856.

L.F. Fieser and M. Fieser. *Steroids*. New York: Reinhold Publishing Corp., 1959.

INDEX

Abeles, John H., 85–86
abortion, 3, 7, 20, 22–30, 43, 77–78, 159
  as fertility control, 22–23, 26, 146–47, 207–9
  legal issues of, 25–27, 29–30, 64
  procedural types, 26–29, 146–47
  related deaths, 24, 98
  second trimester, 27–29, 147
Adams, Roger, 203
adenocarcinoma, 160
adolescent contraception, 16, 18, 153
age and childbearing, 58–59
α-chlorohydrin, 133
amenorrhea, 13–14, 156, 164, 192
Ames test, 53
Amruss, 174–75
Anderson, Jack, 95
androgens, 136–38
anemia, 42
animal models and drug toxicology research, 53–58, 70, 73–77, 86, 107–37, 162, 165
Anordrin, 201–2
Ansbacher, R., 132
antihistamines, 232, 251
Armpitin, 108–19
artificial insemination, 130–32, 164
aspirin, 100
atomic energy, 172–73

Banks, A., 122–23
Beck, Lee R., 104
Benadryl, 251
Berelson, Bernard, 169, 179, 181, 184, 186

Bergström, Sune, 28
Berliner, V.R., 55–56
birth control:
  antifertility vaccine and, 161–63, 180, 196–98
  consumer advocacy and, 217–23
  government-imposed, 169–81
  population-wide contraceptive agent, requirements for, 175–79
  postcoital, 153, 159–61, 201–2
  public information about, 91–108, 119
  technology and, 1, 51, 69, 86, 104, 106–7, 119, 176–77, 190, 200, 210–11, 216–17
  see also oral contraceptives; Pill
Brave New World, 170–72, 227
breast:
  cancer, 58–59, 139
  tumors, 42, 61, 194
Brevicon, 101
Butenandt, Adolf, 233

Caffeine and birth defects, 107–8
cancer, 4, 51–65, 219
  breast, 58–59, 139
  cervical, 61, 122, 246
  endometrial, 155
  and estrogens, 160
  ovarian, 42, 61–62
  the Pill and, 37–38, 51–65, 98–99
  prostatic, 139
  uterine, 60–62, 139
carcinogens, 51, 157, 255
cardiovascular diseases, 38, 46

Cheng Pui-Yuen, 185
children and accidental poisoning, 94–95
China, People's Republic of:
  birth control and, 22, 48, 183–214
  male pill and, 82, 84, 135, 202–5
  medical care and, 184–86
  paper pill and, 154, 198–201
  scientific publications of, 205–6
  vacation pill and, 201–2
chlormadinone acetate, 55, 71–72
cholesterol, 233–37, 242
Church, Roman Catholic, 43–45, 175
Ciba, 232
circulatory disorders, 38, 46, 95
coitus interruptus, 3, 7–9, 14, 127
Colton, Frank D., 249
condoms, 3, 8, 13–18, 35, 48, 127, 153, 155, 190
Connell, Elizabeth, 42, 95–98
Control of Fertility, The, 228–29
Cooper, Theodore, 107
corpus luteum, 144–45, 147, 164
corticosteroids, 230, 232–33
cortisone, 230, 232–33, 237–42
Crotty, J. J., 95
Cultural Revolution (China), 186, 194, 205, 212

Davidson, Julian, 140
DBCP (1, 2-dibromo-3-chloro-propane), 133
deoxycholic acid, 238
Depo-Provera, 55, 72, 154–55, 158, 219
Diamond, Marion C., 139
diaphragm, 8, 18–19, 47–48, 146, 153, 155, 189
Diczfalusy, Egon, 57
diethylstilbestrol (DES), 52–53, 159–61
dilatation and curettage (D&C), 27
Dimond, E. Grey, 185–86
diosgenin, 235, 237
divorce, 22
Djerassi, Carl, 67, 72, 178–79, 215–16, 247–48

Dramamine, 251
drug toxicology research, 71, 134, 152, 162
  male contraception and, 134–36, 203–4
  oral contraception and, 53–58, 70, 73–77, 157, 164–65, 220–22
Doering, William, 173
Doisy, Edward, 233
Dole, Robert, 94, 98–99
Doll, Sir Richard, 39, 42
Dorn, Harold, 63

ectopic pregnancy, 21, 150–51
Edwards, Charles C., 36–37
Edwards, Robert, 150
Ehrenstein, Maximilian, 244–46
Ehrenstein's 19-norprogesterone, 245
Ehrlich, Paul, 228
embryonic development, 159
ergot alkaloids, 159
estradiol, 144, 146, 231–23, 234, 242–43, 246–47
estrogen, 12, 106, 136, 139, 144–45, 152, 154, 156–59, 194–95, 231, 236, 242
  -dependent tumors, 37, 55, 62–64, 160
  and circulatory disorders, 38
ethynodiol diacetate, 253–54
ethynylestradiol, 101, 159–61, 191, 193–95, 247–48
ethynyltestosterone, 247–48

Fallopio, Gabrielle, 14
family planning, 3–5, 9–10, 17, 22, 35, 48, 169–70, 179, 184, 186–89, 195, 198, 212
Feinstein, Alvan, 62
female contraceptives, 121–23, 126, 135, 143
female reproductive biology, 83, 143–46
Fermi, Enrico, 172
Fieser, Louis F., 240
foams, spermicidal, 46, 153, 155
follicle stimulating hormone (FSH), 126, 138, 144–45, 162–63

Food and Drug Administration (FDA), 108, 202
  birth control and, 2–4, 17, 20, 140, 151, 155, 158–59, 224
  drug approval phases and, 73–82, 250–52
  international role of, 71–73
  legal function of, 69–73
  oral contraceptive research and, 73–84, 219
  pharmaceutical industry and, 73–84, 219
  safety of the Pill and, 36–37, 53–57, 64–65, 99–103

gall bladder diseases, 39
Gandhi, Indira, 180
Gandhi, Mahatma, 178
glycoproteins, 126
gonadotrophins, 126, 136, 138, 144–45, 161–63
gossypol, 82, 135, 202–5
Gräfenberg, Ernst, 19
Greenblatt, Robert B., 145–46, 248
Greenstein, Julius S., 108–19
Greep, Roy O., 87
Greep Report, 87
Guillemin, Roger, 125, 166
Guttmacher, Alan S., 91, 165–66
gynaecomastia, 12

Haberlandt, Ludwig, 244, 249
Harkavy, Oscar, 87
Health Education and Welfare (HEW):
  population research and, 3
  toxicology research and, 107
Hench, Philip S., 238
Hertz, Roy, 56, 246–48
hormones, 125–26, 143–47, 152–54
  enzyme systems and, 162–63
  see also specific hormones
Horowitz, Ralph, 62
human chorionic gonadotrophin (HCG), 161–62
Huxley, Aldous, 43, 170–72, 175, 227

hypothalamic releasing hormones, 10, 125–26, 138, 161, 163, 166
hysterectomy, 21

Iman, Guy (Guillemin), 165–66
impotence after vasectomy, 127
infertility, 122, 132
inhibin, 125, 138
Inhoffen, Hans H., 247
injectable, time-release contraceptives, 104–6
International Fertility Research Program, 10
intrauterine device (IUDs), 7–8, 13, 19–21, 35–36, 48, 150, 155, 165–67, 189–90
  research on, 20–21, 151
  side effects of, 21, 51, 151
Investigative New Drug (IND) exemption, 70, 73
Ishihama, Atsumi, 19
17-isoprogesterone, 244

Jacobson, Michael, 107–8
Jacques, Jean, 201
Jaffe, Frederick S., 47–48
Javits, Jacob, 165–66
Johnson, Anita, 219
Jones, E. F., 44
Jorgensen, Valerie, 16

Karow, A. M., 132
Kefauver Amendment, 69
Kendall, Edward, 233, 238
Kennedy, Donald, 2–3, 57, 72–73
Ketchel, M. M., 169–70
Korenbrot, Carol C., 139

Laboratorios Hormona, 236
lactation, prolonged, 8, 10–14, 23
lactational amenorrhea, 13–14, 157
laparoscopy, 150
Lederle, 238
legal issues:
  abortion and, 25–27, 29–30, 64
  birth control and, 3, 99–100
  of the FDA, 69–73
legislation:
  pharmaceutical industry and, 216–17, 220

public knowledge of contraceptives and, 91–100, 108, 119, 166
Lehmann, Federico, 236–37
Lipschutz, Alexander, 248
Loe, James M., 129
luteinizing hormone (LH), 125–26, 136, 138–39, 144–45, 152, 162–64
lynestrenol, 253–54

male contraceptives, 121–23, 126, 135, 143
male fertility control, 68, 121–41, 143, 202–5
    condoms and, 13–18
    inhibition of spermatogenesis and, 133–35
    interference with hormones and, 135–40
    interference with sperm transport and, 126–32
    research on, 82–84
    sperm maturation interference and, 132–33
    sterilization and, 21–22, 122
male reproductive biology, 83, 123–26
Manhattan project, 172
Mao Tse-tung, 184, 191, 193, 196, 205–6
Marker, Russell E., 234–37, 249
marketing:
    condoms, 15, 17–18
    oral contraceptives, 68–69, 71, 79, 84, 97, 106, 249, 251, 253, 255
marriage:
    abortion and, 25–26, 43, 207
    pregnancy and, 43
Marshall, J. F., 155–56
Marxist doctrine, 186–87
McCloskey, Paul, 215
Mead, Margaret, 121
medroxyprogesterone acetate, 55, 72
megestrol, 191, 194
menopause, 13, 62, 165
menstrual extraction, 27, 146, 160

menstruation, 13–34, 54, 56–57, 144–45, 152, 184
    age of onset, 61
    disorders of, 42, 46, 122, 156–57, 192, 194–95, 244, 249, 250–51
Merck, 238, 240
mestranol, 101, 194
metabolism, oral contraceptive influence on, 63, 75–76
minipill, 55, 65, 71–72, 156
Mintz, Morton, 52
Miramontes, Luis, 247
miscarriages, 107, 244
"morning-after pill," 159–61
Morris, John M., 153, 159
Muskie, Edmund, 1
mutagenicity, 107, 133

natural family planning (NFP), 9–10
Nelson, Gaylord, 36, 91–95, 98–100
Nelson hearings, 91–100, 165–66
New Drug Application (NDA), 70, 84, 223
Nilsson, Stefan, 12
noresthisterone, 191, 248
norethindrone, 115, 154, 191, 194–95, 247–55
norethynodrel, 248, 252–54
norgestrel, 157, 253–54
Norlutin, 191, 193
19-norprogesterone, 246–47
Norsigian, Judith, 122
nuclear disarmament, 172–73
nutrition and breast feeding, 12
Nygren, Karl-Gösta, 12

Oppenheimer, W., 19
oral contraceptives, 3, 5, 156, 185, 198–201, 207, 212
    cost estimates in research and, 76–82, 85, 154, 220
    manufacturing and, 210–11
    marketing and, 68, 71, 79, 84, 97, 100, 249, 251, 255
    "once-a-month," 77, 147, 173
    package inserts for, 39, 99–103

oral contraceptives (continued)
  research on, 67, 69, 73–82, 97,
    215, 219, 223, 225
  role of FDA on, 69–82, 85
  role of pharmaceutical industry
    on, 57, 84–89
  side effects and, 14, 79, 93–97,
    100, 104, 106–8, 157
  "tri-cycle pill," 14
  see also birth control; Pill
Orleans, Leo, 198–201, 213
Ortho Novum, 252
Orwell, George, 170
Ota, T., 19
Overbeek, G. A., 56
ovulation,   9–10,   13,   143–45,
    201–2, 249, 251
  detection, as fertility control,
    152–53
  releasing hormones and, 163–64

Parke-Davis,   235–36,   239–50,
    252–54
peptides, 163–64
Petros-Barvazian, A., 11
pharmaceutical industry:
  contraceptive toxicology studies
    and, 57
  FDA and, 84–85, 221–22
  legislature and, 92–93, 225
  oral contraceptive research and,
    84–89, 115, 216–17, 220–23,
    246–55
  patents and, 222–23
Pill, 14, 17, 20–21, 23, 30, 47–49,
    146, 153–54, 158, 165–66,
    172, 191–96
  benefits from, 39–42
  consumption of, 33–36
  early history of, 5, 227–29,
    242–52
  package insert and, 39, 99–103
  religion and, 43–44, 251–52
  safety of, 36–39, 49, 52–65, 69,
    91–108
  sexual mores and, 42–43
  women's movement and, 44–47
Pill on Trial, The, 227
Pincus, Gregory, 227–29, 248–49,
    251

pituitary glands and hormone re-
    lease, 10, 126, 135–36, 138,
    144–45, 152, 162–63
Place, Francis, 8–9
Planned Parenthood, 83
Platt, John R., 177–79
political issues:
  of birth control, 3
  government-imposed birth con-
    trol and, 171, 179–81
population explosion, 4–5, 19, 96,
    166, 169–71, 177, 212–13
Potts, Malcolm, 4, 10
pregnancy, 56–57, 64, 77–78, 96,
    98, 107, 144–47, 159, 161,
    164, 244
premarital sex, 26, 43
preventive medicine, 23, 29, 48, 85
press coverage:
  Nelson hearings and, 92–100
  on injectable   contraceptives,
    104–6
  on oral   contraceptives,   100,
    107–8
progesterone, 12, 20–21, 56–57,
    61–64, 106, 122, 136–38,
    144–45, 147, 151, 154, 156,
    160–61, 164, 196, 202, 229,
    231, 233–37, 239, 241–47,
    255
prostaglandins, 28–29, 147, 164
public policy:
  abortion and, 150
  contraceptives and, 1–2, 72, 89,
    91–108, 119, 166, 216, 218
  government-imposed birth con-
    trol and, 169, 177–78
Pugwash Conferences on Science
    and World Affairs, 173
Pyribenzamine, 232

Ratner, Herbert, 35, 94–95
Reichstein, Tadeus, 233, 237–38
releasing hormones (RH), 125–26,
    138–39, 163–64, 166
religious issues:
  birth control and, 3, 172, 174–75
  the Pill and, 43–44, 251–52
Requena, M. B., 22, 29

research:
on carcinogens, 52–60
on drug toxicology, 53–58, 70–71, 73–77, 134, 152, 157, 162, 164–65, 203–4, 220–22
IUD, 20–21
on injectable steroid contraception, 154–59, 196
on lactational amenorrhea, 13
on male contraception, 127–30, 133–34, 137
on oral contraception, 4, 9–10, 67–69, 71, 73–84, 97, 121, 123, 166, 215, 219, 223, 225
on breast feeding, 11–12
on sterilization, 22
teratology studies and, 77–78, 107–8, 137
rheumatoid arthritis, 232, 238–39
rhythm method, 7–10, 152, 163–64, 172
Rock, John, 249, 251
Roosevelt, Franklin D., 172
Rosenkranz, George, 233, 237, 241–42, 247–48
Ruzicka, Leopold, 233, 237

sapogenin, 235, 237
Sarett, Lewis H., 238–39
Schally, A. V., 125
Schearer, Bruce, 140
Scheuer, James, 67–68
Schmidt, Alexander M., 65
scientific articles, evaluation of, 108–19
Seaman, Barbara, 16–17, 46–47, 140–41, 225
Searle, 228, 249–54
secondary sex characteristics, 144–45, 230–31
Segal, Sheldon G., 166–67
semen storage (preservation), 130–32
sexuality:
birth control and, 7–9, 17, 139, 153
intercourse and, 137–39
the Pill and, 42–43
sex hormones, 52–65, 75, 85, 104, 125–26, 135–40, 144–45, 152–54, 157, 159, 163–65, 170, 233–34
see also specifiic hormones
Shockley, William B., 180
Short, Roger, 10–14, 137–38
Slotta, Karl, 233
Smith, Hershel, 253
social factors:
birth control and, 3, 11–12, 135, 184, 186
government-imposed birth control and, 169–81
the Pill and, 47–48
socioeconomic issues and birth control, 22–23, 30, 169, 179–81, 187, 213
Somlo, Emeric, 236–37
spermatogenesis, 123–26, 132–35
Squibb, 238
Stein, Gertrude, 75
Steptoe, Patrick, 150
sterilization, 7–8, 21–23, 29, 34, 128, 140–41, 146–47, 207–9, 212
chemical, 150–51
compulsory, 179–80
steroid chemistry, 229–48, 253
Stevens, Wallace, 225
Stopes, Marie, 14–15
strophanthidin, 245
swine flu vaccine, 162–63
Syntex, 232–33, 236–37, 239–42, 246–47, 249–54
Szilard, Leo, 172–75

technology and birth control, 1, 51, 69, 86, 104, 106–7, 119, 176–77, 190, 200, 210–11, 216–17
teratology studies, 77–78, 107–8, 137
testosterone, 125–26, 136–40, 145, 191, 231–34, 237, 239, 243, 246–47
thalidomide poisoning, 69
Third World, 2
and fertility control, 19–20, 173, 178–79, 184, 186, 213
the Pill and, 47–48

thromboembolic disorders, 37, 46, 63, 95, 194–95
thyroid hormone release, 162
Tietze, Christopher, 25
tubal ligation, 21, 147, 150
Tyler, Edward T., 115–16, 248

U.S. Congress:
  male contraception and, 140–41
  oral contraception safety and, 65, 67–69, 72–73, 87, 89, 91–100, 215–16, 224
  population control and, 122
U.S. government:
  consumption of the Pill and, 33–36, 154–55
  marketing contraceptives and, 67–69, 84
  pharmaceutical industry and, 84–89, 225
Upjohn, 219, 238, 240–42
urbanization and breast feeding, 11–12

vacuum aspiration, 27, 207
vaginal microcapsules, 151–52
vaginal rings, 158
Van Wagenen, Gertrude, 159

vasectomy, 7, 21–22, 126, 147, 155, 179–80
  reversibility of, 128–30
  side effects of, 127
Vaughn, Paul, 227
venereal disease, 17
Verhulst, Henry L., 94–95
Vessey, M. P., 39, 42
Voice of the Dolphin, The, 174

Weinberg, Alvin, 218
Westoff, C. F., 44
Whitten, Jamie L., 65
Wieland, Heinrich, 233
Wintersteiner, Oskar, 233
Wolfe, Sidney M., 219
women's emancipation, 3, 44–47
World Health Organization (WHO), 9, 33
  birth control and, 147–49, 152, 156–58, 201, 219, 223–25
  steroid studies on male and, 137
  toxicology studies of the Pill and, 54–58, 72
World War II, 172, 238, 242, 247

Zaffaroni, Alejandro, 242, 251–52
Zipper, Jaime, 20, 150